PROJECT AMERICA

Memoirs of Faith and Hope
To Win the Future

By
Marshall Elijah Hatch

Life To Legacy, LLC

Project America: Memoirs of Faith & Hope to Win the Future
By: Marshall E. Hatch, Sr.

ISBN-10: 0984797327
ISBN-13: 978-0-9847973-2-5

All scriptural references are based upon the New International Version (NIV).

Printed in the United States

10 9 8 7 6 5 4 3 2 1

Cover concept by: Shenita Thomas
Cover design by: Tasha Sykes, Legacy Design Unlimited
Back cover photo (King Monument) provided by: David L. Spearman

Life To Legacy, LLC
P.O. Box 1239
Matteson, IL 60443
(877) 267-7477
Life2legacybooks@att.net

www.Life2Legacy.com

TABLE OF CONTENTS

TABLE OF CONTENTS cont.

Presented to:

To contact Marshall Hatch send email to:
Project.America@yahoo.com

About the Author

Marshall Elijah Hatch, Sr. has been the Pastor of the New Mount Pilgrim Missionary Baptist Church located in the heart of Chicago's West Garfield community since 1993. Born and raised in Chicago, Illinois, Marshall Hatch's spiritual development began in Shiloh Missionary Baptist Church under the pastorate of his father, the late Reverend Elijah Hatch. In 1985, he was ordained as a minister, and later in that same year was appointed as Pastor of the Commonwealth Missionary Baptist Church in North Lawndale. In the Summer of 1998, he was selected for one of the most highly coveted fellowships at the Harvard Divinity School, in Cambridge, Massachusetts. In August 2000, Marshall Hatch was appointed to be an Adjunct Professor on the faculty of McCormick Theological Seminary. In November of 2006, he was awarded the Weston Howland Jr. Grant and Award for Civic Leadership from Tufts University in Medford, Massachusetts. In 2008, he was appointed professor of Urban Ministry at Northern Baptist Seminary in Lombard, Illinois.

Rev. Hatch has an impressive history of civic involvement and activism spanning over two decades. He served as a member of the Chicago School Board Nominating Commission from 1989-1991. He served as the Moderator of the Friendship Baptist District Association, and he is the National Director of Religious Affairs of the Rainbow PUSH Coalition. He also serves on the boards of the Academy of Communication and Technology (ACT) Charter School and Christ The King Jesuit College Prep High School. He is a member of the National Baptist Conventions (USA and America), Illinois National Baptist State Convention, American Baptist Churches of Metro Chicago, United Power for Action and Justice, and co-convener of the L.E.A.D.E.R.S Network.

Pastor Hatch has earned both doctorate and master's degrees in ministry and theological studies, respectively, from McCormick Theological Seminary in Chicago, Illinois. He also holds a master's degree in government from Georgetown University in Washington, D.C., and a bachelor's degree in political science from Western Illinois University in Macomb, Illinois.

Marshall Hatch is married to the former Priscilla Murchison and they are the parents of four children: Joyce, Janelle, Marshall and Maurice.

Acknowledgements

These memoirs are, of course, intertwined with my shared life with Priscilla and our children. Priscilla, thanks for your love and partnership. It has been a dream life with you!

Much thanks to the good people of Shiloh, Commonwealth, and New Mount Pilgrim congregations for your love and support. From all of you all, I have learned so much about God's love and grace and the things that really matter in life. I pray that I have helped make your lives better as well.

To my trusted administrative assistant, Shenita Thomas, for your creative design of the book cover and countless hours of "free time," I am grateful. I owe you much.

Bro. Thaddeus Hall, church executive assistant, thanks for "holding down the fort!"

Much love and thanks to the L.E.A.D.E.R.'s Network, especially Pastors Acree and Fields, for being yokefellows in the Gospel and in the struggle.

Thanks too for my "best man" at my wedding almost 30 years ago, Larry D. "Cisco" Harris. You are the brother I never had.

Sincere appreciation goes out to Dr. Dennis Woods and Life To Legacy Books for your diligence in moving this Project to print and electronic upload. You have been a blessing.

To my late mother and father, Helen and Elijah, I have lived to honor your sacrifices. I hope you are proud.

Finally, for my fellow West-siders: thanks for helping conceive a grand vision of 21st century urban ministry and helping to bring back the "spirit of village to the heart of the city."

—*Marshall E. Hatch*
April 2012

Foreword

The first time I wandered into the office of Dr. Marshall Hatch, at the New Mt. Pilgrim Baptist Church of Chicago, I was awe-struck by three things. First, the sheer size of the office. Next is his vast book collection, and finally, his collection of historic photographs. There were many pictures of famous personalities taken from all over the world. The most memorable of these photographs were taken abroad in places like Israel and South Africa; others were taken here in United States.

As I curiously perused these photographs, I noticed several iconic personalities, like Yasser Arafat, Barack Obama, Lady Bird Johnson, John F. Kennedy, Jr., Dr. Henry Gates, Dr. Cornel West and Congressman Danny Davis. However, I couldn't help but notice that even though each picture was different, they all had something in common. Situated in the middle of each picture, was Rev. Dr. Marshall E. Hatch, wearing his engaging vivacious smile.

Sarcastically, I asked Dr. Hatch, "Did you Photoshop yourself into these pictures? With a somewhat surprised look and response, he assured me that all of these were the actual photographs. With my suspicions arrested, from that point forward, I began to refer to that room as the "Forrest Gump" room. Giving his office that name was my way of honoring him, because Forrest Gump was a fictional character who inadvertently affected American culture and whose face accidentally ended up in historic photographs. However, in Dr. Hatch's case, his persona and contributions to American culture are not fictional, nor are his photographs fictitious, but true living legacies.

In Chicago, a city known for infamous gangsters like Al Capone and Jeff Fort, and powerful political forces like Richard "Boss" Daley, Dr. Hatch's Project America, gives an insightful, behind the scenes view of the organizational mechanisms behind some of the most powerful civil rights and political machines of our time. While examining the impact that icons like President Barack Obama, Reverend Jesse L. Jackson Sr. and others have had on our culture, Reverend Hatch thematically weaves in his own life's story creating a multifaceted and colorful literary tapestry.

In a brilliant analysis and literary style, Dr. Marshall Hatch chronicles his own journey from humble beginnings as a youth growing up on Chicago's West Side, through the corridors of power and influence in the academic, political, and ecclesiastical arenas. In his life's journey, Dr. Hatch traverses cultures and continents and goes beyond just rendering mere commentary on historical and social events: he also pays homage to the pioneers whose personal sacrifice and commitment to fellow man, put in motion the kind of opportunities that made a life like his possible.

More importantly, he puts his experiences into historical, socioeconomic and geopolitical context, building his case on America's role in the emerging world of globalization, as she struggles to bring to fruition the hopes of Martin Luther King's "Dream," to all of her citizenry.

The result, Project America, serves as a clarion call to action: for preachers to do more than just preach, teachers to do more than just teach, and citizens to do more than just sit. He constructs a blueprint as to the role that the church can play as a moral compass, to keep us on the road to fulfilling our Manifest Destiny and live out the true meaning of America's pledge as "...one nation, under God, indivisible, with liberty and justice for all."

—*Dwight McKee*
Policy Analyst

Foreword

Project America is necessary, nostalgic, visionary, vivid and discerning. My father weaves together scenes from his personal journey with historical analysis and commentaries to address contemporary public policy issues. He offers his deepest reflections and challenges us to aggressively pursue a national purpose where those who live on the fringes of our society are afforded the same opportunities as the wealthy: "we owe it to our past and our potential to continue the project of perfecting the Union and extending the blessings of liberty."

Project America is timely. The providence of this nation calls our generation to action. The author sheds light on the timeless maxim that "each generation must chart its own course," but he looks to the global vision of Dr. Martin Luther King Jr. to summon the probing question "Where do we go from here?"

How can the changing complexion and future of this nation compete globally if our youth receive subpar schooling? How will the true American values, celebrating diversity and equal opportunity, be bequeathed to "generation next" if they are not at the forefront of our cultural identity? This book delves into these questions and proposes comprehensive strategies that provide the blueprint for "winning the future."

Project America is a spiritual passage. Only an intimate relationship with our Lord and Savior Jesus Christ can inspire the kinds of insights in this book. I continue to be awed by my father's dedication to service; this book is an extension of his profound ministry: "May the things that perturb the heart of God disturb our minds, move our hearts, and stir our spirits to action." I hope that this work touches the lives of countless others as it has mine, so that we may execute and "be about our Father's business."

—Marshall Elijah Hatch, Jr.

Prelude

The American Project is the ongoing experiment with a unique form of democracy that values equality of opportunity for every person above all else. That is an amazing ideal. The founding document of the Republic enshrined a divine mandate to honor the sacredness of human potential in every individual person. The heart of this principle presupposes political rights and economic self-determination. The possibility of upward mobility, the blessings of liberty, and the pursuit of happiness emerged from a new world with new possibilities. The marvelous vision of American ideals is all the more remarkable in light of the inherent contradictions between founding principles of liberty in the context of legal chattel slavery. America's promise is birthed in the midst of America's original sin. The promise and the problem live in such intimate correlation that the nation cannot live out its national purpose without addressing its original sin. The African American legacy of struggle and black America's role in helping to define and redefine our national purpose and national destiny remain central to the American Project. Before the middle of the century, America's minorities will be the majority. That means that the salvation of the nation lies in reclaiming those left behind in ghettos and cycles of cultural poverty. Reclaiming human potential brings us right back to the heart of national purpose. When we live out that national purpose, we give hope to the world.

My life has been a metaphor for Project America. Entering the world in 1958 at Chicago's Cook County Hospital and growing up in a Chicago Housing Authority (CHA) project, I was at high risk for all of the familiar inner-city pathologies. The opportunities to grow and develop that have been afforded me are the direct result of the legacies of my parents, compassionate and effective public policies, and the sacrifices of people who had faith in the ideals and promise of America. From my family's sojourn in the Great Migration of African Americans from south to north, to the substantial contribution of American social reformers, to the legacy of Dr. Martin Luther King Jr. and the civil rights movement, to public investments in public housing and public education, my life is testimony to the invaluable unrealized potential that languishes in disinvested urban centers segregated from opportunity. From these same places of isolation, I have been blessed and allowed to evolve and expand.

As I used this work to reflect on my journey, I could not help but think about the graces and graciousness I encountered along the way. Like many in my generation, I am consumed with the passion of how to redeem the promise and transfer the values of our unfinished Project for a new generation. In the opening decades of the twenty-first century, given our history and present political and socioeconomic challenges, it will be tougher than ever. Our salvation lies in pursuing a vision that contends for our ideals, while embracing the changing complexion of our nation and the emerging new world. One hundred fifty years ago, Abraham Lincoln's America faced the question of our nation's ability to let go of an old world and embrace a new birth of freedom. Forty-three years ago, Dr. Martin Luther King Jr.'s American vision challenged our nation to reclaim its ideals and find a new place in an emerging postcolonial world. This yet new century brings fresh challenges for the American Project: we must reengage our national purpose and mission in the global shifting of a new world order.

Without maximum investment in the future of the new America, the emerging majority of minority and poor children, our nation will have no future. And worse, the world would lose the incalculable gift of the values of a nation whose promise and purpose are found in the embrace of diversity and equality. Out of many, one national purpose can only be achieved by continued perfection of the Union. But the work of perfecting the Union now faces far more complex challenges. Those who have been most abused by the nation's contradictions must be called upon to re-embrace those ideals and take the lead in positioning America to promote universal standards of human rights and self-determination. As my own life testifies, equal access to a high-quality education is the only way we can continue the American Project and work toward our national purpose. We will need local education systems that can compete globally. We will also need to transform our international policy to take full advantage of our diversity as an asset to engage the emerging new world. If we can embrace the new demographics and changing complexion of America, we may offer a new birth of freedom for the world. We may also rediscover our national purpose and help shape the new world that will emerge from the political and economic ashes of the old world order.

This book is offered as a contribution to the dialogue about our national purpose, direction, and destiny. My personal memoirs, blended with the vision of Dr. Martin Luther King Jr., offer insight into our national story. Our vantage point in urban Chicago also allows for public policy directives, and ways we can position our nation to retain leadership in the new globalization. I believe our world will be a qualitatively different place if America devalues its values, loses the future, and withdraws from international leadership. The world will need the leadership and values of a transformed and revived America to continue human progress in the twenty-first century. As Americans celebrate and reflect upon the unveiling of the Stone of Hope Memorial to Dr. King on the National Mall, we must be reminded that King was an American citizen with a thoroughly modern worldview. I believe a true patriot challenges the nation to be its best, true self. Dr. King offers Americans a new and modern way to be an American. King exemplified that our private faith can lead us into the public square as national and global citizens.

Fitting is King's Stone of Hope Memorial in the nation's capital, for it is his vision and worldview that foresaw the possibility of a new American century in an emerging new world. From where I stand, there will be only one way to win the future for our ideals and fulfill our national purposes and place in the world. We must intentionally seek to overcome the defects of our national origins and more fully embrace our national values and ideals. I have benefited from the spirit of Project America in my generation. I am living proof that investments in people and embracing our ideals to make real the promise of America are what it means to preserve the soul of America. In restoring our faith and hope in the promise of America, we will be well on our way toward winning a future that wins the world.

CHAPTER 1

Chicago's Projects and the
American Project: Perishing Vision

"Where there is no vision, the people perish: but people are happy when good laws are established and kept." —King Solomon (970-928, B.C.), the Book of Proverbs.

"I have taught you all things, how that so laboring you ought to support the weak, and remember the words of the Lord Jesus, how he said, It is more blessed to give than to receive." —Apostle Paul, Acts 20:35, Apostle Paul, first century, A.D.

"I have the audacity to believe that people everywhere can have three meals a day for their bodies, education and culture for their minds, and dignity, equality and freedom for their spirit." —Dr. Martin Luther King Jr., accepting the Nobel Peace Prize, 1963.[1]

They are all gone now. The public housing developments that encircled the downtown of Chicago's central city have been swept away in gentrification and renewal. The first large public housing project in the world, named for the early twentieth century pioneer of urban social work, Jane Addams, has been torn down. This was the development my family lived in from 1959 to 1974. Built in 1938, west of downtown and inhabited by predominately European residents, it was a mix of brown brick townhouses and three-story walk ups.[2] The development's one remaining building, at Taylor and Ada Streets, is being preserved to develop and establish the first National Public Housing Museum.

The buildings known as the Robert Taylor Homes, named after President Obama's senior advisor Valerie Jarrett's grandfather, are gone too. Built in the 1960s south of Chicago's Loop, with twenty-seven thousand residents, it was at one time the largest public housing development in the world.[3] Taylor, in his life and times, had fought for decent housing for black migrants on Chicago's South Side. Also south of downtown was the Ida B. Wells Projects, named for the African American anti-lynching matron of the Great Migration. The old townhouses have been demolished to make for a new "mixed-income" development more in line with the upscale profile of new residents moving into historic Bronzeville. In the early and middle years of the twentieth century, every major African American entertainer played establishments in Bronzeville. Black and integrated audiences enjoyed the lively nightlife scene that featured blues and jazz greats. Near Chinatown, southwest of the Loop, were the Harold Ickes high-rises. The Ickes projects, the namesake of the long-serving New Deal Era United States Secretary of the Interior from the Roosevelt Administration, have been replaced by a condo development. To the west of the Loop were the Henry Horner Homes, a collection of high-rises that carried the name of the progressive Illinois governor who passed the state's first income tax to fund social programs during the Great Depression. These were dismantled around 2000.

The last to go, in the spring of 2011, was the internationally known Cabrini-Green Housing Project. Named after Catholic saint to the immigrants, Mother Frances Cabrini, the sprawling collection of CHA high-rises and townhouses sat right in the middle of the highest property value communities in the city. The classic 1975 black movie "Cooley High," filmed in Cabrini-Green, chronicled the crushed hopes and dashed dreams of young blacks trapped in the predicaments of poverty in the middle of prosperity. As the final high-rise was torn down in the spring of 2011, students from the downtown campus of Columbia College collaborated with Cabrini children in a poetry-and-light exhibit. As the buildings came down, flickering lights and copies of the children's poems that were placed in the buildings were ceremoniously buried with the rubble.

Many Chicagoans of conscience recognized that the end of the Cabrini development was the end of an era. The public housing and public schools that served the urban poor had been named after pioneers of America's progressive urban policies. Addams, Ickes, Wells, Horner, and Cabrini left legacies of an American Project and experiment with democracy that dared make real the promise of America for immigrants and migrants to the city. With the tearing down of Cabrini-Green, the CHA had fully carried out a 1996 city mandate to demolish eighteen thousand units of public housing. The projects had first served to settle European immigrants and give them access to the American promise and the American Dream. By the last third of the century, the projects housed black families migrating from the South to the northern land of promise. By the 1980s, the academic and social climate had changed. Urban poverty, and public housing in particular, had been destructively colored with race. In the Reagan era national political leaders effectively coupled race and poverty, and the war against the urban poor was carried out by an aggressive war against urban illegal drug use and peddling. The demolition of Chicago's projects was an indication of the government's disengagement from the American Project, and the disinvestment in social programs for the urban poor reflected a new hostile political climate.

At the end of the twentieth century in Chicago, the times ushered in a new urban policy and the end of old projects. African American families and communities were scattered from the public housing developments and steered into black city neighborhoods and poorer suburbs with federal rent subsidies. The black poor were now being dispersed into communities and suburbs away from the central cultural and political life of the city. Black middle-class neighborhoods, such as Chatham, were destabilized by the influx of fragile and fractured poor black families driven from demolished public housing. Black Chicago, long a mecca of black businesses and cohesive political power, has been disoriented and demoralized by the dispersal of large proportions of its population. The city of Chicago lost about one hundred eighty thousand African American residents from 2000 to 2010.[4]

The urban removal of black project families changed the social and political dynamics of the city in a profound way. The land that they had once occupied is now filled with new urban residents and new upscale communities with new names befitting new visions. The Horner Homes area is now West Haven. The Harold Ickes community is now the South Loop. Cabrini has become known as North Loop New Communities and has an influx of new residents. The old Jane Addams Projects are now replaced by a new vision of a University Village connected to the expanding University of Illinois at Chicago campus. The sprawling large projects for the poor in the central city are now completely gone, a distant memory from an era passed on. The projects are gone, but the promises they held for black migrants remain unfulfilled.

New policy that shifts populations does not mean the end of the problems for America's urban poor, nor does it mean that we can default on America's promise. The premise of this book is that we must fulfill the American Dream for citizens of color, particularly the descendant people of our nation's original sin, in order to fulfill America's purpose and save America's promise for the world. Passing from 2011, at the one hundred fiftieth anniversary of the beginning of the Civil War, our nation is at the same kind of crossroads faced by Lincoln's generation and later King's generation.

In Lincoln's America, free white skilled and unskilled labor, domestic and immigrant, could not compete with the high and low-skilled black slave labor sold and leased. Something had to give. The abolitionists and the advocates for lower-class European immigrants found common cause in fighting to save the Union for the American values of upward mobility. The unionist Lincoln believed that "A house divided against itself cannot stand." In other words, America could not advance in its divisive state—half slave and half free. Dr. King foresaw that we could not win a global future for American values without understanding the correlation between the civil rights and economic self-determination, and the anticolonial movements of the second half of the twentieth century. Legal apartheid locked America into an old, fading world. To win the Cold War, America had to move aggressively to live up to its own values. Recognition of Dr. King's American vision has given him a rightful place among the definers of our national purpose. In our generation, we cannot win the future with large parts of our fellow citizens mired in cycles and cultures of poverty and segregated from opportunity. We cannot survive part educated and edified, and part undereducated and demoralized.

Offering real opportunity to the emancipated, the immigrant, and the migrant is at the heart of our national purpose. The place and time I was born and came of age have given me a unique vantage point to share in the successes of the American Project. My life, and the lives of countless others, are testimony that the promise of America is worth the total commitment of our nation's resources. We owe it to our past and our potential to continue the project of perfecting the union and extending the blessings of liberty.

King's Vision: Moving the Project Forward

Born March 11, 1958, I came of age in the latter Martin Luther King years, and my life story represents a unique part of the American Project. I am a product of the African American great migration of the twentieth century, public housing, public schools, and a public land-grant college. My life has reflected and been impacted by the new birth of freedom ushered in by King and his contemporaries. In the shadow of that movement, I have grown to develop a deep appreciation for the opportunities I have enjoyed and a profound sense of my place in the world. In fact, my life has been woven around the sacrifices of my parents, Dr. King, and others who believed in the ideals of America for me.

The 2011 unveiling of the Stone of Hope Martin Luther King Jr. Memorial on the National Mall affords opportunities to reflect upon how far we've come, how far we have to go, and clear and present dangers to progress and the American Dream. This is not the time to turn our backs on the American Project. This is a time to reengage the legacy of King and his participation in one of America's greatest generations in an age of rapid social change. This is an opportune time to revisit the question raised by Dr. Martin Luther King Jr. over forty years ago in his book, *Where Do We Go from Here: Chaos or Community?*[5] Indeed, King's last years were tense times. It was a time of rapid social change, political uncertainty, and technological innovation. America and the world were at a crossroads. Dr. King made the case that war was outdated, as was the old colonial world order. The mutually assured destruction of the world's superpowers, the U.S. and the U.S.S.R., meant that the cooperation of nations was essential to global survival. Before he was martyred, Dr. King's final testament offered cautious hopefulness. King both warned and encouraged that we had to continue to develop the capacity to live together as members of the human family, or we "would perish as fools."

I believe that time has borne witness to the profundity of Dr. King's prophetic speech, and he has now become the singular American citizen whose life and legacy can help America find her way in the new emerging world order. In the twenty-first century, it is all too easy to overlook the insight and courage it took for King to challenge his own nation's conduct of the Vietnam War in 1967. King accurately assessed the failures of American international policy, and put forth a vision of America's place in the postcolonial world.[6] King's challenge to America is in the same vein as other American patriots who saw the relationship between our unparalleled national blessings and our unique national purpose. Underappreciated in his generation, Dr. King paid a high price for his serious commitment to the ideals and values of the American Project. Forty years plus after Dr. King, in the early years of a new century and millennium, it is time to dialogue about a fresh look at new moral vision and renewed national purpose.

Losing the Soul of America

This conversation is to be had among those of us who still believe that there is yet something universally and profoundly purposeful about a nation founded upon ideals of human freedom and whose Project is perfecting its Union to expand the blessings of liberty. Sadly, today we are at a crisis in the national will to earnestly continue the Project. Between 2000 and 2010, we saw not just the decline of America's industrial and economic prowess,[7] but we have also witnessed stresses on our social fabric and a declining sense of national purpose. We have lost a sense of political civility and hopefulness about the future. We all sense that too many leaders in government and shapers of our national economic course may no longer believe in the promise of America. The heart and soul of America, patriots across the left and right of our political spectrum, are troubled by the prospect that we have been sold out at the highest levels of national industry and government. I am troubled by the evidence that points to an abandonment of the American Project and national purpose. The massive transfer of wealth out of America in the last decade, the huge foreign holdings of national debt and the selling off of American assets, and the conceding loss of our manufacturing capacities: all suggest that people we have trusted to guide and guard our national interests may be anticipating the end of American exceptionalism and global leadership. However, there remain those of us who yet believe that the world needs a revived, strong America to lead the twenty-first century, and that going forward, more than ever, it will need the gifts of our ideals, our history, and our diversity.

What America needs to renew and expand its purpose has often been provided from the ranks and yearnings of its oppressed minorities and immigrants. Today, again, we need a new moral vision. What has been true in the past is yet true. To move forward, America must deal forthrightly with the continual effects of its original sin. We must finally and firmly and thoroughly reject the caste system of racial exclusion produced by the stain of chattel slavery and segregation from access and opportunity. The descendants of these rejected stones have become the chief cornerstones of American survival. All the demographics point to an America that will become "majority minority" by midcentury.[8]

America crossed a threshold in the spring of 2011. For the first time in modern times, the majority of the children born in the United States are nonwhite minorities. The children of minorities are the future of America. These children will have to preserve our values, launch our new industries, pay our national

16

debts, and fund the golden years of our retirees. Preparing this generation for the task ahead requires commitment and resources. Massive investment in mass public education is the tested path to national revival. Without this investment as preeminent public policy, little else we do will matter for the future of the country.

Four Movements: A Symphony of Winning the Future

So, which way do we go at the dawn of the twenty-first century? There are four areas America can master to put our nation on the path for winning the future for our values and ideals. First, we must have a massive investment in education to compete in the global economy. The world's regions will compete in the global economy as regional workforces. Workforce quality will be determined by offering all of our children equal access to high-quality education. The nations and regions of the world with the most developed human resource will emerge as global leaders. Education is the key to global power.

Secondly, we must adapt to the changing complexion of world power. In capital and creativity, there is a monumental shift from north to south in global energy and power dynamics. From the emerging economies of Latin America, to the soon-to-emerge African petro-states, to the wealth transfer to the Middle East, to the Indian subcontinent through the Pacific Basin, to the Far East super economies of China, Japan, and South Korea, hemispheric shifts point graphically to a changing emerging world order. The nations of Europe's past colonial ties and histories to the emerging world may help them navigate the transition, while America must find ways to utilize its emerging minorities and diversity to flow into the new global order. Again, we must look to the latent human potential we have overlooked in order to move forward in national progress and national purpose.

Thirdly, as a postindustrial leader, America must help the world clarify and embrace the challenges of environmental stewardship. The rest of the world will not be able to industrialize without regard to impact on the planet. America's unique cultural influences on the rest of the world help position our nation to help lead the way in protecting global ecosystems. Trend setting American global imaging, especially influenced by American minorities, can lead the way to smart modernizing and recasting an "eco-coolness" for the two-thirds world. We have the cultural influence globally to help make green thinking and environmental stewardship a global project. We must challenge the prevalent corporate capitalistic tendencies to behave environmentally irresponsibly in poor communities. Environmental stewardship means environmental justice. Corporate good citizens must embrace the responsibilities of shepherding the planet through the phases of development for an expanding global economy. Because of our diversity, America has a major role to play in helping the rest of the world stay focused on the big picture.

Fourthly, America must act now to renew faith and reengage the social compact or covenant with the American people. At our core, the spiritual underpinnings of our social contract enable Americans to pursue personal interests in a way that also regards and promotes the common good. Particular faiths cannot rule our government and politics, but people of faith should engage our politics with faith community values. Although our value system allows for class distinctions and unequal outcomes for people and families, our personal faith demands a just society. Our sense of fairness revolts against socio-economic predetermination for children and an intergenerational caste system. Our faith is private, but our fervent demand for justice is public. We have religious differences, but we expect religions and creeds to foster good and gracious citizenship. We require our distinct communities of particular faiths to compete in producing a lived faith that benefits the common good.

All religion at its best inspires a selflessness that fosters civility and sensitivity to the needs of others. The values of our faith can guide in reestablishing a social and economic covenant for the twenty-first century. From Thomas Jefferson's "Declaration of Independence," to Abraham Lincoln's "New Birth of Freedom," to Franklin Roosevelt's "New Deal," to John F. Kennedy's "New Frontier," and Martin Luther King Jr.'s "Dream," to Lyndon Johnson's "Great Society," to William J. Clinton's "New Covenant," and Barack Obama's 2011 vision of "Winning the Future"; we are at a new place to recreate a new social covenant that further perfects our Union and redefines the privileges and responsibilities of American citizenship to the nation and to one another.

If we are up for the challenge, a renewed national purpose will empower us to merge with the flow of human history. Furthermore, we can fulfill our calling to preserve and advance, in our generation, a nation whose gifts and blessings of liberty give light and hope for all humankind. This is a vision of citizenship that can inspire our people to serve our national purpose in the global context. This can be a new moral vision for those of us who have not given up on the American Dream and who yet embrace the American Project.

As an urban pastor, I have chosen a work that has kept me grounded in my community and has given me opportunities to further develop global perspective. This book is structured around the idea that the new millennium has ushered in a twenty-first century symphony of change. For America this means four movements to restoring our national purpose: investing in education; embracing the emerging world; leading global environmental stewardship, and renewing our social covenant and spiritual quest. By moving in concert with the winds of change in our generation, America's future can be as meaningful and purposeful as our past. In the process of perfecting our Union, we can continue to impact the future course of the world.

Historically, the American idea is interactive with the hopes and faiths of peoples all over the world. Oppressed humanity, both inside and outside of the United States, has taken on the task of challenging our nation to live up to its ideals. I count just four generations of my family back into chattel slavery. Our legacy encompasses both the horror and promise of the American experience. As the very first generation of black Americans to come of age post-Dr. Martin Luther King Jr., I am personally and painfully aware that great opportunities come at great sacrifice. The state of grace always brings forth a higher calling. Having received so much, I cannot find it in me to abandon the dream of Dr. King for succeeding generations in our nation and for our world. For me, Project America is both a personal memoir and a call to national purpose.

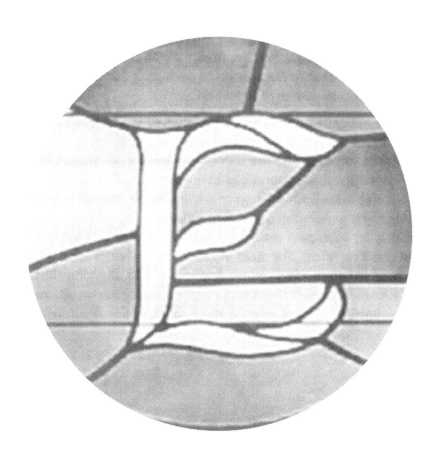

CHAPTER 2

Movement One: Global Education and Opening the Window to the World

"Don't let the world confine you in limitations, but be transformed by the renewing of your mind; so that you can demonstrate God's good and perfect will for your life."—*Apostle Paul, Epistle to the Romans 12:2, first century, A.D.*

"Education, then, beyond all other devices of human origin, is the great equalizer of the conditions of men, the balance-wheel of the social machinery."—*Horace Mann (1796-1859), the first great American advocate of public education.*

"Let us think of education as the means of developing our greatest abilities, because in each of us there is a private hope and dream which, fulfilled, can be translated into benefit for everyone and greater strength for our nation."—*John F. Kennedy (1917-1963), the thirty-fifth American President.*

"Education is the most powerful weapon which you can use to change the world."—*Nelson Mandela (1918-   ), the President of the Republic of South Africa.*

The opening decade of the third millennium has ushered in a new era of human history. In a real sense, we have come full circle from the dawning days when our fore parents emerged out of Africa to populate and dominate the planet.

We began as small families, competing and cooperating for survival, and spread from the connecting continents at the Fertile Crescent. History, as we have written it and read it, has focused upon that migration and evolution and the subsequent re-gathering of clans, tribes, and the emergence of nations. At each stage, with the emergence of larger civil constructs, the levels of competitiveness over resources became more intense between groups. With the emergence of nations and industrialization, the efficiency of war to subjugate a defeated people for dehumanization and exploitation increased exponentially. By the mid-point of the twentieth century A.D., the prospect of mutual nuclear destruction by global superpowers had forced humankind to face the limits of military power as the primary determinant of winning the future of global human competition. Globalization ultimately means that the interconnectedness of humanity requires that our methods of competition and competitiveness be much more sophisticated and complex. This is now seen most clearly in the creation of cyberspace and the intricacies of global social networking. What globalization really means is that the only way we can truly understand anything in the contemporary world is in the widest global context. Everything local is now global, and everything local is affected by what is happening globally.

Few individuals had the late Dr. King's poetic insight and prophetic foresight in understanding the new emerging world in the twenty-first century. In the backdrop of World War II and the atomic bombings of Nagasaki and Hiroshima, and in rebellions against Western colonialism and the apartheids in South Africa and the American South, Dr. King preached nonviolence for social change because he understood that the proliferation of nuclear weapons had placed severe limitations on the utility of war.[9] After King's death, the fall of the Soviet Union and the triumph of capitalism intensified the dynamics of demilitarized economic competition as the primary interface of global human interaction. By the end of the second millennium, nations that escaped through diplomacy and treaty the heavy expense of large standing armies became global economic leaders. Japan, secured under the American military umbrella, became a global economic power by focusing its resources on manufacturing and industrial development. It is quite telling that America, the world's sole military superpower, faces the most severe trade and budget imbalances in its history. The financial meltdown of 2008 and the U.S. bailouts of international banking interests exposed the limits of America's national sovereignty in the global economy.

National economies are dependent upon international creditworthiness and regional economic relationships. America's military commitments and entanglements have become albatrosses. The annual U.S. defense budget is greater than the next ten industrial nations' defense budgets combined. Our military obligations extend far beyond our immediate national interests and drain the precious resources needed to invest in education and the economic development that will help us succeed in the twenty-first century world economy. In the new global economy, the real competition is between the labor forces of the world's regions. The nations and regions of the world that win the world's future will be those with educated, dynamic, creative human resources whose technological abilities attract capital and investment. America's future does not depend on our outsized military, but it will be determined by the quality of education in our public schools. We must begin again to produce Americans who can compete and cooperate with the emerging new world. Our leaders must, in the national interest, have vision that encompasses a U.S.-led North and Central American trade zone of dynamic economic growth that successfully competes in the global economy.

Education: The Civil Rights Issue of Our Time

None of this is possible without reviving the American public school system. President Obama has, since his first budget for 2009, sought to double Department of Education investments in local schools and drive reforms with financial incentives for local school districts. The federal "race to the top" competition has energized school reform movements around the country and helped enliven the conversation about school performance. When U.S. Education Secretary Arne Duncan served as the Chicago Public Schools' (CPS) Chief Operating Officer, he and I shared the realization that access to equal high-quality education should be the top national priority and is the new civil rights issue of our time. When I served as head of Rev. Jesse Jackson's Rainbow PUSH Ministers' Division, Arne and I tag-teamed in rallies around the city to drum up school attendance and school spirit. Through our collaboration, I learned of Arne's mother's commitment to an afterschool program for inner-city children near the University of Chicago. Arne grew up around commitment to urban education. As President Obama considered Duncan for U.S. Education Secretary, I shared a conversation with Duncan and strongly encouraged him to take the post. Although I was aware that he was not a formally trained educator, I thought the President would need a trusted person to implement the education reform

23

agenda he had articulated in his 2008 campaign. At the Martin Luther King Jr. Day Rainbow PUSH breakfast at Chicago's famed Conrad Hilton Hotel's Grand Ballroom in January of 2009, Arne and I discussed the great opportunities he would be afforded to work for real change nationally.

❖❖❖❖❖❖❖❖

There was great excitement in the air. Our hometown guy had won the U.S. presidency. We all had worked hard for Obama's election. Every local Democrat of any significance was there. Although it was a local event, the place was buzzing as the center of the American political universe. I was somewhat disappointed that there seemed to be less of an altruistic mind-set among Chicago's politicians, business people, and even religious leaders. I was consumed with the public policy possibilities of the first American to win the presidency as an urban homeowner. But Chicago politics has always been more practical than ideological. The room had a typical "Windy City-where's-mine" feel to it. There were over twenty-five hundred people working the room and looking for connections and next moves. Every media outlet in town was there. Rev. Jesse Jackson was in his glory. Although it was an open secret that he had been all but barred from any access to Obama or his inner circle during the campaign, Jackson yet basked in the fact that Obama had won the Democratic Party presidential nomination by virtue of the "Jackson Rules." Obama had beaten Hillary Clinton because Democratic presidential convention delegates were distributed by proportion of the primary vote and not according to the traditional state wide "winner-take-all" rule. Those were the primary rule changes that Jackson had negotiated after his 1988 presidential campaign. Rev. Jackson himself was clear about his impact on history. Everyone, including Jackson, worked connections to secure the best available presidential inauguration tickets. I was not necessarily comfortable with the up front "ask favors approach." I was more awestruck by the opportunities to discuss national policies and the influence I supposed we would now have as Chicagoans.

As I worked the room and spotted Duncan a second time, we resumed our conversation about his being tapped for the Department of Education Cabinet post. "You got to do this, Arne; if the President offers, you got to take it. Washington is a tough town," I continued, "and the President will need you on this." In retrospect, I really think Arne had already been asked by the President-elect and had accepted. Yet with good political instincts, he respectfully acted as if he valued my counsel. Duncan asked, "You really think I should?" "Yep," I said, "Washington is a tough town. The President is going to need people he can trust, especially with education reform." The more I thought about it, I was sure Arne was keeping what he already knew close to his vest. He had learned well in Chicago politics: "Act like you know what you don't know, and act like you don't know what you do know." I was impressed with the growth I had witnessed in Arne's political skills set. He was cordial and retained a charming humility. Working through his encounters with me and others, I heard him rephrase questions he did not intend to answer forthrightly. But I was always sure that Arne is absolutely earnest about the issue of education reform and that he is convinced that it is the central issue of our time. There is no more important short and long-term issue in our nation than improving the nation's schools for all of our children.

❊❊❊❊❊❊❊

America's future is at stake. Without the inclusion of urban children in the American Dream and massive investment in their education and human development, our nation has no future. These are the children who must lead our economic rebound and preserve our values and advance our vision. For them and us, education is the only way out of our predicament, and it is the only way to reclaim the promise of America and win the future. I have only to reflect upon my own life story to see that children of ghettos and barrios and rural towns possess all the potential to take hold of our promise and preserve our national values. What these young people lack are real opportunities to develop and grow. I am grateful that I was given opportunities early in life, even though I did not always have the capacity to fully appreciate them at the time. With the patient faith and the continuous support that all young people need to reach their potential, I was able to rise from public housing to achieve multiple academic degrees and live a productive and fulfilling life. The truth is, however, it was not just my personal perseverance and hard work that saved me, but it was also compassionate public policies and gracious personal investments of others that gave me space to mature to learn the lessons of life and the values of citizenship.

Coming of Age in a Chicago Project: Looking Out from Within

I am a product of the Great Migration of African Americans who moved from rural towns to urban cities.[10] Both of my parents were migrants from the South who settled on the west side of Chicago at the end of World War II. My father, Rev. Elijah J. Hatch, was a Baptist preacher who moved to Chicago from

Amory, Mississippi, in 1939 at the age of thirty-three. He came to Chicago in search of a church, employment, and a wife. He is listed in the 1930 U.S. census as living within the household of his mother, Anna, and cousin, Richard Pegues. Elijah had been born out of wedlock on November 17, 1906. He never had a relationship with his father, Mr. Donaldson, who had his own wife and family on the other side of the plantation in Aberdeen, Mississippi. My dad's schooling terminated in the sixth grade.

In 1939, my father's older sister Mary won the Chicago policy number racket. It was not a legal operation and was probably controlled by organized crime. With her winnings, Mary sent for her younger brother, Elijah. Upon arriving in Chicago that year, Rev. Hatch was elected pastor of the Shiloh Missionary Baptist Church, an upstart church with just seven adult members. The secular job he found was as a meatpacker for Swift and Company at the stockyards on South Halsted Street. In 1945, Rev. E. J. Hatch married and baptized Helen Holmes Jackson. Helen had moved to Chicago from Memphis, Tennessee, with her African Methodist Episcopal (AME) minister father, Rev. Marshall Jackson, and stepmother, Jennie. Helen's natural mother had died when she was two years old and her father remarried. Helen was a bright high school graduate who was fifteen years younger than Elijah. They met in Helen's father's small store under the public transportation elevated train ("L") tracks on Forty-Third Street in Bronzeville. In our family lore, as they say, the rest was history.

Once, as a young minister in my mid-thirties, I tried to scold my Aunt Mary, then in her nineties, about regularly going to horse races to gamble. She reminded me of how she had sent for my father from Mississippi with winnings from her policy number, and how my father met my mother at Rev. Marshall Jackson's train station store. "Marshall, honey, policy is the reason that you are in the world." She added, "Baby, the Father **(God)** is in everything!" That was the end of my moralizing with one who knew my personal history better than I did.

My parents were married in 1947, and my sisters—Rhoda, the twins Joyce and Joan, Anna, Jennie, and Nancy—were born in rapid succession. By 1958 I was born, the seventh child and only son. My youngest sister Josephine was born in 1964 when my father was fifty-six years old. Unusual for his time, my dad started having children in his early forties. He seemed to relish making up for lost time. Whenever someone would mistakenly refer to my youngest sister Josephine as his grandchild, my dad would recoil with mock indignation.

He would step back and say, "You better take another look at her; ain't no grand there, that's mine!" With Josephine's birth, all ten of us lived in a three-bedroom apartment in Jane Addams public housing, at 835 South Ada Street on Chicago's Near West Side.

Chicago's Jane Addams Project

As a child, I had almost no concept of being poor or cramped. We lived at 835 South Ada Street in a double apartment, #102-103. We had good project heat in the winter, long summer vacations of playful days, and good neighbors. A distinctive concrete "animal court" playground was at the center of the cluster of row houses and three-story walk-ups. Our project enclave was surrounded by the remnants of an old neighborhood of bungalows and two-flats called "Little Italy." The legendary First Ward Democratic Organization has always controlled the politics in the community, and elements of organized crime have always had great influence in the ward organization.

This community had been disrupted in the late 1960s as Mayor Richard J. Daley had claimed large chunks of the neighborhood for his newly built University of Illinois at Chicago.[11] That University has become a major part of the Daley legacy. It has been transformed from its original design as a concretized commuter college fifty years ago in the shadow of downtown, to an expanding residential academic institution of higher education with student and faculty housing creating the University Village neighborhood in the central city. The old Italian community leaders of the early 1960s waged a passionate fight, but Daley won and many homeowners lost their homes. There were old families who never forgave Daley.

I did not realize then that the projects we lived in were initially built for Italian immigrants. By the 1960s, the demographics of the Jane Addams Projects had shifted to almost 100 percent black. These projects were now our world. We did not venture far from our development. We were content to live, play, and go to our designated school, segregated from working-class Italian families who lived just a block away in all directions. In the fifteen years of growing up in Jane Addams, I cannot recall being personally acquainted with a single young person from the adjacent Italian community. Although they lived a few feet away, I had almost no knowledge of their cultural customs, the schools they attended, or their churches or religious practices. We patronized their businesses along Taylor Street, but that interaction was the extent of the relationship. There was little to no social integration. Our world was focused inward. We had only vague notions of what it meant to actually live near the Chicago Loop, the center of a great metropolis. The downtown buildings we glimpsed every day from our projects seemed worlds away.

My mother Helen was a well-read woman with literary tastes that spanned from Charles Dickens to Ernest Hemingway and Edgar Allen Poe. Her high school education gave her a great appreciation and love for all things classical. The bookcase was in the living room. She read stories to us from classical works, and she saved money to take us on family outings to Disney movies, the museums, and other cultural attractions. What substantially changed the trajectory of my life was my mother's wise investment in a set of World Book encyclopedias, complete with the World Book's annual Year in Review. I remember spending hours upon hours engrossed in these books. It was in these books I first learned of a place called Soweto in South Africa. I read about the new republic of Ghana, and the ancient nation of Ethiopia. I read about politics, geography, and science. It was as if the whole world was opened to me. In those days, these books were the equivalent to having a computer and Internet in the home today. My mother had actually bought the set of encyclopedias one or two at a time, using a layaway payment system. It is all testimony to my mother's foresight and the southern black traditions that place high value on education. Helen was also particularly intentional about building the self-esteem of her children, I suspect because all of us tended to inherit her dark-skinned complexion. When someone called us "black" as a put-down, we were taught to say, "The blacker the berry, the sweeter the juice." We were taught to make up in character what we lacked in resources and social standing.

In retrospect, I have a deep appreciation for my mother's skilled parenting and the ways she built strong and positive self-image in her children. We were fortified early on that we had great worth in spite of the color caste system that operated outside and inside the black community. As I learned about politics, geography, and science from the World Book Encyclopedia, and learned from the cultural excursions with my mother, I would have no inkling that my days with her were numbered. Yet, in a few short years, early in my childhood, it would be my mother who was the first to pass away.

My mother died suddenly of a massive heart attack during the great Chicago snowstorm of 1967, just two years after giving birth to my youngest sister, Josephine. In late January, Chicago experienced a twenty-three inch snowfall within twenty-four hours. As the city had been brought to a standstill, my mother passed out coughing in the washroom during the wee morning hours on January 28th. Mounds of freshly fallen snow prevented the fire department ambulance from being able to get down our side street on Ada. I was told that the first responders and my dad and neighbors had to carry the stretcher through the snow down Ada Street to Taylor Street. By the time I woke up it was all over. I had slept through whatever commotion there had been. I awoke to the wailing cries of my thirteen-year old sister, Nancy, jumping up and down, screaming, "Momma's gone, Momma's gone!" I opened my eyes to a world that was quite different than the world I had fallen asleep in. "What's wrong with Nancy?" I thought. There was something about the look on everybody's face that conveyed to me that something had gone terribly wrong. I thought about what Nancy was saying while the others stood in silence with blank looks. Slowly, it began to sink in: "Momma's gone?" Even though I was a child, I remember starting to process that the "gone" my sister was screaming about meant finality. My mother was gone for good.

Strange thing was, as soon as I contemplated the finality of my mother's death, I immediately thought about what had happened the night before. Before going to sleep, there was some disappointment on my part about being overruled on what television program we would watch on our one small black-and-white set in the living room. I slept on the living room couch, so when my mom or someone else wanted to watch television at night I was forced to watch as well. I remember wanting to watch a Western (I always wanted to watch Westerns), but my mom insisted upon watching a symphony performance on the local Public Broadcasting Station (PBS) station. I remember pouting some, but I was much too young and disciplined to verbalize disappointment. The next day, in my grief, I was consoled by the realization that I did not get my way. I was glad that my mother got to see the program she wanted to see. I would have felt guilty otherwise. Just a month-and-a-half shy of my ninth birthday, I began to feel a deep sense of obligation to honor my mother with the rest of my life. Young and motherless, I was filled with a sense of unique purpose and left with the legacy of a mother whose bright mind endured the fate of a brief life of forty-seven plus years lived out in early marriage, eight pregnancies, a clerical job with the Internal Revenue Service (IRS), church duties, and a project apartment. I was pretty clear that she had given up much of her own life to be a mother and a minister's wife. Given her intellect, she had to have forgone her own ambitions for this life. Dying with a two-year-old meant that her life had come full circle.

Helen's own mother passed when she was just two-years-old as well. I still had my dad and older sisters, so we did what families do. We went on and worked together to fill in the gaps. After the funeral our routines returned, and I went back to third grade. I remember the teacher scolding me the first week: "Don't think you can cut up just because your momma died." Without my mother, childhood seemed to go fast.

Raised in Church and Being Kept Out of the Streets

My mother's death left my father at age sixty-one with five minors and three daughters in their early twenties. My father would never remarry. His life revolved around pastoring Shiloh Missionary Baptist Church. The congregation had grown to about two hundred fifty poor southern migrants who settled on Chicago's West Side. Most of the church consisted of several extended families who had come from small towns in Mississippi, Arkansas, and Tennessee. The Varnados, the Sanders, the Finners, and the Haleys; all had stories of their northern trek to a promised land of opportunity. Over time the children of the families married and intermarried and drew other families into the fold. That was how the congregation grew, slowly and steadily over decades.

The old, red brick church structure in Chicago's East Garfield Park community, at 3162 West Monroe, resembled a small, country church building in the heart of the city. The congregation purchased the building in 1953 for $25,000. The average adult member paid about two dollars a week in dues. My dad had served the congregation as pastor since 1939, and purchasing this building that seated about 175 people was the fulfillment of a vision for him. The families of Shiloh were an extension of my world. For members of the congregation, family life revolved around the Sunday church services. Even time itself was measured by Sundays. Special programs were held on specific Sundays of the month, and it made each Sunday a sort of day-long retreat. The first Sunday of the month was the longest Sunday of the month. Sunday School began at 9:00 a.m., and a three-hour "morning service" followed at 11:00 a.m.

We had five choirs: a children's choir; youth choir; an inspirational young adult choir; an older adult gospel choir; and an elderly group of a cappella singers who sang old American shape-note hymns. Every choir would sing every Sunday, and there was always a joyous competition as we looked each week to see which choir the Spirit would use to lead the congregation into a dancing and shouting display of spiritual ecstasy. My dad would preach in the old African

American sing-song "whooping" style, a biblical, dramatic storytelling custom that drew the congregation into a frenzy of call-and-response. The preacher did not simply recite the passages, but the expectation was that the preacher would act it out. It is an unforgettable drama. The people literally would help the preacher get the message out. It is really a glorious experience that climaxes in shouting, rejoicing, and dancing. "Getting happy" or overcome with emotion in the Spirit is the sign that God has visited us and favored us with His divine presence. Typically, after morning worship, a potluck meal attended by all church members was served in the lower dining hall. Soul food was always the order of the day. The dining together melded all the families together. It also meant that folk outside of the main family clans were grafted into the church fellowship through this weekly free meal; that everyone was welcomed to eat was an inviolable community norm.

After dinner there was always some sort of scheduled 3:30 p.m. program, anniversary, or engagement at a visiting church that almost never began on time. We lived in the city, but our culture was still rural. Sunday was not a day for hurrying. After the afternoon service, Baptist Training Union (BTU) was at 6:00 p.m. The training program had a different purpose than the early Sunday School Bible Study format. The BTU drilled participants in Bible scripture memorization, held training for holding offices in church organizations, and emphasized learning church procedures and etiquette. First Sundays of the month also meant a 7:30 p.m. testifying and Communion service. Sunday, and especially first Sundays, could be a very long day! In addition, several weeks out of the year, we would have weeklong anniversary or revival services on weekday evenings. As a child with no other basis of comparison, it all seemed like a natural course. Our most meaningful relationships were within the congregation. When we described ourselves as being "raised in the church," we almost meant that literally.

Church was designed to fill our time and keep us out of the world, away from Chicago's street life, a deadly urban culture that sapped the spirit and life out of its victims. Church was literally a sanctuary from the clear and present danger of the city. Some young people drifted out into the world. For migrant families and the first-generation urbane, church life was designed to fill the time of people so they had little time to be caught up in the streets. I was Rev E. J. Hatch's only son, and I idolized my father and his stature in the church world. Being my father's only son gave me a definite identity and place of being. My family, our church, the projects, and our local school, Jacob A. Riis Public

School, were my world. Because my life was full, it was not the Chicago street life that captured my imagination; rather, it was the encyclopedias at home and television news that began to open my mind to the struggle taking place in a wider world. The first major public figure to fully capture my attention was the Baptist preacher from the South, Dr. Martin Luther King. I would later learn how King had come north to Chicago as a community organizer and activist, residing briefly on Chicago's West Side.

As a child, I remember a poster in the small vestibule of our church advertising a Chicago King-led rally at Soldier Field. The year had to have been 1966. That was the year Dr. King launched a Chicago open housing campaign to nationalize the civil rights movement to address the discrimination and institutional racism in the North. It was this latter part of his work that transformed him from a southern regional civil rights activist to a national leader. Chicago would be emblematic of stifling urban decay. The Southern Christian Leadership Conference Chicago open housing campaign exposed the fault lines of the American promise in the North. Daley's Chicago would test King and eventually frustrate and disappoint him. I was too young to understand that King had actually lived briefly on the West Side in Lawndale at 1550 South Hamlin. He would find the West Side ghettos so disconnected from Chicago's power dynamics that its people would have the least to lose in challenging the Daley Machine.[12] As it was, I would learn much later that much of the community organizing for King's Chicago campaign for open housing was concentrated in the communities near Jane Addams and near Shiloh, my dad's church. King was not welcome in many of Chicago's black churches and communities in 1966. I don't remember my dad taking a role in any of the organizing, although it was all around us. I do remember hearing one older church sister remarking, while riding in my dad's car, that King should leave town because everywhere he goes "he causes trouble."

The Assassination of King: "Shoot to Kill" in Chicago

In April of 1968, with the spring assassination of Dr. King, I remember the somber silence in our project apartment as my father wept during the broadcast of the martyr's funeral service. At ten, I was impacted by King's "mountaintop" prophetic speech delivered at Mason Temple Church of God in Christ the night before he was killed in Memphis. The whole week after the assassination had been tense in our community. The Chicago version of the riots surrounding King's death occurred mostly on the West Side, in the two particularly desperate communities he had worked in diligently in his 1966 open housing campaign. The Near West Side community we lived in near Jane Addams on Roosevelt Road erupted in flames, fueled by residents from the cluster of public housing projects known as ABLA (Addams, Brooks, Loomis, Arthington). The businesses on Roosevelt, mostly owned by nonresident entrepreneurs, were burned to the ground, while just three blocks to the north on Taylor Street, Italian resident businesses were untouched. The other riot area was thirty-two blocks northwest on Madison Street at Kedzie Street, one-half block from my father's church in East Garfield Park. National Guard troops in military vehicles with bayoneted rifles patrolled the streets to restore order.

In the midst of the riots, Mayor Richard J. Daley had issued a "shoot-to-kill" order aimed at individuals police suspected as arsonists.[13] Daley had great difficulty admitting that blacks in Chicago had not been sufficiently pacified. With incredulity and anger, Daley took license to judge, convict, and order the execution of arsonists and rioters. He could not possibly appreciate that the West Side black communities most isolated from his regime and the most exploited by the power dynamic were primed to respond to King's assassination with profound grief and violent rebellion. The isolation from economic and political power that had made West Side communities ripe for organizing by King's Chicago social justice campaign, also caused people from the West Side to feel more deeply the pain of King's assassination. In fact, many folks in these communities had met and interacted with King personally during his 1966 Chicago campaign. King had spent much time with street gang members in the Lawndale community attempting to mentor and teach tenets of community organizing and nonviolent social change. Less than two years later, the man West-siders knew as a neighbor himself became a victim of violence, and people in the community took out their rage against the most accessible targets of their oppression. They rioted in lawless rebellion and burned the businesses of absentee owners. To this day, as the Near West Side has gentrified, the Far West Side has not recovered. From 1968 to the first decade of the new millennium, the communities surrounding Garfield Park still bear the marks of the violent response to King's murder.

Taken by the swirl of events around King's assassination, I would follow the events of 1968 with much fascination. The June 6th murder of presidential candidate U.S. Senator Robert Kennedy (D-NY) added to a sense of the world becoming unhinged. Later that summer my family took a front row seat to the nightly news of Chicago's violent hosting of the 1968 Democratic National

Convention and the nomination of Senator Hubert Humphrey. There was blood on the streets, and downtown's Grant Park was the focal point of protest. It was fascinating to see televised footage of Daley's Chicago police beating young, predominately white protesters. It was a treatment by police that black people in Chicago were accustomed to, but now the whole world saw how oppressive and monarchial the city's administration was. I, however, was more drawn to the larger political story. By then I knew we were Democrats, and Humphrey was the civil rights candidate. From my bed on the couch in the living room, I followed the November 1968 election night like a sports junkie follows a championship game. As the tallies came in from around the country in the wee hours of the morning, Republican Richard Nixon squeaked out a victory. The decade of the 1960s was coming to a close and, even in my preteens, I knew that there would never be another like it. For one locked into a world of church and a Chicago project, somehow the world seemed to come to me at the very time I contemplated going out to discover it.

Jacob A. Riis School: Lifeline to Project Kids

In elementary school I had inklings of the rapid social change around me. My passport to knowing about a rapidly changing world was the World Book Year in Review editions in our home. From the independence movements in the Third World, to the anti-apartheid protests in Soweto, to the growing civil rights movement and black militant emergence around Chicago, I began to develop a personal identity as to who I might be in the wider world. Of course I could not fully grasp that my local public elementary school, Jacob A. Riis,[14] was my lifeline to opportunity and the promise of America. Riis, at 1018 South Lytle, just one-and-a-half blocks away from our home, was where we received discipline by sturdy male educators and nurture by committed educators who prepared project children for a place in the world.

I remember an African American dean of students named Mr. Dukes who made every disciplinary encounter a terror-filled experience. By junior high school age, most boys were already as tall, or taller, than Dukes, whose disciplinary strategies were legendary and fierce. Dukes stood about 4'11". Dark-skinned and muscular, Dukes sported a small, pencil-thin mustache, bushy eyebrows, a close-cropped crew cut, and thin 1950s style tie. He carried himself like a drill sergeant. One of Dukes' favorite tactics was to stand on the shoe top toes of a wayward boy and stare him down eyeball-to-eyeball. Then he would snarl the last name of the miscreant, prefaced with the handle "Mister." Spewing tobacco-breath funk he'd say, "Mister Hatch, you want trouble, my friend? I can give you plenty of trouble." Dukes never smiled, but he often managed a smirk when he knew he had some young tough guy's heart racing. That's when he would smugly ask, as he drew even closer, "Are you okay, my friend?" The man had a serious Napoleon complex. I don't know of a single soul who ever tested Duke's bluffs. Mr. Dukes was never, ever out of character. He was always on and at the top of his game. The threat of Dukes standing on our toes kept us on our toes. Yet strangely, we somehow felt both terrorized and safe with Dukes. With Mr. Dukes as the person at the end of the disciplinary line, boys were always clear at whose office the buck stopped.

While Dukes evoked fear, the stability of the school environment allowed many other opportunities for warm and fuzzy interactions. Through the omnipresent terror of Mr. Dukes and the tenderness of other teachers and staff, we felt cared for and protected. Our education mattered to our families, faith communities, neighbors, and school officials. In my junior high school years, I spent time in band and enjoyed field trips to Chicago's vast offerings of museums and other cultural attractions. By eighth grade, I had enjoyed a trip to the Lincoln sites in Springfield, our state capital. Finally, amazingly to benefit a group of project kids, our teachers and families invested in a class bus trip to the nation's capital.

Almost forty years later, I am yet moved when I think about how the adults—our teachers and parents—followed through on the investment of an eighth grade trip to Washington, D.C. In a fairly diverse neighborhood, Jacob A. Riis Elementary School was clearly the school exclusively for black project children. Most of us had never been to the East Coast. If any of us had traveled at all, it was down to southern states for summer vacation. But I had not even taken a trip like that. The honest truth was that we were a terrible group to travel with for a long fifteen-hundred-mile round-trip bus ride. God bless our veteran teacher, Mrs. Kellogg, for her patience with us. We were so mischievous that, in one instance on the trip, we reduced her to tears. And God bless the soul of that poor, white bus driver, too. We were loud, uncouth, and had very bad manners. We had especially bad, long-bus-ride bathroom manners. Goodness! But for me, this trip was absolutely life-changing. It was testimony to the long curve of the transformation of travel and exposure. It was on this trip that I fell in love with Washington, D.C. and the nobility of the American story.

We stopped in Gettysburg, Pennsylvania, on the way home, and I became enthralled with the heroism of the Civil War. We toured the battlefield and experienced the retelling of the battle inside an exhibition theater with surround sound seating. At Gettysburg I began to process the centrality of the struggle of black Americans and the continuing universal themes of the war between the American states. There was something about the sacredness of the battlefield that moved me. For years afterward my most prized possession was a souvenir Union infantryman's hat I had purchased with the limited money I had to spend. The trip took me on journeys through space and time. My passion for politics and the quest for social justice was now melded with a love of history.

Riis was an educational outpost amid the isolation and challenges of the projects. The public school investments in my development immeasurably enhanced the quality of my life. I graduated in 1972 as the president of my class. I reveled in the charge to deliver the class farewell speech. It would be a proud day. In practicing my parting speech, I told my best friends and fellow classmates, Robert Bingham and Charles Hawkins, to watch my hand. In the last sentence of my speech, I would wave my hand like Dr. King had at the end of his 1963 "I Have a Dream" presentation. I don't have any idea of what I said that day, but I do remember going for style points with my Kingian gesture. The legend of who Dr. King had become, and the historical and global impact of his heroism and prophetic witness, had struck a chord with me. It had been four years since his death and, though I had never personally met him, I sensed that King had been in my vicinity. Isolation is not easily overcome in an inner-city environment. But I was able to embrace a unique sense of purpose and place in the world. Home, church, and school altogether made me feel that I had some unique obligation to those in and beyond my community whose sacrifices gave me reason to believe in the promise of America for my own life. While I felt blessed and too filled with a sense of destiny to be distracted by street culture, I was also discovering that the good fortunes of extraordinary opportunities that came my way in the inner-city were exceptions, not the rule.

Within four years of our eighth grade graduation, my friend Robert Bingham's brain had been destroyed by drug and chemical abuse. For the rest of his life he would be a mere shell of himself. By age twenty, my other friend, Charles Hawkins, had been killed in a fight by the hand of a Jane Addams neighbor. During our high school years, Charles had been a star quarterback for the Crane Technical High School football team. Crane was near the Henry Horner Homes Project.

Robert and Charles were unforgettable classmates of mine and great guys. Charles Hawkins had been especially good to me. He had a large family in the projects and older brothers. Charles helped defend me several times from bullies who knew I had no brothers or family members who could help me fight back. The guy had a kind heart and helped me survive a tough environment. I knew that I certainly was not better or smarter than Robert, Charles, or any of my friends. I knew I would never forget the goodness of many of the people who were perishing in the entrapments and intergenerational cycles of segregation from opportunity. I got breaks, and the older I got, I grew to appreciate the special graces that opened doors for me and gave me exposure beyond my wildest dreams. I was never, however, comfortable stepping over the bodies of friends to find paths beyond the pitfalls and limitations of the project world.

"The Club": An Oasis and an Opening to the World

Across the street from Riis school on Lytle stood the local Old Town Eisendrath Boys Club. With a gymnasium, bumper pool tables, and table tennis games, the "Club" was the after-school and summer vacation hub of activity. A boy's most prized possession was the necessary Club membership card that was needed to gain admission. One of the most respected and feared men in the community was Club Director Mr. Pete, who ran the Club with strict rules and high expectations. He seemed like a rather typical working-class white guy with black-rimmed glasses and a paunchy waistline that served as a backdrop for the wide utility belt which carried bundles of keys. Pete was in constant motion, always busy and often huffing, as he worked long hours monitoring activities and repairing equipment. The last thing a kid wanted to do was get on Mr. Pete's bad side. He had the ultimate power to do the one thing that would make a guy the most pitied soul among our peers. If Mr. Pete were to revoke a kid's Club card for misbehavior or breaking too many rules, not a soul alive wanted to be in that kid's shoes. When the offender's punishment of suspension ended and Mr. Pete let the kid back into the Club, it was a privilege he never wanted to lose again.

In the summers, the Club sponsored our local Little League baseball team, the Cubs, coached by Mr. Daniels, a Chicago policeman, who also was a surrogate father, counselor, and truant officer. No one wanted to cross Mr. Daniels either, since he had the power to remove a boy from the team (another unspeakable disaster). Thanks to Daniels, we were enrolled in two to three different summer league tournaments around the city. I settled into the position of second baseman. What I lacked in great natural ability, I tried to compensate for with grit, courage, and sportsmanship. The most important thing that won respect for an infielder was to stay in front of the ball, while the worst thing we could do was attempt to field a ground ball from the side. Staying in front of the hardball and letting it hit off the body was the manly thing to do. I prided myself on a high-pain threshold. I did not have the best natural ability, but I would never run from the ball. Showing heart was how I got a starting position on the team as a preteen. Mr. Daniels would transport the team from game to game in a worn, white-and-yellow van. We felt like a major league team, playing in different diamonds around the city and returning to our home field and our neighborhood fan base. Graciously, at the end of the season, Mr. Daniels would treat the entire team to McDonald's for a hamburger, small fries, and courtesy cup of water. The Club was another oasis that gave us discipline, structure, and exposure to a wider world beyond the projects.

I have no idea how I was selected as one of two high school sophomores to represent Illinois at the 1974 Hugh O'Brian Youth Leadership Government Seminar in Washington, D.C. O'Brian has held these seminars annually for decades to inspire new generations of young leaders to engage the nation and the world with a sense of mission and service. I remember Mr. Pete, or someone from the Club, having me write an essay expressing interest in attending the seminar. There could not have been much that was special about my application or essay. I say this because it felt more like my selection was a foregone conclusion. Someone somewhere had decided that a West Side kid from the projects would get this grand opportunity to attend this ten-day seminar in the nation's capital. What a break! It would be my first time on an airplane. The first lesson of air travel I learned is one I have never forgotten: pack lightly. I over-packed and paid a burdensome price as I dragged luggage through the airport. That I was overly excited is an understatement. Counting my eighth grade class trip just two years before, this unexpected and anonymous benevolence had me back in D.C. again.

It was a whirlwind week-and-a-half. We toured every major federal government facility, including the White House. We had lunch with Lady Bird Johnson and heard lectures by black four-star General "Chappie" James and insurance tycoon W. Clement Stone. I visited Capitol Hill and met with Illinois U.S. Senator Charles Percy and West Side representative Congresswoman Cardiss Collins (D-IL). I even met with the first black U.S. senator since the Reconstruction, Edward Brooke (R-MA). We had dinner at the Iranian Embassy one night and were entertained in a stunning mirrored-and-full-floored Persian rug reception room. O'Brian used his personal influence to obtain access for us with every conceivable department of government and available political figure in Washington. It was indeed a big deal, bigger than I could have imagined. As the week wore on, I looked for opportunities to make some sort of big splash for the folks back home.

Chicago Sun-Times columnist Jack Anderson did an article on a question-and-answer session we had with a group of U.S. senators. I knew what the stakes were, so I raised my hand to ask Senator Percy a question that I calculated would make me look smart and land me in Anderson's column for our local paper. "Senator, do you support increased funding to expand our local Regional Transit Authority (RTA)? It would help inner-city people access jobs in the suburbs," I asserted. I recall that the Senator answered affirmatively. But what really gave me joy was the fact that my publicity-seeking strategy had worked. The question I asked landed me in Anderson's column: I had made the paper! I was beginning to think that maybe I was as smart as teachers at Riis told me I was, and that maybe I was as special as folks in the church made me feel. I had distinguished myself among young people from all over the country and from around the world.

I made friends that week with young people from diverse backgrounds. My closest roommates were Brent Ray Childress from Oklahoma and Hussein, an Iranian citizen when the country was an American ally under the Shah of Iran. As the seminar came to a close, we were all well aware that it was unlikely that our lives would ever intersect again. We also knew that our views of the world had expanded, and that the relationships that we had enjoyed meant that the world itself would seem smaller and more personal. The last social gathering before we left was rather tearful. The atmosphere was more profound than the good-byes shared at the end of a summer camp session I had experienced earlier in life. We had all spent a lot of meaningful time together in the centers of national and global power. We were representatives of countless others in our generation. The closing party was a bitter-sweet experience that was more sweet than bitter. The last song the disc jockey played was Gladys Knight's, "You're the Best Thing that Ever Happened to Me." There were tears of amazement and joy and one last dance. There was a sense that we had been honored with a unique privilege, and our charge was to go back to our respective worlds and help change the world. It would seem a tall order, except in reflection, it is clearer that the change we influence does not have to be earthshaking to have local and global impact. Change begins with change agents and creation of the critical mass. Over the years, as news reports of the Iranian Revolution and other political instability in the Middle East unfolded before the world, I have wondered what became of my friend, Hussein. In life before Internet social networking, we assumed that these kinds of experiences and relationships would become distant memories in still photographs.

For over fifty years, Hugh O'Brian, the 1950s star of the "Wyatt Earp" television series, has brought young people together, investing in the future and exposing youth to the larger issues of the world. His youth leadership development work (HOBY) has now become a global project with over three hundred seventy-five thousand alumni from all over the world. I am proud to have benefited from this foundation in the early years. O'Brian has faithfully served in this life mission, and I am certain the world is a better place for this investment in human capital. All that Mr. O'Brian has requested is that seminar participants write him annually. It took me thirty-seven years, but I e-mailed my first letter in 2011. I deeply regret that I had not done so before then. Though I knew and was appreciative of my good fortune, learning to maintain networks and fully appreciate the breaks that came my way are lessons I learned better much later life. In 1974 after attending the youth leadership government seminar, I returned to my neighborhood with a much more profound sense of my place in the world. Thanks to Mr. Pete, the Club, and Mr. O'Brian, my reflection on our national story had greater depth. Special investment and privilege have a way of intensifying the call to serve and creating a passionate sense of obligation.

Dunbar Vocational High School: Moving Up and Out

Providentially, the brief time I played clarinet in the Jacob A. Riis Elementary School band I was impacted by two student musicians who would graduate to high school a year before I did. When I graduated in 1972, I followed Rodney Battles and Barry Mitchell to Paul Laurence Dunbar Vocational High School on the Near South Side of Chicago. The namesake of the famed late nineteenth and twentieth century African American poet, the school was located on Dr. Martin Luther King Jr. Drive in the old historic "Black Belt." This was one of Chicago's oldest black communities.

Dunbar attracted nearby project kids, as well as students from middle-class black communities farther south. At Riis, Rodney had played trombone and Barry had played trumpet. They had gone to Dunbar because they were serious about their instruments and the school had a legendary marching band.

I went to Dunbar because I was following my friends, the school was out of the neighborhood, and I passed the admissions test. I never did play in the high school band. Our neighborhood school, Richard T. Crane High School, was about a mile-and-a-half northwest of Jane Addams, and I would have had to the cross gang territory near Henry Horner Homes. That was the school Charles Hawkins and most of my friends from our neighborhood attended. Dunbar seemed more upscale, as it was selective and safe. Although Dunbar was vocational and not particularly suited to my liberal arts interests, going there gave me the opportunity to traverse the city daily. My decision to attend Dunbar was another life-changing and life-saving break. In high school I would encounter another set of disciplinarians who would further nurture and challenge me with high expectations.

By the end of my sophomore year, in 1974, my father and older sister Joyce purchased a single-family home in the Austin neighborhood on Chicago's Far West Side. African Americans who had migrated from the South in the 1940s and 1950s were moving farther west. My family's move to 4909 West Huron was part of a blockbusting dynamic as Austin and other West Side neighborhoods changed rapidly. In a decade, Austin changed from white working-class to black working-class. Real estate sales companies made handsome commissions, and mortgage companies profited from front-loaded loan fees. Whites moved to western suburbs, and blacks moved into racially re-concentrated communities of isolation. The processes of economic redlining and segregation from opportunity would turn this once-proud neighborhood into a new ghetto. On the Far West Side, seventy percent of the employment base evaporated in fifteen years: General Electric, Sears and Roebuck, Aldens, Brach's Candies, and others folded.[15] While businesses and banks moved out, crack cocaine and revolving incarceration moved in.

However, in 1974, Austin was still the "promised land" for us. We had moved from the projects into a nine-room, two-bathroom house that cost us $17,000 with a monthly mortgage payment of $217. Our West Huron Street home would be the only house my father would ever own in his entire lifetime. Compared to Jane Addams, we had finally arrived (considering square footage and the vast space difference between the two addresses). At one time in Jane Addams, all ten members of the Hatch family lived in a three-bedroom apartment, and I slept on the couch in the living room. The move to Austin at age sixteen meant that I would sleep on a bed and have my own room for the first time in my life. It also meant I traveled almost the entire breadth of the city

41

on a daily basis. I could wander through the Palmer House Hotel at the midway point downtown and walk State Street or Michigan Avenue when I transferred from bus to train. In my choice of a high school and now my family's move to Austin, I had been further delivered from the limitations of a neighborhood.

I did not have an interest in a shop or trades major, so in my junior year at Dunbar, I chose "distributive education" as my major. I don't know if I ever knew what distributive education meant, but I chose it mainly because the program meant the school would arrange a work-study job in the dietary department at the nearby Michael Reese Hospital. We worked in the kitchen, serving dinner and doing cleanup for the third shift. We passed trays, pulled carts, ran dish machines, washed pots, and professionally mopped floors. We made good money, and working kept me out of shop classes (instinctively I knew I would never be good at mechanics or the building trades). My first and second shift weekend workdays also gave opportunities to opt out of marathon Sunday church services. The rotating off-days of hospital work gave me a schedule that liberated me from regular church attendance my last two years of high school. I found that freedom from church also gave me the ability to party at disco clubs on weekends with a clear conscience. In working thirty or so hours a week and on most weekends, I was able to buy my first car from a coworker of my sister's for a grand total of $265. My car insurance was twice that every six months. By the end of my junior year, I was driving my beat-up 1969 AMC Rambler to school every day. Driving my car was a special adventure. First, the driver's door didn't open, so I entered from the passenger side. It made going on dates interesting; I couldn't practice much chivalry. Next, after a while, my defrosters stopped working, so I had to drive and wipe the windshield on rainy, humid days. Finally, my taillights failed, so I had external lights mounted on the rear trunk. Still, as raggedy as my car was, driving to school put me in the elite at Dunbar. Any car in any driving condition brought high social status.

I loved school, even though my work and social life were great distractions from academic performance. By my senior year, I went to school every day because it was a fun place to be. Pep rallies, cheerleaders, marching bands, the Wendell Phillips High School rivalry, school dances, drama club, and loaded weekend outings: all of that meant that the action was in school. The few folks I knew who had dropped out of school at Dunbar were a distinct minority. I would never have imagined today's urban drop-out rates at fifty percent. For us at Dunbar, dropping out of school was for dopers or losers. And nobody I knew wanted to hang around losers. That's not to say we didn't get in trouble, because we did, and we had to face the disciplinarians. Females had to worry about Mrs. Dawson and what corner she would turn up at next. Just her presence caused girls to scamper and clear halls and washrooms. Athletic coaches and shop teachers used the carrot-and-stick technique with most guys. Since, I was in distributive education, I reported to Mr. Kaplan, who taught distributive education and was faculty advisor for my major. Kaplan sold us on getting a job. His first-period class was a joke. He read the paper, fudged the attendance, and rewarded those of us who knew how to look busy when we had an occasional class observer or visitor. I thought it all clever until I realized that old Mr. Kaplan had such low expectations of us that he'd decided to just coast to retirement.

In the early part of my senior year in late 1975, I must have been guilty of some infraction (memory fails me now) because I ended up in the Dean of Students' office. Mr. Estelle, a straight-shooting, older black guy with professorial wire glasses, summoned me from the waiting area into his office. Smugly, I took a seat in front of his desk. It felt kind of cool to be in a little trouble. I hadn't been in here before, but I knew people who had faced the dean for infractions that were much worse than whatever it was I'd been hauled in for. I was sure old Estelle had some long, drawn-out case to make as he talked me through my discipline problem. I was expecting a tedious lecture. I figured he would give me a good talking-to in order to get me back in line. But to my surprise, Mr. Estelle's spiel was short and sweet. He leveled with me and said, "Hatch, you're a smart guy, probably too smart for your own good. There are a lot of guys who think like you. As it looks, at the rate you're going, you'll probably outsmart yourself." That was it. My being-in-big-trouble trip to the dean's office was over. Mr. Estelle had two thousand students and the worst of the lot to attend to; he had very little time to coddle me. I don't know that I said anything after Estelle's brief reprimand. I was approaching eighteen years of age, and I had begun anticipating the responsibilities and higher expectations of adulthood. I think I got Estelle's point: "Don't be too smart for your own good. Don't be so smart that you miss the point. Smart is good, but insight is better." I was smart alright, without a clue or a plan. I had opportunities that I obviously did not fully appreciate or understand. Even up to that point, my life experiences suggested that I was blessed to have people who were investing resources and time in me that I really didn't deserve. The more I thought about how old Estelle handled me, I think I concluded he was the real wise guy. He got my attention with a few choice words.

Going into my last semester, my main extracurricular activity in high school was the drama club with Mrs. Cargerman, an English teacher. Acting became my little claim to fame. I was pretty good at it, and I knew it. We did not do full-length plays, just vignettes and skits for small groups, and we performed in a small room off the main lobby. One of the deficiencies of our public vocational high school was that there was no full-fledged fine arts program with an annual theater production to showcase and develop our talents. I didn't know then that I was missing so much. For me, acting was my way to attract the attention of girls (I kind of wished I had found this niche earlier). There were some very pretty girls who thought being good at drama was attractive. That was all the motivation I needed to hang out with the drama club. Mrs. Cargerman was a lot more passionate about my talent and the craft than I was. She suggested that I consider a theater major in college (at the time I would have been more interested in law, politics, or history). I of course had no idea on how to follow through with my interests and devise an action plan. In time, Mrs. Cargerman took a more personal interest in me and filled my head with thoughts that I was smart enough to look at "selective colleges" like "Harvard or Princeton." She even brought me an application for Princeton that I never completed. The fact was, I didn't know how to complete it. Dunbar was primarily a vocational school and administrators did not invest heavily in college admissions counseling. Furthermore, no one in my family or circle of friends had ever gone away to college. I knew nothing about the college admissions process, and no one I knew had a clue. My ACT score, the one time I took the test, was probably in the mid-teens. Most of my high school friends were looking for jobs in factories and trades organizations around the Chicago area related to the shop classes they had majored in. I was already working almost full-time (longer hours during holidays) in the dietary kitchen at Michael Reese Hospital. The only way I was going to go to college right away was if someone found me and took me by the hand. Then, providentially, a college recruiter from Western Illinois University came to our school in the late spring of 1976.

Recruited for Western Illinois University: Looking for the Lost

What I mostly remember is the prospect of getting out of class early that afternoon. The visit of a Mr. Rudolph V. Womack from Western Illinois University (WIU), whose apparent job and mission was to recruit students with potential from inner-city high schools, was announced over the intercom. According to the announcement, Womack was eager to meet seniors who wanted to go to college immediately after graduation. The "carrot" was that this was a one-stop opportunity. WIU was looking for students who could benefit from a sort of Head Start program for the summer. It sounded good, plus I was able to get out of a class by responding, so I went with my buddy Larry Harris, another distributive education guy. Truthfully, Mr. Womack did not look hard at any of the group who'd reported to the lunchroom for this one-stop college opportunity. Womack had obviously made the rounds in Illinois urban schools before and had developed a presentation that was abrasive and charmingly dismissive. It went something like, "Y'all don't know nothing about going to college, but I'm going to get you in. If you want to go to Western Illinois University, shut up, sign up, and don't worry about money." He was confident and mostly correct that most of us had family financial profiles that qualified us for free state tuition and federal Pell grants that would constitute a full ride. Womack's offer included starting college in the summer term to take a few lightweight courses to get our feet wet. It was beginning to sound like a sweet deal, even beyond escaping class.

My high school buddy Larry Harris still lived in the projects off Roosevelt Road with his mother and two sisters. We had grown up in the same old project neighborhood and we had started hanging out together in our last two years at Dunbar. He also worked in the kitchen with me at Michael Reese Hospital. Talking about our kitchen jobs, Larry would make fun of the white dietary uniforms we wore. He also would sarcastically recall how we learned to sing while washing pots, and how we had been trained to glide rhythmically with the mop to cover the whole floor. Larry had a wicked sense of humor about the racial subtext of the Michael Reese system. Whites and foreigners dominated the administrative and medical professions, while blacks sang with pots and danced with mops in the basement kitchen. Hearing Womack's WIU presentation, Larry said, "Man, I'm ready to go today!" I agreed. Working long days at the hospital and having no other concrete plans for my future, Womack's offer was too good to refuse.

I was excited about going away to college now that I had some guidance, hands-on support, and a definite time of departure. Opportunity had come and found me and had taken affirmative action. Within two weeks after graduation, I was enrolled in the university and was building up my confidence, thanks to a program and support system put in place by the WIU Office of Academic Services. That was the beginning of my journey through predominately white institutions. Over the years, Mr. Womack never let Larry forget that he recruited him and had to send him a paid Amtrak train ticket for his first trip from Chicago to Macomb, Illinois. Womack says when he picked Larry up from the train station in the summer of 1976, Larry had made the one hundred seventy-mile trip with his belongings in three plastic Jewel Foods' grocery bags. Larry's family, who still lived in the projects, did not even own a piece of luggage. Womack had a way of reminding all of us who'd matriculated successfully that we were rescued by his forays into the inner-city. He kept us humble.

In retrospect, it is clear that I benefited handsomely from the compassion and affirmative action of a nation still grieving and reacting to Dr. King's assassination eight years prior to my high school graduation. I have always been conscious of the fact that a large measure of the educational opportunities I was afforded were directly attributed to King's blood sacrifice. The only reason I got to go away to college was because I was recruited; the only reason I could afford college was because of public financial aid. The backdrop of all this was the spirit of the civil rights movement and King's Dream, and the project to make the promise of America real for kids like me. As much as my family loved me, they were limited by their own experiences and limited resources. Through a public system of education and community institutions, I had access to adults who guided, chastened, and inspired me. By 1976, with very little foresight of my own, I found myself in a government land-grant, state-sponsored institution of higher education. I was excited, although I found my first year quite unremarkable and not overly challenging.

At Western I learned reflectively and quite thoroughly that intelligence was pretty evenly distributed among racial groups in the human family. Even more than extraordinary intelligence, I observed that what mattered most for success in college was opportunity, exposure, and hard work. These were the essential things, in that order. I had naturally intelligent friends from the neighborhood, immersed in Chicago street culture, who were much smarter than kids I sat with in classes in Macomb at WIU. What those inner-city kids lacked was real opportunity and exposure to the wider world. When we moved to the Far West Side in Austin, I made friends with Steve Broxton and Sylvester "Moses" Bolds. These very smart and street-savvy, good-natured guys introduced me to drinking cheap wine, neighborhood disco lounges, and party hopping. Sadly, they had been exposed to very little outside of the neighborhood. They attended neighborhood schools, dated neighborhood girls, and frequented neighborhood bars.

After high school, I came home from college, hung out a little bit, and vanished for long stretches. Communicating new developments and knowledge

I had picked up over the semester to my West Side buddies was always challenging. I remember telling Sylvester Bolds in 1978 that I had pledged the Phi Beta Sigma Fraternity (a predominately black national fraternity) at Western. I explained that frats functioned sort of like street organizations, but for college guys. I added that the most important value of the group was the way we used step show performances to attract girls. Sylvester did his best to process my report without any understanding of Greek letters or fraternities. He blurted out with excitement, "You guys are the Far Better Men, right?" He had translated the Greek letters "Phi Beta" to "far better." That sounded good to me; so good, in fact, that I took Sylvester's translation back to Western and included it in a new step show routine. I found new ways of processing my own identity by becoming a translator between the urban and the academic. I felt I lived in a special place between two worlds and had a unique capacity to interpret each world to the other.[16]

What my friends at home would miss, and what I would pick up in my undergraduate and graduate school years, was critical access to relationships with people from the dominant society. I discovered a truth that cannot be overstated. As a general rule, in order for a black person in America to overcome the barriers of race, that person must have a nonblack sponsor or mentor who vouches for their exceptionalism to the dominant society. My opportunities at Western allowed me the graces to remediate and overcome the handicaps acquired in under-resourced inner-city schools. Two of my first three quarters at Western I made the Dean's List for achieving quarter honors. I spent the first semester of my sophomore year at Georgetown University, earning a 2.8 quality point average. Returning to Western and completing my degree program in political science and history, I graduated in the spring of 1980 with semester honors. Going away to school gave me space to develop greater independence and to grow intellectually. I traversed between the worlds of academia, the inner-city, and my father's church of southern migrants. In the larger world, I sensed retreat from the momentum of the civil rights movement in the years since King's death. The Supreme Court in 1978 sent down a game-changing ruling in the Bakke case that defined reverse discrimination against whites.[17] I discerned that I had gained entrance through a ten-year window of opportunity from King's assassination that was closing for others as soon as I had walked through. That part of my life journey was clear to me. I was grateful and sad at the same time.

The Ronald Reagan-led conservative surge in American politics recoiled from the kinds of social and human capital investments and affirmative actions that had found me and opened windows to the world. By the end of undergrad in 1980, it was clear that the America that I had entered into college with in 1976 had undergone regressive transformation. With the defeat of President Jimmy Carter and the election of Ronald Reagan, the modern reconstruction of black America was over. The nation had suffered a severe case of "Negro fatigue." Moving forward, the national government would officially disengage the great Project of righting the wrongs and repairing the damage of America's original sin. The business of America would again be business, not some idealistic movement to perfect the Union. Deregulation and union-busting would be the new order of the day. Greed would be good, and unfettered laissez-faire capitalism would resume. The prevailing economic and social ethos would again be the survival of the fittest. Intellectuals in elite academic institutions would provide the philosophical and intellectual basis for ethical and moral accommodations to high rates of poverty and wide wealth disparities. President Reagan signed the Martin Luther King Jr. Holiday Bill in 1983, and that further facilitated misappropriation of Dr. King's core messages and vision of beloved community. Reactionaries declared fulfillment of the goals of the civil rights movement and the effective end of the relevance of race and racism. I could not possibly have grasped how profoundly these changing moods in the nation would affect the dialogue and direction of the country years hence. Looking to go back to the East Coast, back to a Reagan-led Washington now moving in full retreat from dealing with poverty and race, I would indeed encounter a different world than the one I had come from.

Georgetown Graduate School: Thinking in Two Worlds

After graduation from Western Illinois University, I gained admittance to the Georgetown University graduate school's department of government. It was the first time in my life that I actually had definite academic plans. My goals were to finish a Master of Arts program at the graduate school as preparation for Georgetown Law School. At Georgetown I picked up important mentors in what was for me an alien environment. I had met Professor Roland Flint in the fall of 1977 in a sophomore English class. He became Georgetown's longest-serving English professor, and he became an invaluable critic of my work ethic as he pointed out my inattention to detail. He once pronounced my paper on a Flannery O'Connor short story both brilliant and careless. I can still see his red markings all over the paper. Flint became the poet laureate of Maryland, as his specialty was writing brilliant and white-folk soulful poetry.[18] He featured my poetry readings in a campus wide event in the fall of 1977. It was a high honor, allowing me to get some exposure among the student body and school faculty. Over the years we became good friends, and years later, my family stayed at his home when my children were small. He became their favorite "Uncle Professor" Flint. Upon his passing in the fall of 2000, at his personal request, I delivered a eulogy at his memorial service in February of 2001 at Georgetown's Dahlgren Chapel.

Also impactful for me at Georgetown was the Vice President for Minority Affairs, Samuel Harvey. Harvey was a constant resource, advocate, and ombudsman for me and other students of color. On a campus where many of the students were privileged through legacy, political, or diplomatic connections, Sam Harvey was the poor, black kids' version of a well-connected father and friend in high places. For me, Harvey became another reflection of grace. I had gained admittance to the Georgetown University graduate school in the spring of 1980 on a letter of reconsideration. My first application had been rejected. I had thought I could get right into Georgetown's grad school because I had previously attended the undergraduate school in my sophomore year and had graduated from Western with honors. When rejected, I found the humility to phone Professor Flint looking for a favor. Flint advised me to call Sam Harvey. "Do you remember me?" I asked Harvey over the phone. "How could I forget a guy with the name Marshall Elijah Hatch," he answered. Harvey had indeed retained fond memories of me in my sophomore semester and my socially conscious poetry. In fact, he said he wanted to use this instance to "teach me a lesson." I had tried to apply without checking in with him first. His lesson: "You always use your friends." I wrote a letter of reconsideration, and within a couple of weeks I had a letter of admission to the Georgetown graduate school for the fall of 1980. I thought deeply about Mr. Harvey's lesson: relationships matter. Harvey's point helped me to understand how the world outside my world worked in the valuing of relationships. It is instructive to note the kinds of investments schools like Georgetown made to help even the playing field for students with disadvantaged backgrounds. Sam Harvey's position in the school gave him tremendous leverage to advocate and support us. Harvey's position and mission in the school's structure helped Georgetown's black student body navigate through cultural shocks and university power dynamics.

I cannot overstate the intentionality of the investments mainstream academic institutions made to welcome and accommodate black American students in the years after Dr. King's assassination. At that time, schools, Georgetown included, had intentionally created space for black students to gather on campus. The place went by many names, but on most white campuses the space was essentially a "black house," a place where black students could go to for refuge from the stresses of being a minority. In that space, the whitest school felt like an HBCU (Historically Black College and University) for black students. This space was a standard "demand" on campuses nationwide through the student movements and campus agitation that occurred during the Civil Rights Era. The existence of a "black house," "black studies," and black vice presidents on major campuses were the living legacies of the student protest movements of the 1960s and early 1970s. These investments were won in hard-fought battles, campus by campus. Sadly, these black student hang-out places rarely exist in these schools now. Schools now have "diversity" centers and "inclusion" officers that serve all groups defined as minorities.

Times have changed. I don't know, however, that the unique needs of a critical mass of black disadvantaged students from the inner-city attending predominately white campuses have changed with the times. In 2012, college enrollment and matriculation by lower-class blacks are down all over the nation. If the retraction of an intentional welcoming strategy for promising black students from the urban centers is not a major cause of the declining enrollment and matriculation, the retraction is certainly not helpful. I am grateful for the support system that was in place for me in the late 1970s and early 1980s. Years after I had completed the graduate program, Professor Flint remarked that he was amazed that I had succeeded in navigating the graduate program and the conservative worldview of the majority of the professors in the department of government at Georgetown. Flint did not express his concern until after I was almost done with the bulk of the program. The truth is, it was not easy, and the environment was not hospitable. In fact, I found it necessary to have and utilize both academic skills and street savvy.

My first graduate school paper in my American political theory class contrasted the political thought of Martin Luther King and Malcolm X. I thought it wise to rework a paper I had done in undergrad that had gotten a superb grade. I knew the subject matter, had new insights, and was passionate about the ongoing King-Malcolm X dialogue on the meaning of America and the influences of black political thought in defining that meaning. I received a low "C" on the paper. I knew then that I needed to improve my understanding of what was expected in grad school in general and this class in particular. I asked and received an emergency consultation with the course instructor, Dr. Victor Ferkiss.

At the outset of the meeting I was informed that the main problem with the paper was that the subject matter was not "relevant or appealing." I was stunned by the bluntness of the comments. I also quickly picked up on the fact that this was not going to be a long meeting with free-flowing exchange. Across the desk Ferkiss was classically professorial, wearing a black three-piece suit and sporting a gray-and-black goatee. Clearly agitated by my presence and avoiding eye contact, Ferkiss rustled papers into his briefcase and added, "History is about the winners." That was that. It was an interesting retort, I thought. The statement was dismissive and instructive. Clearly, I was at Georgetown and not at Howard.

In Ferkiss' class, we had excellent texts on the development of the American notions of egalitarianism and Manifest Destiny from the founding of the Republic through the rise of contemporary conservative intellectuals. In the professor's opinion, the figures I had chosen to write about were not in the mainstream of the ongoing conversation between the American "winners." What I learned from Ferkiss' response was to develop the capacity to write and frame things in ways that would be sanctioned by the dominant culture. The prescribed "winners" had a dialogue across generations that defined what was relevant. The "winners" of a dominant culture defined relevancy as a world at which they remained the center stage. In their final analysis, the "winners" have the prerogative to determine that what really matters is their interests and what holds their interests.

Once I got Ferkiss' point, it allowed me to process how I would move through the program successfully. The point was that I could think critically only within the predetermined parameters and, in the end, give back to the professor terminology and thought processes sanctioned by the academic community. Creativity can only be accommodated within institutional and discipline parameters. This would be the first graduate school survival skill I learned. Old Ferkiss helped me resolve that the best approach to this graduate program was to strive to make grades, not waves. I was financing graduate school with student loans that I would later have to repay. I was a full-time student, but I had other things on my mind. The graduate school Department of Government context was only one of several worlds I had to navigate and process.

As a graduate student, I walked the streets of Washington to Georgetown from Columbia Circle several days a week. My one-room basement apartment

51

at 3301 Brown Street, NW, was a sanctuary for work and reflection. Three days a week I worked at Cardozo School near Howard University. I loved the history and beauty of the Georgetown campus, but I had great difficulty relating socially and making friends. I didn't exactly fit in around students whose families had substantial resources or who were second and third-generation Hoyas. My family had only recently moved out of public housing, and I was not particularly skilled at the social graces of the affluent. I attended a few parties with international students. Some of them had similar stories of working hard, so I found some commonality with students who saw Georgetown as an escape from a life of poverty. Living off campus, I felt more at home in my multicultural working-class neighborhood than in Georgetown. Columbia Circle was a mix of blacks, some whites, Hispanics, and blacks from the Caribbean. It was gritty, and the people were scrappy. On the weekends, neighborhood bars were enlivened with live band music and exotic dancers. Washington in those days had a way of feeling sleepy and wide open at the same time. I was over twenty-one and free to indulge in everything my little neighborhood had to offer. I made a few cross-cultural friendships that centered around weekend bar hopping, and I maintained one steady relationship with an older lady friend.

Although I was not piously religious, I had begun attending Sunday services at Canaan Baptist Church, a half block from where I lived. Though I had wandered far from viewing church attendance as central in my life, black church culture and my relationship to my father's congregation still shaped a large part of my personal identity. I always said my prayers every night. The worship at Canaan seemed to feed my soul, and the Sunday service gave me a taste of home. The minister, Pastor Carter, seemed genuine. His message was basic and biblical, just as I needed and liked it. I loved the way the choir sang and swayed around the altar during collection time. I liked being able to enjoy church service without the pressures of being in the pastor's family. I normally sat high in the church balcony, and never sought to meet anyone after service. When church was over, I simply headed home to enjoy sports programs on television and Sunday afternoon beers.

During the summers, I returned to my summer job driving Chicago Transit Authority (CTA) bus routes through the inner-city on the night shift. I was part of a cadre of college students who had been trained to operate the bus, and who could work the summer months while regular drivers vacationed. The pay was excellent. The job was adventurous and often dangerous. The three summers I drove the bus, 1979-81, gave me an interesting vantage point from which to process higher education. Although I had access to academia and famed lecturers at Georgetown, I never felt far removed from the struggle of working and poor people. I knew that the people on Chicago's West Side had the same challenges and aspirations as those who lived near my Columbia Circle apartment. Their struggle, our struggle, to make real the promise of America, was the one I was sure I could never abandon.

What I did not fully comprehend when I came home to Chicago from Washington was that I was in the midst of a coming-of-age season of life. My worldliness and personal reflections on God's amazing graces; attending school semesters in the nation's capital and driving the bus in Chicago; relating struggles of the people from Washington's Columbia Circle to Chicago's West Side; the physical distance from my family; and my father's deteriorating health—all these were one contrasting and interconnected reality that interacted in the processes of my developing a more mature sense of personal purpose.

Coming Home with a Calling: Following the Voice

By the summer of 1981, my father had battled prostate cancer for over five years. He passed away at age seventy-four on July 28th after having served as pastor of Shiloh Church for forty-two years. My father's death was the one thing I feared more than anything. I loved my dad more than anything in the world. I think that because he was so much older than me, we had difficulty relating personally. From my junior high school years forward, I did not have daily adult supervision. My father had a habit, from our days in the projects, of leaving home early in the morning and coming back very late at night. He would do his pastoral care work and be available to the members of the church from his office at Shiloh. He and older deacons hung out at the church on a daily basis. I never knew him to spend daytime hours at home until he became ill late in life. I don't think we ever had a full-fledged father-and-son conversation. My sisters and I received our instruction from his pulpit sermons like other members of the church. That was his way, but I revered him. I always thought he had done well as a father, given the very limited relationship he had with his own father, and given his own personal limitations. I lived for his affirmation. I could hardly fathom my life without Daddy. Losing my mother early in life felt like abandonment. My father had been my emotional crutch, and he was now gone. I spoke at his funeral about how every generation must chart its own course. Within a month after his death, I finished my summer bus-driving job and headed back to Washington.

In late August of 1980, I took the shuttle bus from downtown Chicago to O'Hare Airport. I flew into Washington National and caught a cab to my basement apartment. When I entered my place, I dropped my bags and closed the door behind me. It was the first time I would confront my new reality in the place that I had spent so much time alone in my thoughts and saying my prayers. I felt like an orphan, and abandoned again I sobbed, "Oh Lord, now my father's gone; who am I going to lean on now?" Strangely, I heard a voice from within answer my question with a question: "Who do you think he was leaning on?" I really did not expect so direct an answer. I was certain this question that answered my question was a voice from within that was not my voice. The voice within was so clear that it could not have been more clear had it actually been audible. It was not my ear that the voice had spoken to. It was my heart. I knew that the point was that my father, who did not even know his natural father, had come from a Mississippi plantation to a Chicago pulpit because of his faith in God. Of course, Daddy leaned on God. I processed the voice's question and obvious answer as assurance that the same God who my dad had depended upon could help me, too. That moment in time, crossing the threshold of my apartment, was an epiphany. It was not the first time I had heard the voice. In fact, I had felt that I could sense the presence of divine providence from my early baptism as a child, especially after my mother's death. Now, however, I felt a greater sense of urgency to follow the lead and trust the direction of the voice from within.

As the days and weeks of the semester wore on, my life felt open-ended. I was still in bereavement, but I was not despairing. I was praying more, not from a place of grief, but my prayers were a wrestling with my life's purpose. Upon my father's death, I initially felt that I was now free of others' expectations that I should follow him in ministry and inherit his church. As an only son and as a brother with seven sisters, it was a burden I had carried all my life. I had resisted ministry as a vocational option because I just did not want to be a preacher. Although I loved my dad and respected his commitment, the church world seemed so limiting. I saw local congregational dynamics as stifling and at times humiliating for the pastor. It seemed as if pastors were forced to function within constraints that allowed people who were not so nice to take full advantage of them. My father's tender heart and trust in God had enabled him to suffer slights and antagonisms with reserve and patience. I wanted be an attorney and politician with the freedom to fight back and stand up to people. In spite of the congregational challenges I saw my father face, I had great love and respect for the people and the community they created. I marveled that the black preacher and black church culture created a womb that nurtured young people like me and fortified us for interaction with a hostile outer world.[19] I was proud that my dad had been a faithful servant in the institutional black church.

What had also captured my imagination from childhood was the public ministry of Rev. Dr. Martin Luther King Jr. I knew that I had directly benefited from the long march of social justice. I was attracted to the sacrifices of faith-filled people whose private faith led them to engage public policy. That fall semester after my father's death I pondered how I could be of service to the people who were close to the heart of God. Our religious tradition had always presented God as the Liberator who took the side of the oppressed. In Bible stories and in the drama of worship among the southern migrants, God met the people in their struggles. Jesus came from among the dispossessed and demonstrated that God is not neutral in world affairs. God suffers with the suffering. In my basement apartment on Brown Street I had intense nights alone in prayer, stirred by an active subconscious dream life. Although I was not a formal and active part of a faith community in Washington, I attended church at Canaan Baptist more intentionally each Sunday. Over the course of that fall semester in 1981, alone in my thoughts, at age twenty-three, I accepted a life calling of ministry among people in the inner-city.

In our church culture it is called accepting a divine call to ministry. I had reasoned in my wrestling, that the best way to help people help themselves is to help transfer the timeless values and virtues that sustained the community that nurtured me and launched me into the world. It was a gift I wanted to give back. My call acceptance coincided with my conclusion that the church—organized religion—was a vehicle to do God's work among the exploited and oppressed. And so it was, while in Washington studying government, I made a personal and private decision to embrace the ministry. Once I decided to become a minister, I was also determined that my work should be on Chicago's west side among the people in the inner-city. My heart was at home. My dad's church had already selected his forty-three-year-old assistant minister, Rev. Ferdinand Hargrett, as the new pastor. Hargrett had grown up under my father's leadership and had been seasoned and faithful. I knew very little about the political and power dynamic of our local church. I was in support of the new pastor, and I believed it best to come home and learn all I could under his leadership. My greatest personal asset was that I was entirely clear on how little I knew about what it would take to be effective in ministry. I was young, naïve, eager, and broke. I just wanted to do God's will, learn the work, and develop as a young minister.

55

Returning to Chicago from Georgetown in December 1981 meant that I had been away from home for over five years. I was amazed at how much of an outsider I had become and how little I understood some of the more important nuances of the evangelical black church world. Although my father had been pastor, I had not been an active member of the congregation since my early teens. I did understand, however, that it would not be wise for me to make a public announcement of my call and intention to preach upon my arrival. There would be little reason for church members to trust my motives with such an announcement. I took a few months in the new year to re-acclimate myself before sharing my intentions with the pastor. With Pastor Hargrett's blessing, I made a public announcement to the congregation in early April and preached my first sermon on April 25, 1982.

There was great excitement at my first sermon because of my father's extraordinarily long legacy on the West Side. Local pastors and elders were present to wish me well. I preached a sermon entitled "The Permanent Fixture: God's Word Will Stand Forever," from Isaiah 40:1-8. "Everything and everyone else may fail us, but God never will." I think it went rather well. Truly, any decent sermon I would have preached that night would have been well received. However, after that highlight event, it was clear to me that I would have to start at the ground floor of ministry. There were three other associate ministers in training, and Pastor Hargrett would have to demonstrate fairness and impartiality. The members of the congregation knew my sisters and their commitment to the church, but they did not know me. I figured my level of commitment would be suspect. I had been home less than six months and already I was a minister-in-training. My time line challenged credulity. I would have to work hard in the areas of assignment that demonstrated commitment and brought little glamour.

I found my place in the Sunday school and the Saturday morning house-and-street witnessing teams. My evangelism work in the streets on Saturdays gave me serious evangelistic credibility among the most outgoing saints and more confidence in pulpit ministry on Sundays. I soon became a pretty good worship leader (also known as the set-up guy who made sure the service was high-spirited before the pastor's sermon). Worship leading, public prayers, and scripture reading were practice opportunities in preparation for appointments to preach at home or away. Our congregation did not have ready direction and supports for young ministers to attend seminary as a part of ministry development. The expectation was that upstarts would learn ministerial work by working in the work. If one's ministry demonstrated effectiveness over the course of time, then that happenstance would be evidence of divine favor and an authentic call. I would not consider this an efficient and effective way to develop trans-generational institutional leadership. I was disappointed to discover firsthand that one of the great weaknesses of independent black Baptist churches is the lack of formal processes of ministerial training and development.

Building Urban Ministry and Family: Working in the Vineyard

In January 1985, within three years of my first sermon, I was ordained and elected to pastor a small congregation of about twenty-five people. My first assignment was the Commonwealth Missionary Baptist Church in Chicago's West Side Lawndale community. This was the community where Dr. King and his family had resided during his 1966 open housing campaign. Although the congregation and the church building were small, at age twenty-six, this was a great opportunity for me to gain some experience and earn a reputation as a church leader. My election by the congregation was engineered by my pastor and several other pastors who had been friends of my dad and leaders of our local Friendship Baptist Association. My inheritance was not money, but my father's rich legacy. My rapid rise upon my return from school was certainly due more to me being my father's son than the reputation of my preaching ability. As a young inexperienced preacher I struggled with content, rhythm, and singing ability. All of these would be essential to an increase in demand for engagements and for progressing in black clergy networks. I had an uncommon head start and more youth day appointments than I deserved based upon my preaching ability. Nonetheless, I took every appointment I could garner, and dove into my pastoral work with enthusiasm and a young family.

Priscilla Marie Murchison, my wife, had grown up and been baptized in my dad's church. She was a year younger than me, and her family had been one of the largest and most loyal families in the Shiloh Missionary Baptist Church congregation. Her grandfather and grandmother, John and Rosie Sanders, had migrated in the 1940s from Grenada, Mississippi. John Henry Sanders was a respected church patriarch at Shiloh, and he served as chairman of the church deacon's board for twenty-five years. Priscilla and I courted the last year of my father's life, and in that time she won my heart with her faithfulness and character. It did not hurt matters at all that her caramel-colored round face had the prettiest smile and set of dimples, and that she had maintained her high school cheerleader figure with long slightly bowed legs. She gave me a lot to think about. We had a long-distance relationship while I was away in Washington, and we grew closer through letter writing and expensive long-distance calls. Priscilla was my link to home and to our local church. Since her family was large and influential in the life of the congregation, I gathered that I had to be serious and earnest about this relationship. I did not have the usual latitude of the casual relationships to which I had grown accustomed in my travels. Priscilla was a friend of the family and like a younger sister to my older sisters. They all sang in the church choir together, and my sisters had recently coached her in the art of church solo singing. At the outset, we talked about commitment and marriage. It was a conversation nurtured by the lonesome, longing intimacy of long-distance conversations about love, life's hurts, and wrestling with understanding God's direction.

Priscilla and I were married on August 6, 1983, less than two years after I had returned to Chicago and became a preacher. Priscilla told me later that her grandfather advised her to stick with me because I would need the help in ministry. I always thought she felt a little sorry for me in the ways that translate into love. When we got married Priscilla had a steady job in administration at the local Hines Veteran's Administration Hospital, while I was pursuing preaching with little income. My heart was full of idealism and thoughts of helping the people. We had our first child, Joyce Ann, and in January of 1985, answered the call to ministry at the tiny Commonwealth Missionary Baptist Church in Lawndale.

At its height, our Commonwealth membership grew to about seventy-five active members in the eight-and-one-half years we served there. The church building was an old synagogue in the middle of a residential block at 1318 South Keeler Avenue. It had a small sanctuary that sat about sixty-five people. With no parking, there was limited capacity for growth. At Commonwealth I learned that long-term members of small churches have tendencies that enforce congregational dynamics to ensure that the flock stays small. They are not interested in growth and are often intimidated by too many new faces. They can be highly committed to the church, but they also tend to be very much satisfied with their level of ministry and impact. They are members of small congregations because they enjoy the intimate relationships. Commonwealth was not well known in its surrounding community. In fact, it was barely acknowledged on the block that the church building sat in the middle of. Looking back, however, it is interesting to see how things lined up in our favor. It was providential that we were able to survive and thrive in a place where we could have easily been isolated, forgotten, overlooked, and never heard from again.

In 1985 when I became pastor, I also had worked at the local public elementary school as a substitute teacher. It was the first steady job I got after coming home from Georgetown in the recession of the early 1980s. The Charles Evans Hughes Public Elementary School was one-and-one-half blocks away from Commonwealth. Since my job was to fill in daily for absent teachers at all grade levels, it meant that I got to meet children of all grade levels from all over the neighborhood. As a teacher and now local church pastor, kids would see me at school in the day and in the evenings in the community near my church. Within a year, Priscilla spiced up our Sunday School program by serving pancake breakfast meals before classes. We quickly began attracting children from all over the neighborhood. We fed them, she taught them, I preached, and we started lining up baptismal services for the new converts. Of course, we had to get the parents' permission to baptize children. That meant we now had an increase of adult visitors for these high-energy events.

We soon also took in adult family members in the neighborhood as new joiners. The successes we had at Commonwealth were not the result of an intentional strategy on our part. I had taught four months at Hughes, beginning in September of 1984, before I even knew I would be appointed at Commonwealth in January of 1985. It was one of those states of grace that is unexplainable. My life and our ministry could have easily fizzled at Commonwealth in Lawndale. Our reputation and enthusiasm could have died on the vine. All of the small church dynamics, the limitations and inherent frustrations, were present in this assignment. Priscilla and I have often reflected on the irony of what bailed us out in that first church appointment. I had a good family name and an advanced degree in my favor. I had learned to preach better sermons with classic black preaching delivery. All of that was great, but what really carried the day for us in the Commonwealth years were pancakes and children's baptisms. Pancakes and Christ attracted children, and the adults followed their children. When community families joined, we taught Bible lessons and the congregation grew in unprecedented ways. One year after Joyce Ann was born, we added another daughter, Janelle, in 1985. My first son, Marshall Jr., was born in 1988. Life was good. My family, my congregation, and my reputation were growing from the small place that gave me a start in ministry.

Citizens Against Desert Storm: Finding a Public Voice

A year or so before Saddam Hussein sent his Iraqi army to invade Kuwait in 1990, my oldest sister Rhoda's son, Wesley Marshall, enlisted in the military. His goal was to serve a few years and earn benefits to attend college.

As President George Herbert Walker Bush presented ultimatums to Iraq and began the drumbeats to war, a growing antiwar movement emerged in Chicago and around the country. In our congregation, my sister and two other mothers became concerned about their sons in the military and the coming war. My focus had become local church ministry, and with that, I left my passion for politics and my political science background behind. I was working hard and nurturing relationships with church members, but the issues of the war arrested me through the concerns of members of the church. As a pastor I helped my sister and the other parishioners and families form a group called Citizens Against Desert Storm. I helped the mothers articulate one of the themes that surfaced because of the all-volunteer military: minorities and the poor would bear a disproportionate share of the risk and sacrifice of the coming war.

It seemed unjust and unfortunate that the sons of these mothers and the children of families like theirs would be the frontline troops of a "blood for oil" premeditated war of choice. To increase the effectiveness of getting our message out, I drew from my political science training. Although antiwar groups were bubbling up in pockets all across Chicago and connecting to a national movement, I knew having the consciousness to form an antiwar group with an articulate message would be "news" when it emerged from Lawndale. When the protest came from black, poor families with their local West Side church base, it would heighten the newsworthiness. That level of consciousness from such a blighted community would be news. News editors are predisposed to project the unexpected. Our group was small, but it emerged as one of the high-profile antiwar groups in the Chicago area. Several times the local television news programs led with live shots from our small sanctuary. Good turnouts packed in a small place made good television. We joined a national protest in Washington, and our mothers were profiled in national publications and news stories. By the launch of the attack of the American-led Coalition's forces against Saddam's Iraqi army on Martin Luther King's birthday in 1991, the Chicago Sun-Times had a reporter embedded in my living room to gauge my reaction. With location, message, visuals, creative energy, and coalescing with the larger antiwar movement, we had maximized our impact on the national dialogue from our small place of ministry.[20]

The antiwar movement fizzled with the successful and efficient prosecution of the war. In building and projecting our anti-war group, I had earned some distinction, at least in some West Side circles, as an activist minister. Some local politicians took notice that I had shown some organizing skill and a social justice conscience. I believed our positions were thoughtful and responsible. I do think that there is such a thing as a morally justified prosecution of war. War in the modern world, however, has very limited utility. As we have seen in the years after the 2001 9-11 tragedy, wars of choice should be conducted very judiciously with precise effect. Without a clear vision of the endgame, war can cause problems much more complex than the problems it solves. In the first Gulf War, I never quarreled with the danger Saddam's ambitions presented to American interests and stability in the Middle East. History has shown that the first Gulf War was prosecuted efficiently and excellently. Saddam was pushed out of Kuwait, contained without the ability to threaten Iraq's minorities or its neighbors, and his regime was left in place to account to his people for the economy and making the trains run on time. We broke Saddam's stranglehold of power without breaking Iraq.

My concerns were and are the moral questions that are present when young people without live options in civil society are called upon to risk their lives in military service, while young people of privilege are not. The all-volunteer military was put into place in response to the social unrest and the unpopularity of the Vietnam War. If we are not thoughtful, we will use our national all-volunteer force in ways in which we would not use our national army if every citizen knew that every part of our national family was on tap to pay for the full costs of war. When every family must bear the burdens of war, politicians are extra careful to narrowly define vital national interests worthy of the sacrifices. In the wars in Iraq and Afghanistan after 9-11, politicians gave the wealthy tax breaks and sent an all-volunteer force to fight. Few members of Congress had an immediate relative in combat zones. Our recent war efforts, arguably wars of choice, have asked for neither financial sacrifice nor service from the most privileged Americans. I was concerned in the case of Gulf War I, and remain so today, about how disproportionate sacrifice in the time of war affects the soul of our country.

My nephew Wesley fought in Iraq and survived the war. By the spring of 1992, he was stationed at Fort Hood in Killeen, Texas, to finish his stint in the military by the end of the summer. Mother's Day that year was a day of horror for my family and my sister in particular. Wesley was murdered in the early morning at an off-base motel. He had been summoned to a motel room by the girlfriend of a fellow soldier. Apparently, what he did not know was that his friend had been shot and thrown out of a car on the other side of town by criminals apparently involved in illegal drugs. From what we know, the men took motel room keys from the victim, and went to the location and found the young lady in the room. Fatefully, she called Wesley out of fear. When Wesley responded and entered the room, two Jamaican gunmen ordered him to lie face down on the floor. He was shot through the back, and a single bullet entered his heart.[21] The young lady was unharmed. Wesley's twenty-one-year-old friend would survive his injuries, but would have to live with permanent paralysis from the waist down. We never knew the full details of the incident. In fact, we were too grief struck to inquire further. We also didn't know much about the murderer, captured by police at the home of relatives in Buffalo, New York, two weeks after Wesley was killed. The girlfriend's eyewitness testimony sealed the case, and the gunman received a thirty-nine year sentence for manslaughter in a plea bargain with the State's Attorney.

The military personnel and the prosecutors were extremely sensitive to our grief and walked us through the legal processes. I traveled to Killeen with my sister Rhoda a few weeks after the funeral. It was therapy for us to visually see the base and meet the young people Wesley had served with. His fellow soldiers seemed so young, many barely out of high school. During the trial, phone contact with the State's Attorney was enough. Rhoda had decided that it was best in the long-run to have no visual of the man who was convicted of the murder. I thought that was wise. In the end we were satisfied with the result. From that personal tragedy, I have never been an active proponent of broad use of the death penalty. We had closure with the justice system's determination. I think the death penalty may be warranted in particularly gruesome cases, especially those with child victims or peace officers. But I can honestly say that the death penalty for Wesley's murderer would not have improved the quality of our sense of closure. We accepted and appreciated the work of the judicial system and went on with our lives.

I had thought at the onset of my life as a minister that I would have to forgo my passion for politics and my interest in public policy. The intimate ways the issues of the war engaged our congregation forced me to pick up and utilize my political skill set. I mentioned in follow-up media reporting the sad irony of our family's personal tragedy. Wesley had survived war in the Persian Gulf, but he had succumbed to the violence in American civil society. Wesley's death helped me more fully embrace my own mortality. It gave me a greater sense of urgency for my ministry. We had been very impactful in making a contribution to the dialogue about the war. My organizing and speaking on our concerns about the Persian Gulf War rekindled my passion for engaging ministry as a blend of evangelicalism and activism. We could not let our personal loss be the end of engagement of public policy. There was a great need to address many other issues that affected families of my congregation and the needs of our community. The antiwar organizing helped me find a public voice of prophetic ministry to go along with my growth as a church leader. At this time, at least in West Side black church circles, I had begun to distinguish and define myself and my ministry as a West Side activist pastor.

New Mount Pilgrim and McCormick Seminary: Growing in Grace

Exactly one year after Wesley's death, in May of 1993, two developments occurred that would further change the course and expanse of my ministry. First, I had been recommended for a seminary program for inner-city pastors at McCormick Theological Seminary, a Presbyterian school on the Hyde Park campus consortium of the University of Chicago. Community organizer and The Woodlawn Organization (TWO) founder Leon Finney had entered the ministry and seminary. His doctor of ministry thesis made a case that training black pastors who were practitioners was a strategic way to foster and further community revitalization. Finney set up the African American Leadership Partnership and got initial grant money from the MacArthur Foundation. With a master's degree in government from Georgetown and eight years of pastoral experience, I was a prime candidate for the program. I was accepted and began a five-year master's of arts and doctor of ministry program in May of 1993.

Secondly, also in May of 1993, one of my late father's dearest pastoral friends, Rev. James R. McCoy, died at age seventy-five one month after moving his congregation from a storefront building in East Garfield Park to a massive, old Catholic facility in West Garfield Park on the West Side.[22] Pastor McCoy was a real southern gentleman and had migrated from the same hometown as my dad, Aberdeen, Mississippi, in the delta. When I returned to Chicago to enter ministry, he had taken me under his wing. Through his counseling and mentoring, I learned the practical sides of ministry. His was a homespun wisdom. Once, he counseled me not to take a church about forty miles from Chicago in Gary, Indiana. I was not yet thirty and wanted to move faster and assume a larger church than the one I had. Pastor McCoy did not know of the specific church in Gary, but he was an expert on church dynamics. The church had just built a new building and had a large board of elder deacons, made up of retirees from the Gary steel mills. Gary's economy was dead, and young people with promise and drive abandoned Gary in droves. The major businesses had moved out of the predominately black city and had taken the jobs and tax base to Merrillville, Indiana, eight miles south of the city. In pastoral strategic reasoning, that appointment would have been a dead-end. Location and timing would be important considerations in successful pastoral moves. I was young and green. The church elders would not need me to do anything but preach, and a young pastor would be at their mercy. At some point the seasoned board of deacons would have eaten me alive. I did not understand any of this at the time. "No one knows you there," Pastor McCoy cautioned. I was eager and wanted a bigger church, but I was also afraid to ignore my mentor's counsel. In the spring of 1989 we decided against a move to Gary. We stayed put at Commonwealth and worked with Priscilla's pancake ministry and children's baptisms.

A month after Wesley's death in 1992, I quit my job as a City of Chicago auditor to devote my energies to full-time pastoral work at Commonwealth. Elder pastors had impressed upon me over the years that my ministry would only be blessed as I lived by and exampled my faith. That meant quitting secular work to work for the Lord at a small church. I wrestled for years with that move and then finally obeyed the voice by leaving my city employment in one act of risky faith. One year later, in May of 1993, after serving twenty-eight years as pastor, Pastor McCoy died. This could not have seemed more untimely. Pastor McCoy was in the midst of a major transition, literally, in both a physical and contractual sense. Physically he was moving his New Mount Pilgrim Missionary Baptist Church congregation from East Garfield to West Garfield Park. Contractually, he died in the middle of a gentleman's agreement with Catholic Church officials to occupy the properties until a mortgage was secured. After Pastor McCoy's death, the contract was put on hold while the congregation worshipped in the building and began the pastoral selection process. They would need a new pastor who could close the $400,000 mortgage deal, build the congregation, and launch ministry in a new community.

I did not initially realize the wise ways my mentor kept me before his congregation, preaching Annual Day celebrations and revivals and teaching workshops and seminars. As we labored at Commonwealth, Pastor McCoy had remarked to my wife and me that I "was too good a preacher to be in the out-of-the-way place" location that I was in. "Boy, you need to be on the Boulevard," he'd said with his unique chuckle. His remark actually hurt me. It was even more hurtful at the time he had said it, when I considered how he had counseled me out of moving to a more substantial church in Gary. But in his wisdom, he kept me before the people in his church. The day he died, May 17, 1993, was on the third day of my first class at McCormick. I had visited him at Mother Cabrini Hospital the day before, and he was alert, upbeat, and seemed to be recovering from a serious surgery. Mother Cabrini Hospital was just two blocks away from where I had grown up in the projects on Ada Street. When Priscilla picked me up the next evening at school in Hyde Park around 9:00 p.m., she said, "Pastor McCoy passed tonight." At that instant, I felt an immediate burden for his church. At that point in my work, I knew enough about black Baptist church politics to know that succession dynamics would begin immediately.

After Pastor McCoy's funeral, I had heard rumors and potential plans about filling the pastoral vacancy. I attended the funeral but was not on the program. Those honors would be reserved for senior pastors and ministers of great reputation in the church world. Before he started preaching, Pastor McCoy had been a great singer and was part of a gospel quartet. That music tradition lay at the core of New Mount Pilgrim. The early evening funeral service, held on a Sunday, drew a massive crowd from the black church and gospel-singing worlds. I sat in a side pew, insignificant among church greats in a high-spirited, massive audience of about fifteen hundred people. The next morning, by spontaneous selection, a senior pastor and old colleague of my father's called upon me to perform the committal rites of Pastor McCoy's body at the gravesite in a west suburban cemetery. That was a high honor. From there, I had little idea of where things would go next. I did not have a pipeline into the congregation. There were several ministers who had served with the late Pastor, and I was sure that all of them had to be given the courtesy of consideration by the selection committee. I was a little disappointed that almost three months had passed and I had not heard anything about the status of the succession process. I was beginning to resolve I was not in serious contention to succeed my mentor.

The first word I heard about being under consideration was while riding as a passenger in the back of a van in Harare, Zimbabwe. It was the second year I had traveled with a group of black pastors to fellowship and support the work of a group of evangelical Christian churches there. The indigenous churches had broken away from a white Wheaton, Illinois, sponsoring group of evangelical congregations. Zimbabwean church officials had complained that the white evangelicals had placed white missionaries over their churches as a condition of receiving financial support. The white missionaries appointed pastors and held financial and administrative control over the pastors they appointed. To Zimbabweans, a dozen years removed from Rhodesian apartheid, this arrangement smacked of old colonialism. They rejected the arrangement, and a group of American black pastors stepped in to fill the gap. Several older Baptist pastors with substantial congregations had taken up the cause of fellowshipping annually with the Zimbabwean churches—gathering and shipping resources, and empowering local pastors with no strings attached. The story impressed me, and I was also eager to travel to Africa, do missions work, and build relationships. I rallied the members of my small church, and I traveled on my first three-week mission in the summer of 1992.

On my second trip in 1993, I was riding in the back of a van with the president of our Illinois Baptist Convention, Reverend Stephen Thurston. Thurston is a third-generation pastor in Chicago and had risen to the top spot of our state convention. He lived in Chicago, and New Mount Pilgrim church officials had reached out to him for guidance, asking about me in particular. Thurston said he had given a good recommendation. He informed me, "You should expect a call when you get back home. Remember, Pilgrim is a big ship. If you turn a big ship too quickly, you will upset the passengers, and some will fall overboard." Thurston counseled, "If you turn it slowly, folks will stay on board for the ride, remain on the ship, and not mind that they are going in a different direction." It was a good word for the reflection I would do while in Africa.

Within two weeks upon my return, in August, I preached my candidate sermon at New Mount Pilgrim and was elected pastor of the two-hundred-plus-member church on September 22, 1993. Not every faction of the congregation agreed with the decision. The chair of the selection committee was formerly a member of my dad's old church, Shiloh. I had allies in people who had relationships with my dad, and who thought Pastor McCoy's desire was that he be succeeded by an "educated preacher." Pastor McCoy had almost no formal education, yet he valued it greatly. Most of the people in the congregation also had the same kind of southern black reverence for formal education and training. So a new chapter for us was unfolding in this West Side congregation. We had a deal to close, facilities to rehab and manage, a congregation to build, a vision to cast, and ministries to launch. Some members from Commonwealth joined us at Pilgrim. Although we welcomed them, I wanted Commonwealth members to stay put so the ministry work there could go on. I was thirty-five, and I believed that we could impact our world locally and globally with the Good News of God. I had a new and challenging assignment in the inner-city, and I commuted weekly to seminary at McCormick in Hyde Park.

Our little family had grown. We had three children under ten years old. The story of how we had been faithful with a small church and moved seemingly seamlessly to a larger church had become an example for other young pastors. I had come home, worked hard, married up, and emerged, not in my dad's church, but in his legacy. Pastor McCoy had made one last daring move to set up the purchase of the Old St. Mel Catholic Church properties and, in his passing, had handed off the invisible baton to me in the middle of the transaction. In our little private celebratory dinner after my selection, Priscilla and I marveled at the journey we had made and the challenges we now faced. This was altogether an infinitely more complex appointment than our first church appointment. "Well Marshall," Priscilla remarked, "Pastor McCoy done put us on the Boulevard!"

By 2011, New Mount Pilgrim has blossomed to over eight hundred members. We rolled up our sleeves and went to work. We refurbished the facilities, replacing some of the European-featured stained glass art of the Old St. Mel congregation with African American icons and themes. In 2000, we unveiled a twenty-five-foot in diameter representation of the "slave ship" icon as a tribute to those who did not survive the horrors of the Transatlantic Slave Trade. The window, "Maafa Remembrance," is the largest display of the slave ship packing icon in the world. It is quite spectacular. In 1999 we unveiled a "Family Child Dedication" that has a North Star depiction and honors the courage of the antebellum "Underground Railroad" and the Great Migration. These art themes helped make an old Catholic facility feel like an African American church home. Our guiding mission has been "Building the Spirit of Village in the Heart of the City." The congregation has developed a wide range of ministries in an urban community of great challenge: affordable housing developments, after-school programs, educational support projects, parent training workshops, mentoring programs, employment, and on and on. I think one of our proudest legacies has been inspiring and supporting scores of young people from our congregation to attend colleges and universities across the country.

Our wonderful faith community has allowed Priscilla and me to grow and expand in ways we only dreamed of in early years. By the late 1990s I had led mission teams on several trips to Zimbabwe. Sharing housing with Zimbabwean families allowed us to donate rental stipends to the families. Our goal was always to transfer as much of our expense resources as was possible directly to families. New Mount Pilgrim also provided a platform to develop the kind of social justice and advocacy and community development ministries that helped fulfill the political and public policy impact interests connected with my particular life calling. A premier urban ministry in the heart of Chicago's West Side, this church has afforded many opportunities to live my boyhood dreams of relevant ministry and substantive public service. In 1996 our last child, Maurice, was born, completing our set of two girls and two boys.

Jacob A. Riis Elementary School, Kindergarten Class of 1963-64, Marshall Hatch (second row from bottom—3rd from left)

My Mother Helen and Father Elijah as new parents to baby Josephine, 1965. Mother Helen dies in Jane Addams Project, 1967

Me and Josephine in our project apartment on Easter Sunday, 1972

8th grade Graduation and 1972 Class President at Riis Elementary School

Marshall Hatch with Hugh O'Brian and Lady Bird Johnson, 1974

With Hugh O'Brian in Washington, D.C. in 1974

With Senator Brooke (R-Mass) 1974

Phi Beta Sigma Fraternity "Step Show" at Western Illinois University

Dunbar Vocational High School Graduation, 1976

With my Haitian host family at 3301 Brown Street N.W.I lived in their basement as a Georgetown University Grad Student

Being wed to Priscilla Murchison, August 6, 1983

Pastor's Anniversary at Commonwealth Baptist Church Family picture: Joyce, Janelle, and Marshall Jr., circa 1990

Wedding Party with Priscilla's Parents at Shiloh Baptist Church, 1983

Faith Based Westside Isaiah Plan Affordable Housing Construction, with Mayor Daley, 1989

With Pastor James McCoy at New Mount Pilgrim Baptist Church, circa 1987

"Maafa 2000" Window at New Pilgrim Baptist Church, the largest display of the "slave ship" icon in the world. Recreation of Tom Feeling's "Middle Passage."

Harvard University Sabbatical: Private Faith and Public Service

While growing and developing our family and church, by 1998 I had completed my seminary degrees at McCormick: a master of arts in theological studies and the doctor of ministry. My academic successes made me restless within the confines of the local pastorate. In conversations with a couple of local politicians, I contemplated a run for the Illinois General Assembly from the West Side's Eighth Legislative District. They thought, and I initially agreed, that electoral politics could be an extension of my ministry. Black pastors serve as elected officials all over the South. That was not so true in Chicago, where the black church has been tightly controlled and used as a power base by the Democratic political machine. It was an agonizing decision. I was in, then I bowed out. It was something I really wanted to do. I had often swayed in my ministry model from the prophetic King, to the political effectiveness of Harlem's Abyssinian Baptist Church's late pastor, Adam Clayton Powell. I filed petitions for the Democratic Primary, but finally decided against it. I backed away after considering that the church was about one year away from paying off the first mortgage on the sanctuary. In the end, I acknowledged that the church had a momentum I did not want to see dissipated by a political run. I was still new enough at Pilgrim, and I had not yet built the levels of trust and infrastructure that would adequately support the move into electoral politics. I thought not running was the right decision for the church, but I felt personally limited by the decision I had made.

After the 1998 campaign season had passed, I was yet stirred by the prospect of involvement in influencing and impacting public policy. As a sort of consolation, I applied for a fellowship sabbatical semester for local pastors at the Harvard Divinity School for the following year. I knew I had a strong application. I had succeeded in building an impactful indigenous inner-city urban ministry. I had secular and seminary advanced degrees. I enlisted two recommendations: (1) from my U.S. Congressman, Danny K. Davis, a friend and mentor from the early days after my return home from college; and (2) from retired Georgetown professor and Maryland Poet Laureate, Professor Roland Flint. In the late spring of 1998, I was accepted as a 1999 Merrill Fellow at Harvard Divinity and awarded a stipend for expenses. My first call was to Flint to share the news. I was happy about it, but not overly enthused because I was still wondering if I had made the right decision by passing up a run for state representative. In fact, I was very regretful. Flint, knowing me as a sophomore project kid in his 1977 English class, gave me a little insight as a career academic. He was ecstatic with my selection.

I said, "Professor Flint, it's only a semester-long stint at Harvard. Is it really a big deal?" Flint returned the fire: "Marshall, ANYTHING at Harvard is a big deal. OKAY?" It pays to have a mentor who not only helps one to succeed, but who is also able to help a person process the magnitude of the success.

I obviously did not realize how transformative four-and-a-half months of sabbatical in the intellectually charged environment at Harvard could be. First, I had not realized the distinction of being identified by my campus ID, not as a student, but as an "officer." It meant that I had access to almost everywhere in Cambridge. It also meant that I would be up close and personal with renowned faculty and guests from around the nation and the world. I lived one block from the Harvard Law School and could walk to anywhere on campus. I would end up spending more time at the Kennedy School of Government than the Divinity School, my official host. I found conversations about ethics and politics just as interesting as theology. It was Harvard, indeed, and people everywhere were fascinating. There were sessions with Dr. Peter Gomes, the brilliant Baptist preacher and scholar; and Preston Williams, the gentle spirit of the Divinity School. There were brown-bag lunch sessions with Dr. Henry Louis "Skip" Gates at the Department of African American Studies. At the Kennedy School, in lectures and exchanges with former New York Governor Mario Cuomo, former Arkansas Governor David Pryor, former Wyoming Senator Alan Simpson, former Illinois Governor Jim Edgar, and others, my assumptions were confirmed about the interconnectedness of ministry and public service.

Governor Pryor, in particular, was available at the Kennedy School the entire semester and was genuinely passionate about the notion that the joy of politics was the ability to help people have a better life. It was amazing to watch how animated this southern politician became as he described a ribbon-cutting event that celebrated bringing indoor plumbing and electricity to remote parts of Arkansas. "That's when you know all of the unpleasantries in politics are worthwhile," Pryor assessed. I learned that good people could enter politics for all the right reasons. Resisting the temptations of arrogance, greed, power, and insulation and isolation from reality was a daily struggle. But what I suspected was reinforced, public service was a noble ambition. I always thought it wrong and unhelpful to label all politicians and politics itself as inherently tainted and crooked. That viewpoint is too cynical for my tastes and simply not true.

I had read many biographies and noticed that many politicians had once considered ministry, and the clergy I admired most had ministries in the public square. Pastors whose work had benefited my life the most, like Martin Luther

King and Adam Clayton Powell, were unafraid of the rough-and-tumble world of politics and public discourse. Harvard confirmed my belief that authentic, forward-looking faith serves the common good and advocates for progressive public policy. For me, the Divinity School and the Kennedy School of Government were the perfect complement for my blend of ministry and public service. The separation of church and state was a conversation designed to free people of diverse faiths and the nonreligious to participate in the development of public policy without the partiality of imposed, established state religion. The U.S. Constitution was designed to protect freedom of religion, not create a litmus test for public service that required freedom from religion. The Constitution always facilitated the contributions of persons who respectfully serve the common good in the name of a particular religion. What the Constitution promotes is service to the common good irrespective of religious persuasion, but religious persuasion does not take away the right and responsibility to engage in our mutual work of perfecting the Union. Harvard Divinity School, founded as a school for training Baptist pastors, was the perfect place to explore faith-based public service.

One evening while strolling through Harvard Square, I ran into Dr. Cornel West walking alone. He was on sabbatical himself and was not teaching formal classes on campus that semester. West is one of the most popular public theologians and political scientists in America. Running into West was a stroke of good fortune for me, and I tried to take full advantage of it. He was dressed in his usual three-piece black suit and sported his 1960s untamed-style Afro and unkempt beard. West was strutting through the Square with the peculiar gait of a street-savvy African American male. He was gracious and seemingly unhurried. He had to be headed somewhere, but for a while he engaged in a conversation with me about Chicago. He said he had only recently been through the city and had spent some time talking to some "brothers on 63rd Street." Our conversation turned to black music and black life. Professor West is a profound musicologist who loves to reflect upon how positive, conscious cultural music helps families—everyday people—overcome and transcend the onslaught of corporate hegemony. Conscious artists identify with and seek to inspire the working poor in their daily struggle. Wholesome music about love relationships helps nurture and flavor the kinds of families that help build strong communities. Keeping romance and love in family life is the frontline of daily cultural and spiritual warfare against the dehumanizing effects of capitalism and the greed of the global oligarchy. Families and communities around the world are losing the battle for the souls of humankind. Prophetic voices must sound the alarm that raises moral issues and projects the interests of the least of these. Good music with love themes provides the soundtrack of the daily spiritual struggle.

Dr. West has made the point as a musicologist that the music of folks reflects and interacts with their culture, revealing values and how they live their lives every day. We know we are losing the spiritual warfare and battle for the soul because much of the "sweetness" has been wrung out of black urban culture with the decadence and hedonism reflected and projected in contemporary music and music videos. In the intimate relationships that create family, we have gone from music that serenades lovers in bonds of commitment to music that degrades women and devalues people. When black folks controlled the means of musical production in our own community we were conscious in our efforts to edify the people. Black-owned Wattstax Records in the early 1970s produced the Staples Singers singing the hit "Respect Yourself." Popular music is a soundtrack that can reflect the best of who we are, and it can also influence the quality of our cultural life. The BETization of black America has not been helpful. Over a thirty-year span, Robert L. Johnson's Black Entertainment Television's cable television rap and R&B video images have reflected and projected the debauchery of urban subculture. BET was eventually sold to corporate interests for three billion dollars, and it continues to add to the poisoned pathologies of black urban America.

In the conversation with Dr. West, I felt a unique kinship to this public intellectual and self-described philosophical bluesman and jazzman. West has a great mind and an even greater heart. My charge has also been to help sustain people with the good news of the Gospel through the unspeakable horrors I have witnessed as an urban pastor. My presentation of the Good News has to be jazz-like—spontaneous and extemporaneous. Talking to West that day, I reflected upon how hard I worked in what was my charge. This sabbatical allowed me opportunities of reflection that could keep my Gospel approaches cutting-edge and fresh. The chance meeting with Dr. West was refreshing and indicative of the kinds of serendipity that only occurs in Cambridge.

The longer I stayed at Harvard, the clearer it was to me that I had to maintain a regimen of self-care when I returned to Chicago. I could not afford to burn out because my inner-city assignment meant that I had to stay in a place of prayerful, critical thinking and positive energy. From the vantage point of Harvard, I marveled that I had survived and thrived against great odds. I was not born for Harvard. This season of life was a part of a grace that fosters a twist of fate. Oddly, as the semester wound down, I became even more discontented with the inequalities and economic violence that helps create the pathologies of inner-city America. I was a pastor, not an artist, and returning to Chicago to help people cope with pain would not be enough to address my dissatisfaction with injustice. Given the context, my pastoral ministry must be priestly and prophetic, and my charge required that I enlist the powers of private faith into the cause of public service and social justice.

Toward the end of my sabbatical, the Harvard School of Education hosted an Ira Berlin lecture where Berlin spoke about his powerful book and cassette tape recollection library, "Remembering Slavery."[23] Berlin's work codifies the recorded testimonies of former African American slaves who had been interviewed in the South by Works Projects Administration (WPA) workers during the Great Depression in the 1930s. I had dinner with Berlin in the faculty club, and I asked what he would have us take away from his work. He responded by saying that he had lectured at the School of Education because "we will not be able to adequately address issues of urban education without engaging our history." Slavery is so recent in our history that Berlin had the ability to capture tape-recorded eyewitness testimonies as part of his book. The number one thing former slaves wanted to communicate for posterity was this truth: "Slavery was a living nightmare."[24]

Our enslaved fore-parents did everything in their power to resist dehumanization. They knew that the goal of the slave system was to break their spirit, so they were conscious and intentional about the energy they put into celebrations. They were often mistaken for "happy slaves," but their "celebrations" were less about their complacency, and more about their resistance to their oppression. Even chattel slavery could not destroy the human spirit and the will to make the best out of the worst. Their capacity to rejoice was something they determined that no human master could take away. But the predominant theme of the recorded testimonies of former slaves was that slavery itself was hell on earth. And after emancipation and reconstruction they faced a string of broken promises of repair and requite. They never received forty acres and a mule, nor did they receive any other compensation for themselves and their families. Less than one decade of Reconstruction was followed by almost ninety years of a reign of terror and legal apartheid. Berlin's point was that the pathologies that we seek to address in the present are rooted in the not-too-distant past. Inner- city pathologies are the product of multigenerations of disadvantage, disenfranchisement, and segregation from opportunity.

Reflecting on this at Harvard disquieted me on a personal level. A place like Harvard is filled with people who benefit from multigenerational legacies of advantage. When I considered the black rage among males on the west side of Chicago with Berlin's work in mind, I better understood their response to their predicament. The streets are filled with angry, young, black fatherless men who have become menaces to their own community and to society-at-large. There I was at Harvard, becoming more disturbed by the week. As I interacted with people of privilege, I began to bemoan my lack of a material and tangible inheritance. In making it to this place of privilege without family connections, I pondered what my life would have been with a better head start. I knew on some level that what I was thinking and feeling was ungracious and a little out-of-pocket. My thoughts were not necessarily gracious, but they were authentic. The place I was in helped me understand the uncontrolled rage of inner-city black young men better. The world that runs by network and legacy is a cruel joke to a fatherless black male trapped in the ghetto and segregated from opportunity. I understood that pain a little more profoundly as I prepared to leave Cambridge.

The irony was, the longer I remained at Harvard, the more disturbed I became, and the more I wished I could stay for good. I felt both alien and at home, much like the duality expressed in W. E. B. DuBois' Souls of Black Folk. I was asked a few times if I was ready to go back to the pastorate, rested from my sabbatical. "Am I ready to leave Harvard, and go back to Chicago's West Side?" I thought it was a strange question, but I was earnest every time I was asked some variation of it. My answer was, "Not only am I not ready to return, but it would be like leaving the mountaintop experience and going back to the valley." The mountain was a more peaceful place to be, but it was not the most purposeful place to be. The mountaintop was a place for reflection, but the call to labor was in the valley. If I was seeking comfort, I would have sought a career change. But it was not comfort or career that drove me, it was the calling I had sensed most of my conscious life. My inner vision had been formed in Jane Addams housing projects and by the images that Dr. King's 1968 funeral seared in my ten-year-old mind by the flickering black and white television in our crowded project apartment. The voice that I was determined to heed was the one I heard in my one-room Washington, D.C. apartment in my last semester at Georgetown. It was time to return to Chicago and get back to work.

Rainbow-PUSH Years and the Jackson Vortex: From the West Side to the World

In the summer of 1999 after returning from Harvard, I participated in another three-week missions trip to Zimbabwe. While I was in Africa, Priscilla called to inform me that Rev. Jesse Jackson and some West Side pastors had appeared in a local television news story about Chicago police abuse issues. I had never formally met Rev. Jackson, although in earlier years of ministry I would visit the PUSH Saturday morning forums to be inspired by the national radio broadcast from Jackson's headquarters, Dr. King's workshop. By late August, Jackson had his emissaries looking for a West Side early Sunday service preaching spot. Jackson had a way of scouting for new organizing territory and new clergy recruits for his organization. One cannot fully understand black Chicago without understanding the disconnect between the West Side and South Side African American communities. The West Side and west suburban black population is about one-tenth the population of blacks on the South Side and southern suburbs. National black political figures from Chicago's dynamic South Side base will travel the country and world, and almost never venture to the city's West Side. West Side blacks grow up with a major chip on their shoulder that South-Siders have difficulty comprehending. West Side blacks are so disconnected from the African American South Side community that, although Jackson lived in Chicago and had a weekly forum at his headquarters in Hyde Park, Jackson's visit to my church would be the first time that many of my parishioners would meet him in person and hear an unfiltered live sermon from the civil rights icon. They had heard speeches on television, but not a church sermon. There is a profound difference.

That late August Sunday, Rev. Jackson preached a message challenging us "to follow Jesus Christ and not just admire him." People were pleasantly surprised that one whom they had thought to be exclusively political had a profound biblical message. Then Jackson, while in high-preaching gear, made a grand departure in concluding his sermon. It was vintage Rev. Jesse Jackson, whirling in high-drama stagecraft. For his own sense of urgent purpose, he must always be in motion, off to the next appointment. Jackson bounded out of the pulpit while in preaching gear and went down the center aisle shaking hands campaign-style as folks leaned out of the pews to make a connection. My staff put a packet of information about me and the church in his hand before he left. In the following weeks, I started regularly attending the Saturday Operation PUSH forum.

By October, Jackson invited me to be the keynote speaker of the forum broadcast while he celebrated his birthday away in Los Angeles. I had training in political science and theological studies, plus I was an experienced pulpit communicator with urban ministry expertise, and so my speech went well. Upon Jackson's return, I was debriefed by the PUSH leader, and became a fast-rising favorite on the broadcast platform. As is said in PUSH circles, I was drawn into the "Jackson vortex." I was to find out that this "drawing in" can be as dangerous as it is exhilarating. Specifically, one can lose sight of one's own personal mission and assignment through the unceasing whirlwind of life in Jackson's world. Rev. Jackson has a way of investing time and lavishing attention on the next potential clergy protégé, well aware that a substantial pastor pulled into Jackson's circle will provide his organization a talented self-funded staff member. I soon figured out that there are scores of PUSH alumni who serve for a season and move on. Rev. Jackson will never slow the pace of his activism. His organization survives from the aura of constant motion in search of momentum from the social justice causes of the day. His pace is one few other people will have the personal resources to sustain as a staff member or volunteer. People who do not plan an exit from the "Jackson vortex" eventually leave feeling bitter and used by the experience. My goals were to be helpful to the remnants of the movement that PUSH represented and help in any way I could, that is, for a season.

By November of 1999, I was a leading clergy participant in the Rainbow PUSH Decatur, Illinois, campaign to address the expulsion of seven African American males who had participated in a fight at the local high school. They had been kicked out of the public high school for the fighting infraction for two full years without any offering of alternative education. There were no weapons or injuries in the altercation. It happened at a football game at the predominately white school for less than two minutes. The administration of the school and district issued a most severe sentence for the infractions. The fact was, as we examined the case, that these young black males were given group or "mob action" justice, not individual due process. "Mob" is thinly veiled code for out-of-control young black males. Each of them could not have been just as guilty as the other and altogether equally worthy of a two-year expulsion. A "mob action" charge, the equivalent of group justice, meant that each defendant would be denied individual due process.

In the end, after national media attention and court challenges, the decision stood. PUSH had to help the families obtain alternative education options. The officials in that community dug in their heels, fully aware that the power of the local school district to expel students in the name of public safety would rule the day. In my work as a social justice activist, I have seen a lot of this type of racial profiling. The stereotype of the dangerous, violent black male negates the fair administration of justice in countless cases. We cannot claim a post-racial America as long as this racial stereotyping and profiling are ingrained in the power, social, and legal dynamics of American society. We yet have a long way to go to realize Dr. King's Dream of color-blind America. What I have learned in degree programs and fellowship opportunities has been invaluable and has educated and shaped me, but I have to singularly credit Rev. Jackson for his intentional investments in leadership development. He mentored and taught me and a generation of black activists and leaders to conduct the kind of critical social and political analysis that will continue to be essential for our community going forward. Jackson's PUSH alumni have been spread across the American political, social, and economic landscape over the twenty plus years since his brilliant presidential campaigns of 1984 and 1988. That he had intentionally invested and poured into many will be a part of his living legacy for years to come. I am proud to have worked as a volunteer PUSH official and to have served as one of Jackson's choice clergy lieutenants.

There are many sides to Rev. Jesse Jackson. Some of the negatives we know all too well. There have been some insightful biographers who have uncovered Jackson's weaknesses, especially his inordinate craving for validation and attention. We should know that any man whose identifying mantra is "I Am Somebody" is likely a person who has wrestled with profound personal identity issues. Jackson is a person who, by his own telling, embraced three different surnames in his youth. He was born as Jesse Burns, with his teenage mother's maiden name, but he longed to wear the Robinson name of his natural father, the middle-aged married man who lived next door to the Burns family. After his mother later married World War II veteran Mr. Jackson, young Jesse adopted his stepfather's name. The enigma that is Rev. Jackson is that while he is extremely confident of his gifts and abilities, he has wrestled with personal validation and identity.[25]

Rev. Jackson's passion, vulnerability, and his obvious charisma make him a unique type of leader and minister. For Jackson, there is a distinct disconnect between private and public morality. While we all struggle privately, what we do publicly and with public office impacts the quality of life of many other people. Jackson's public ministry has focused upon public policy and social justice, while his private struggles have at times become public. The impact of Dr. King on his life, while young Jesse was in his early twenties, has been lifelong and profound. Jackson's aggressive personal ambitions, however, did not endear him to King's family and many of King's close associates.

I always thought Rev. Jackson a logical successor after King's assassination, given Jackson's drive, gifts, and commitment to the work of carrying out King's human rights work and prophetic ministry. From 1968 there was clearly room for growth. But he was surely shaped in the spiritual womb of the civil rights generation. From his early years in the movement, Jackson caught the breadth and breath of the spirit of the age. He understands King's vision of the American Project. He knows that the promise of America is upward mobility, equal opportunity, justice, and high national moral purpose. Jackson has carried the mantle of King, but that does not mean he has absolutely embodied the powerfully humble character of King. King's unique era and sublime character were blended to create living prophecy and poetry. Jackson's life, like our lives and the life of our nation, has been impacted by the quality of King's life and the depths of his commitment and sacrifice.

As one who has studied and admired both Dr. King and Rev. Jackson, I have discerned profound differences in the biographies and leadership development of the two men. King was self-effacing, formally educated and patrician, a true prince of the institutional black Baptist Church. History and duty called him; he reluctantly answered and faced a tragic and heroic fate. King's was substantially a religious calling, and the confluence of history and personal courage offered a life that was transcendent and transformative. On the other hand, Rev. Jackson has been aggressive, ambitious, and self-consciously charismatic. His life has been much longer than King's brief life, and Jackson has often been irresistibly tempted to own what is political over and against what is prophetic. That is not to say he has not done a good work. He has carried on the work of King and has been infinitely more impactful in the nation and the world than he is given credit for. Jackson's national and global impact is as a disciple of King. As has been the case with many others, I was drawn to the work of Rainbow PUSH because I saw it as an extension of the civil and human rights movement. My work at PUSH blended my own passion and interests and, I thought, fit my skills set too.

By 2001, I regularly helped conduct the Rainbow PUSH national radio and television Saturday broadcast. As the National Director of Religious Affairs, I did the keynote addresses rather frequently when Rev. Jackson was away. One of the great advantages of this work was the number of political, business, and entertainment figures who visited PUSH and sought the favor of Rev. Jackson and his surrogates. I had the pleasure of introducing then-Illinois State Senator Barack Obama on a PUSH broadcast the year he ran his losing congressional race against First District U.S. Congressman Bobby Rush. Rev. Jackson was present that day. He wanted to allow Obama use of the platform without jeopardizing the relationship he had with Congressman Rush. Rev. Jackson had known Rush from his Black Panther days. In fact, Rush had surrendered to Jackson on the PUSH platform during the broadcast in December of 1969, after Panther leaders Fred Hampton and Mark Clark were killed by Chicago Police in the infamous early morning raid led by the Cook County State's Attorney. Rush was given high-profile protective covering by Rev. Jackson in that case, and Rush went on to serve in the Chicago City Council and the U.S. Congress. Standing for reelection, he had street credentials and was widely known and popular.

Everyone knew that Rush was going to handily win reelection to Congress. Rush was also known to have developed considerable political skill, with a long political memory to match. I was unknown enough in South Side political circles to get the deed done of introducing Obama with a minimum of risk to PUSH and Jackson. Obama was relatively unknown, but clearly restlessly ambitious. He lived in and represented the Hyde Park neighborhood and was a fairly regular listener and observer of the PUSH broadcast. Later, when Obama rebounded from losing his congressional race, I had the privilege in 2004 of introducing him in the S.E.I.U. (Service Employees International Union) sponsored final rally of his successful campaign for the Democratic nomination for the U.S. Senate. Of course, I had no idea that this young, rising political star would, in a few short years, become the first African American President of the United States.

The PUSH platform provided great opportunities for networking and exposure. For me, it was a perfect blend of religion and politics. The community saw the broadcast as a religious service with political overtones and impact. Local and national pols saw the forum as an opportunity to reach black voters. They came around constantly before and during election seasons. This was true even after the challenging hit PUSH suffered after the disclosure of Rev. Jackson's marital infidelity (resulting in his fathering a child). The organization remained influential, and the resilience of the PUSH leader was apparent. While there was some diminished power domestically, Rev. Jackson remained a very well-known and highly respected voice abroad. Facing a tense situation at home, it was fortunate that Jackson was able to access the honor that comes outside of one's own country. The PUSH president had a trip to Israel on the docket in the summer of 2001. Within days of departure, I got an invitation to travel to the Middle East as part of a peace mission led by Rev. Jackson. Acceptance would require that I rearrange my already scheduled travel plans for an August missions trip to Zimbabwe. It would be my second trip to Israel in two years, but this time I would travel with a delegation as an official guest of Middle Eastern religious leaders and the Israeli government. There was no way that I was going to let this opportunity pass.

In August of 2001, our Jackson-led clergy peace mission met up in Zurich, Switzerland, and from there we flew on to Israel. Upon our arrival, we were greeted at the Tel Aviv Airport by Foreign Minister Shimon Peres, and then ushered to a meeting with a full council of Israeli defense officials in an airport conference room. Days and evenings were filled with receiving visitors, taking tours, and engaging meetings with various groups and factions. Two days after arriving, we traveled by land to meet with Palestinian Liberation Organization (PLO) Chairman Yasser Arafat and members of his Cabinet. Officially, we were the guests of the Jerusalem Council of Churches. In both settings, Jackson led the discussions. He articulated an ambitious vision of an Israeli-Palestinian peace march led by religious and government officials through the streets of Jerusalem. It was Jackson's attempt to use the imagery and inject the moral authority of the American civil rights movement into this volatile Middle Eastern conflict. In separate settings, both sides were challenged to forswear retaliation against the other and become the initiator of peace in the conflict.

Laying the groundwork for a Jerusalem peace march was a very ambitious vision within this mission's eight-day time constraint. It was idealistic, and perhaps not even Jackson himself seriously thought we had the time or means to lay the groundwork for the march. I thought it was ironic that as we met separately with Israeli and Palestinian officials, offering the vision to each side, a representative from each group spontaneously offered the same facetious response to our approach, "Are you trying to get us to behave like black Christians and turn the other cheek?" When an Israeli defense official raised a variation of the retort on the first day, I did not feel comfortable enough to speak. Two days later in the Palestinian session when one of the PLO officials raised the "behaving like black Christians" question, I felt inspired enough to pound the table and respond, "Precisely!" But really, I understood their point. This was clearly not the American South in the second half of the twentieth century. This was a clash between worldviews and religions—an ongoing, intimate conflict for land—and resources and holy sites. Each side made the point that they had little latitude in this conflict. They could not and would not respond with nonviolence like

African Americans in the civil rights movement because non-retaliation in their context is dangerous.

In light of the religious differences, mistrust, and the history of the conflict, they may negotiate, but neither could afford to capitulate or turn the other cheek. My hope is one day we Americans can challenge Middle Easterners to a high calling. I would submit that negotiation requires a certain level of trust and graciousness. America has had the capacity to earnestly broker between Israelis and Palestinians because we have had leverage on both sides and, given our own national transformations, a good measure of moral authority. The hope of the Middle East, as is true in resolving conflict in many areas around the world, is grounded in the restoration of a principled America, leading and collaborating as a powerful and principled democratic champion of human rights, peace, and prosperity.

Our peace mission was to end abruptly, as we got tragic news while we were en route to Gaza for the second time. While traveling southwest on a coach bus, we received word that a terrorist attack against civilians had occurred at a hotel on Mount Scopus in Jerusalem. That spurred an emergency mobile phone call to Rev. Jackson from Secretary of State Colin Powell. We were about thirty minutes from a meeting with Sheikh Ahmad Yassin, the spiritual leader of Hamas, the militant Palestinian faction claiming responsibility for the bombing. Secretary Powell strongly urged reconsideration of the meeting and expressed serious concerns for the safety of anyone in the Sheikh's immediate vicinity. It was a very tense situation. It was also probably the beginning of the end of any hopes we had for a productive peace mission. We knew enough about our context to know that the warning was urgent and the threats were real. Without real options, we abandoned course and headed back to Jerusalem. It was a two-to-three hour journey back our quarters in the Roman Catholic pontiff's hotel complex right outside the West Gate of the Old City.

Our team included a conservative Catholic priest from Boston and a liberal Jewish rabbi from Los Angeles, two other Protestant clergy, as well as about four PUSH support staff people. The complexities of the Middle East had gone from the abstract to the realities of escalation of violence and concern for our personal safety. We experienced the ancient and modern worlds, the historical and the immediate; it all came together in one swirling humid day of travel, meetings, violence, warnings, and threats of retaliation. That night we spent hours on the hotel's roof overlooking Jerusalem, conversing about theologies and our American traditions of tolerance and diversity. Out of all we Americans have gotten wrong, we have somehow created a civil culture that allows us to be our particular faith-filled selves in wholesome relationship with other particulars.

The bombing on Mount Scopus was the backdrop of this frightful night and, after eight days in this Holy Land, we knew that some form of violent retaliation would be Israel's necessary response. So much for the vision of a King-style peace march. Our hopes of helping by challenging the combatants to move to higher ground would have to wait. Two days after the bombing, Rev. Jackson and the delegation left together, heading back to the states. I stayed behind an extra day to pick up my original itinerary to join my church members and missionary colleagues in Zimbabwe. I would leave Tel Aviv a day later for a flight to London and then Harare. I spent my last day in the Holy Land that summer walking the old city of Jerusalem alone for hours on end, pondering and reflecting on how the "City of Peace," with intersecting religions and sects, had become the focal point of one of the world's most volatile conflicts. Little did I know that in short order, the volatility of this land would be so tragically exported to the United States and change our way of life forever.

After we returned home in late August, the tragic attacks on American soil on September 11th that year forever changed our sense of security and detachment from the dangers of international terrorism. As I watched the attacks on the New York City Twin Towers and the Pentagon, I knew our world was changing in fundamental ways. The complexities of our mission of peace in the Middle East had followed us home. I reflected deeply upon my journey from public housing to pastoral and social justice ministry. The world was changing and, with increasing capacity, I was able to process the interrelatedness of my local ministry in the global context. With my work in the inner-city as a pastor and activist, and with my travels, I had experienced the fulfillment of doing what I always dreamt from the days of admiring and studying the social gospel ministries of Martin Luther King Jr. and Adam Clayton Powell. Chicago's West Side has provided a valuable vantage point from which to view the world as I reflected on our nation's entry into the new millennium. When I look back at my family and the community that nurtured me and the public school educators who inspired me, I see renewed faith and hope for America to win the future. The fight against terrorism is only one part of preserving the Project of America. Going forward, we must preserve the promise of America to preserve an America worth fighting for.

CHAPTER 3

Reforming Education Policy:
Working What We Know Works

"Be diligent to teach the children, instruct them at home, and when they are on the road with you, and instruct them from the time they rise up early in the morning until they lay down at night."—**The Book of Deuteronomy 6:7, ancient author, date unknown.**

"The school is the last expenditure upon which America should be willing to economize."—**Franklin Delano Roosevelt (1882-1945), the thirty-second President of the United States of America.**

"I never cut class. I loved getting A's. I liked being smart. I liked being on time. I thought being smart is cooler than anything in the world."
—**Michelle Obama, the First Lady of the United States of America, 2011.**

As an urban activist pastor, much of my advocacy is driven by my reflection on the graces that found me on the journeys of my personal story. My childhood in public housing was a part of Project America that made decent housing a citizenship right and family-friendly public policies the chief aim of government. My experience reflects what public schools are at their best: an oasis of opportunity for at-risk children in challenging environments. In retrospect, no one was more at risk than I. Access to public schools and subsidized state universities saved my life. Public education was my lifeline. I did not simply go to college, but a land grant college found me and embraced me. Left to my own devices and our limited family resources, I was not going to be a high achiever. People were placed in my path every step of the way. I have always understood how this grace has been my salvation, so I have worked to give back as one who has received much. My personal journey can provide insight for our current dialogue about education reform.

In West Africa among the Ghanaian Akan people, there is a "Sankofa" symbol of a bird whose neck stretches back to look behind itself. The symbol illustrates a proverb that means that in order to move forward, sometimes a people must look back and reclaim the values that have been lost. For Black America and America at-large, I think the answers to where we go from here are found in the wisdom of Sankofa. We must reflect in order to move forward. I have sought to use my personal memoirs to guide a reflection on moving forward from the morass of inner-city pathologies. We need to move with a wisdom that recognizes that some of the things we have left behind are things we will need to move forward. These are the things I believe we must embrace to help provide opportunities for millions of young people of color suffocating in ghettos and segregated in cycles of poverty in our inner cities.

Family-Friendly Public Policies

The American Project is a national vision that supports intergenerational sacrifice for individual and family upward mobility. The well-being of families must again become the cornerstone of public policies. I am a product of the Great Migration of African Americans who, due to oppression and lack of opportunities in southern states, trekked north. My family benefited from the national policy of investment in public housing. The political consensus that spawned public housing was the understanding that our nation can only be as strong as the families that produce and rear our children. Family-friendly policies are defined as public policies that support the healthy development and economic progress of families with children. When I lived in public housing at Jane Addams, the community norm was still a two-parent household. The severe crises in the black family, particularly disappearing fatherhood, was yet a couple of decades away.

If there is one single factor in perpetuating the violently unstable wasteland urban black America has become in the twenty-first century, it is the devastating effects of fatherlessness as a way of life.[26] In my years of urban ministry, what has troubled me most has been the absolute disorientation of fatherless black boys, and the mothers who were oblivious to the dysfunctional relationships they had with their children as a result of these stresses. I fear that among inner-city blacks, we have allowed a critical mass of the masses to become dysfunctional and debased. Yesterday's abnormal has now become the norm in the subculture. Chaos in the home has been internalized and manifests as violence in the streets. Young people exposed to violence prepare for funerals and not futures. Ultimately, we cannot ignore what festers in urban America. What we have allowed to happen in urban America is a precursor to what is in store for the rest of the nation without focused pro-family public policy. Given the stresses on all families and the disappearance of fatherhood for millions of children, what are the strategies for reversing the trends? In the current economic crisis, men have been disproportionately adversely affected. Blue-collar jobs for men are disappearing, and very little attention and address are being given to how this radical change in the economy impacts family households with children. That we have not seriously engaged these developments says much about our disregard for the importance of viable fatherhood in the lives of children.

As I have pondered the early loss of my mother, I consider myself extremely fortunate that I retained in my father the essential parent for life preparation. Much of my life's drive was to seek my father's affirmation. To get affirmation from Elijah Hatch, I had to earn it. From my childhood, I understood that having my father at home meant I had retained the one parent most essential to my becoming an adult and contributing citizen of society. Even in that case, my dad was only able to keep our family together because we had family-friendly undergirding public policy. We did not call it such at the time, but my widower dad was a "single parent," and his provision for our family was supported by public housing until my mid-teen years. In time, my sisters had become employed, and my family, as it was constituted, moved up and out into the American Dream with a mortgage backed by the Federal Housing Authority (FHA).

I don't know that we fully comprehend what the diminishing American Dream in the twenty-first century economy is doing to the soul of America. The economic crisis that came to a head in 2008 was, and is, fueled by the defaults in home mortgages and depreciating home values. Books and studies abound on the economic costs of this crisis. Of more concern to me is what this crisis means for families, and the human and spiritual costs. Jane Addams, Mother Cabrini, Harold Ickes, Robert Taylor, Ida B. Wells, and others knew that an America

---

91

without individuals and families in effective pursuit of dreams and opportunities is a nation that has lost its promise, its passion, and its purpose. From America's westward push and Manifest Destiny, to the Civil War and Reconstruction, to immigration, industrialization and the New Deal, to the civil rights movement and democratizing cyberspace: Americans are a people in pursuit of a piece of the nation's promise and a place to call home. We simply must recommit to providing the hope for families that the land belongs to all of our families and that, even at public expense, every family deserves decent housing. We have made great social and economic progress when we have engaged directly in class political warfare, fighting for the economic well-being of families. At the center of that fight is the right to a place to call home in the national commonwealth.

This history of Project America is part and parcel of the history of homesteading and public housing projects for immigrant and migrant families pursuing the promise of America. Decent housing as a citizenship right, with a striving to upgrade the stations of life, is the heart and soul of the American Dream. We cannot afford to shy away from public housing and assisting families in upward mobility as the core mission of government. Families raise the children who carry on our collective legacy, and public policy should reflect that family units do the good work of reflecting our values and projecting our future.

Equitable Funding in Public Education for Poor Children

We must begin again by viewing educational funding as an investment in America's future and not as an expenditure in the budget. As my narrative makes clear, Jacob A. Riis Public School, a school in the middle of the housing project, saved my life. High-quality public schools are essential to the future of America.[27] In view of the global economy, the public education budget must be as sacrosanct as we have believed the defense budget to be. Historically we have viewed defense spending as a non-negotiable necessity for national security and national survival. Without rescuing the lives of inner-city youth, going forward, there will not be much left in America worth defending. I have worked with education reformers to restructure the way we fund public education in Illinois. Our state has some of the widest disparity gaps between rich and poor school districts in the nation.[28] The disparity between rich and poor public school districts in Illinois approaches almost $20,000 per pupil per year. The disparities between poor public and rich private schools are even greater. Yet, all young people take the same standardized tests and compete for the same limited placements in colleges and universities.

I am always amazed how passionately people whose children attend well-resourced schools can be in making a case that money does not matter so much in the offering of quality education in schools in challenged communities. They blame poor communities, poor parents, underpaid teachers, and teacher unions for the failed educational outcomes. For sure, many of these criticisms are well-founded. There is a culture of poverty and bad parenting in poor communities, as well as poorly trained and poorly motivated educators in poorly performing schools. Nonetheless, I have never met a high-end-funded school parent willing to trade places with the poor families and students they critique. We also know that poorly paid teachers all over the nation work diligently every day with the calling to teach in the toughest environments. The truth is, in spite of the social analysis and politics of the "blame game," money and resources do matter. The mission of public schools has always included specializing in kids who come from varied places of disadvantage and family dysfunction. The noble mission of public schools and teachers is to offer real access to the promise of America for all of our children. As a motherless child in public housing, my future hinged upon what I encountered daily in school. Thankfully, I had publicly funded educators who undertook their vocation as public service and a call to national service. That mission today is just as necessary and more urgent. As long as the quality of education is tied to zip code and property tax, poor children will get a raw deal. That is not good for the future of America. All children must receive equal access to equitably resourced, high-quality public education.

Training and Supporting Strong School Leaders and Teachers

Training and supporting strong school leaders and teachers must be a top national priority. Children from disadvantaged backgrounds benefit greatly from school structure and the stability facilitated by strong school leadership. This is more important for poor children from stressed families than for children from more stable homes. School principals in challenged communities are on the front lines in the battle for the future of the country. We must train, equip, support them, and hold them accountable and reward them for effective performance. Properly compensating strong school leaders is a major reason money matters in education.

The greatest school resource is the human resource. Great schools begin with great principals. Especially in the inner-city, school leadership is the difference between a succeeding and a failing school. As we built West Point and military academies for national defense, we must create national school leadership academies for national offense against failing schools. Leaders trained to control and direct public schools in every environment are the new four-star generals of America's future. In my coming-of-age experiences through public schools, I was never confused as to who controlled the school and the environment around the school grounds. All children deserve that level of stability, security, and certainty concerning the direction and mission of the local school. School leaders must be allowed to select their teachers and school team. Similarly, they should be held accountable for succeeding (or failing) in any community environment.

All of us recognize the incalculable impact great teachers have on students. Our national movements to demand high performance and commitment from educators must be complemented with our own commitments to properly compensate performance and sacrifice. Teachers are paid too poorly for us to get the quality we demand. The best modern teachers are adaptive, and master the use of modern technologies for diagnostic teaching and personalized learning. Computers in the classroom help skillful teachers deliver customized instruction, improving the learning performances of students in classrooms and scores on standardized tests. In the adequately resourced districts, great teachers are better paid. We need to get the best talent where it is most needed with financial incentives. Teachers' unions must be open to reforms that evaluate performance, and help fast-track processes to remove underperformers.

We need not waste time Waiting for Superman, but we all must accept the high calling for investing our resources and ourselves in restoring greatness in the classroom. It will not be enough to play the blame game against one another in the crises in American education. Considering the radical creative reform that is needed, we must not be interested in fixing blame, but fixing problems. Folks who are not totally invested in this battle for our future can no longer be taken seriously as American patriots. Winning the future for American values will be accomplished by the developed minds and critical thinking skills of our nation's children.

Recruiting Male Educators for Public Schools

We need to intentionally recruit male educators to serve in our public school system. Recruiting males is a case that U.S. Department of Education Secretary Arne Duncan has consistently made during his tenure. Arne and I worked closely staging back-to-school rallies together when he served as head of the Chicago Public Schools. In inner-city schools where fatherlessness is a tragic epidemic, only two percent of our public school teachers are black males. Black males are less likely to encounter images of themselves in positions of authority in public education than any other student demographic. In the narrative of my story, I shudder to think where I would be had it not been for my single-parent father, and the male disciplinarians I encountered in school, such as the snarling Mr. Dukes in elementary school, and the wisdom of Mr. Estelle in high school. These men got my attention. Perhaps more than in any other context, the presence of male discipline by male educators matters in inner-city public schools.

In Chicago, a network of urban prep academies for high school-aged young men has had much early success attending to the particular needs of at-risk black males. Chicago Urban College Prep Academy for males, one of the first public schools of its kind in the nation, is producing an attractive track record for gaining acceptance of its graduates into four-year colleges and universities. In 2010, the first graduating class retained 100 percent of its entering students, and 100 percent of these graduates had acceptance letters to a four-year college or university.[29] School founder and Georgetown alumnus, Mr. Tim King, set out to prove that male imaging matters in our battle for the minds of urban young men. His inaugural class in Chicago's tough Englewood neighborhood was kept intact for four years, starting out together and finishing together with college acceptance letters. No young man was left behind. We are rediscovering that all-male or all-female school options may be helpful in addressing some aspects of the crises in urban education. These kinds of single-gender school options have always been available to advantaged and well-connected families. The trends toward public school variety and choice are hopeful signs of real education reform.

Intentionally seeking males for school leadership and teaching is not meant to disparage strong and powerful professional woman educators who work miracles in schools on a daily basis. I am simply emphasizing that in times of crisis we need all hands on deck. Male neglect of the challenges and call of public education leaves our nation severely handicapped. In modern armies we would never restrict or discourage a woman's right to serve beside men in national defense. In war we want access to the fullest contingent of our best solders. In our war against ignorance and national decline we need the same breadth of vision. We need women and men altogether on the front lines of education, in the battle for the minds and souls of America's children.

Education as Windows to the World

We must view schools as vehicles of exposure and opportunity and windows to the wider world. My first travels were in my mind on the living room floor of our project apartment as I spent hours captivated by the World Book encyclopedias my late mother had invested in. The investments in school trips in my early years also helped fundamentally shape my identity as a citizen of America and the world. I still marvel at the sacrifices of the parents and educators who had the foresight and wisdom to take our junior high school classes on bus trips to the state and national capitals. Today in times of budget limitations and limited vision, very little of this kind of investment in exposure is made for poor children. Complex layers of education are brought to bear within and outside the school environment. Internet access is a great tool of the modern classroom, and bridging digital divides is important for educating the disadvantaged, but there is no substitute for the wonder of physical travel and field trips that connect young people to our common heritage.

In my life story, at Lincoln's home and tomb in Springfield, history's expanse of time and place came alive. It was on the hallowed grounds of Gettysburg on the bus trip from Washington, D.C. at age fourteen, that I pondered the cost of liberty, the nobility of the American experiment with democracy, and the ongoing work of perfecting the Union. That experience helped give me vision and perspective. We still need to count exposure and visiting national sites as important parts of education. Affluent school districts still provide for these civic lessons, but sadly, poorer districts do not. Lack of exposure to the wider world is a major handicap that disadvantaged students face. To level the playing field, poorer school districts need resources to offer travel opportunities and exchange programs. The segregation from opportunity of poor children is exacerbated by isolated schools. The culture of poverty is reinforced by a lack of exposure. In a view of life from the projects, I have learned that travel is part and parcel of the culture of wealth. All children deserve exposure, and thrive when they have access to the wider experiences of our world.

Extracurricular Activities Are Essential

We must value the investments in extracurricular activities for our young people, especially in high school. My high school attendance at Dunbar Vocational was never an issue, even though I had very little daily supervision from my father throughout my teens. My dad was fifty-two when I was born and in his late sixties during my years at Dunbar. He did not have the know-how or energy to monitor my school attendance as I traversed the breadth of Chicago every day for school and work. I went to school daily for one main reason: school was fun! It had pep rallies, sports, dances, drama club, music, friendships, and girls. My school had over two thousand students, and there was always a lot of fun stuff to do. I do not want to overstate the obvious, but I have learned that the profound is often simple. Extracurricular activities are not expendable, but they are an essential part of the high school experience. Extracurricular activities are what make school fun, and making school fun and attractive helps win the battle against increasingly high school dropout rates.

When we debate urban school budget issues, the things that make school most attractive are the first things we cut from the school program. We almost never fully appreciate the correlation between cutting extracurricular activities and the increasing dropout rates. School districts with high property values would never consider sending young people to schools without the needful things that make high school so fulfilling that students show up daily, and so memorable that adults show up to reunions a half century after graduation. That many charter schools are in makeshift facilities with limited extracurricular programs should cause us to pause and ponder whether these schools can fully replace the large public high school equipped for all kinds of students with all the bells and whistles. That only one in five charter schools outperforms regular public schools means that we have not found a panacea in privatizing education. Charter and contract schools may fulfill needs for school choice and innovation, but it is wrong to do this at the expense of the larger public school mission to serve all kinds of children. Young people generally are not born valuing education, but they can grow to value it. All of our children deserve a stimulating school culture and the space to grow. When they and their education are our primary concern, it is reflected in our budget priorities. We cannot afford to cut out the extracurricular activities and program enrichments that are the soul of education. To save the soul of our nation, our high schools must be fully funded with all the things that build the character and constructively unleash and guide the passions of all our young people.

Vocational Education

We must have real career and jobs training opportunities for urban young people. Not only do we need traditional curriculums that lead to higher education, but we also need opportunities for vocational education and access to apprenticeships and trades. In the years I attended Dunbar Vocational High

School, students had shop classes that introduced trades and helped connect education to economic viability. With vocational training and job prospects in the Chicago area, I knew many young men and women whose dream was to work, marry, and build families as a matter of course. Those kinds of post-high school dreams have dried up with the disappearance of vocational education opportunities. Inner-city youth are effectively shut out of labor unions and building trades in American cities. Large state budget capital programs and private sector construction projects are essentially "white breadwinner union jobs." Blacks are locked out of employment programs in cities like Chicago. There are really no explanations for this exclusion except nepotism and race-based segregation from opportunity. The predominately white trade union's perpetuation of this reality has done much harm to the historic relationship between African Americans and labor unions. The racial breach between working people and the divisions between workers in the public and private sectors has been politically exploited by corporate interests, and has pitted folks with similar economic interests against one another.

Today shop-style classes should be supplemented by vocational tracks in computer technologies, service industries, medical and hospital professions, and work opportunities in the emerging green economy. Education must be linked to economic opportunities, allowing students to envision a gainful future for working hard and graduating. Junior colleges and post-high school vocational schools should be a direct pipeline to substantial careers. We should not simply offer alternative vocational options after students have failed at high school. High school must be a place we track aptitude and interest. For students at the high school and community college level, it will be clear that it pays to stay in school when education leads to specific employment opportunities.

College-Bound Must Not Mean College Cost Bondage

We must embrace a moral obligation to subsidize undergraduate education for under-resourced college-bound students. Upward mobility in America should not require debilitating debt accumulation. In 2010, total student debt in the U.S. passed credit card debt.[30] College for too many young people means guaranteed high levels of debt in an uncertain, flat-lined job market. We will not win the future for America with this wide gulf between aspiration and reality. When I went to college in the mid-1970s, federal Pell grants and Illinois state scholarship programs paid for the total costs. The bulk of my student debts were accumulated in graduate school. By graduate school, however, I had already

98

benefited from the heavy investments in the Illinois state university system. Graduate school program costs are more manageable because the number of classes to complete an advanced degree is much less than for undergraduate programs. By graduate school, my life foundation was set, and I was well on my way toward overcoming the handicaps of my early education years. Having an undergraduate foundation gave me the tools I needed to compete with people from more advantaged backgrounds. The public institutions of higher education did for me, and students like me, what they were designed to do: provide a further gateway to the world for those who had the aptitude to expand their horizons and make a larger contribution with their gifts and abilities.

The original mission of land-grant state universities focused upon opportunities for first-generation college students. In their genesis, these colleges served mostly white families and provided substance to the hope of immigrant families for a piece of the American Dream. Our nation is founded and fueled by the promises and principles of fairness. For higher education to be treated as a luxury of the wealthy diminishes the brightness of America's light to the world. While great private universities flourish with donors and endowments and impressive financial aid, government must support state university systems for the masses of working families, the poor, and the new immigrants.

College Support Systems for Urban Youth

Finally, we must reestablish support systems in predominately white college and university settings for disenfranchised urban youth. In my life narrative, I wanted to clearly reveal the ways I was preserved as I persevered in colleges and universities where I was a distinct minority and educationally and culturally handicapped. Rudolph Womack at Western and Samuel Harvey at Georgetown were employed for kids like me. Their positions and missions were the fruit of the black student movement demands in the 1960s and early 1970s for address of minority cultural isolation on white college campuses. There was a real sense of commitment to making the way better for those coming behind. Academic institutions responded by establishing black studies departments, staff and program supports, and "black houses" for cultural space on campus. Looking back, having advocates, academic supports, relevant course options, and a particular space on a campus were saving graces for students like me. These things were not extra helps for minority black students; they were equalizers in our interactions with students from the dominant culture and privileged backgrounds. These equalizers were the fruit of a movement that responded to generations of specific discrimination against a court-protected class of citizens crippled by the legacies of America's original sin.

These supports were not to overcompensate or relish in black victimization, but the support systems were clear-headed realism that the nation and its institutions had compacted to respond to the legacy of slavery, and that colleges and universities would lead the way in enlightened address of painfully obvious obstacles that have to be overcome. The consensus was that opportunity had to be real and tangibly reflected in outcomes. It was an awesome season for America. I benefited from it greatly, as did others, including the likes of Supreme Court Justice Clarence Thomas. Sadly, I remember the feeling that doors for others like me were closing as I passed through these institutions in the late 1970s and 1980s.

By 1978 the Bakke Supreme Court embedded the concept of "reverse discrimination" in American jurisprudence. I felt sad, because I sensed I was passing through doors that would leave behind countless kids in our urban centers who had backgrounds similar to and worse than mine. Tragically, I was right. The national mood turned regressive right after a small window of opportunity of less than ten years, from 1969 to 1978. From that brief window of opportunity, I have had to live with seeing many black youth swallowed up in cultural poverty and in the morass of socioeconomic pathologies. I have had to admit to myself that I really did not go to college, but gracefully, college came and found me. The joys of my life have been tempered with the bittersweet recognition of the different life that I would have had without the favor of unsolicited opportunities. When I watch the continuing saga of the nightly news in urban America, I have to wonder but for the grace of God, there go I.

In the forty plus years since the death of King and the old black student movements, there has been almost total retreat and retraction by majority institutions of higher education from the commitments to students from the black urban centers. Some black studies courses remain, while minority affairs college and university officers have been long phased out. "Black houses" are now multicultural and diversity centers. It all feels eerily like post-Reconstruction and benign neglect. In the face of this withdrawal from commitment to domestic African American students among college educators, receiving and retaining black students is a major concern. Of course super-talented students of all backgrounds will succeed in almost any context regardless of the barriers. I'm more interested in how schools help those like me who need the kinds of supports my family and community could not provide. With resources to make the environs equally user-friendly, more kids from isolated places in America could make it through educational institutions and into the wider world. If we hold that the future of our nation will be determined by developing the full potential of urban youth, then we must re-embrace the passion and programs that sought to bring the disenfranchised into higher education and blessings of America.

❖❖❖❖❖❖❖

Creating Zones of Opportunity in the American Educational Landscape: A Vision of a West Side Corridor of Educational Opportunity

Our nation's participation in the world economy depends upon creating a pipeline of opportunity through inner-city elementary and high schools to welcoming environments in colleges and universities. My work on Chicago's West Side has been directed by this local focus and global vision. The children of our nation must compete in the world economy, and we must all take responsibility for giving them the tools they need. Properly funding and maximally investing in an equal high-quality education that is accessible to all children is a thoroughly American value and project. America is not America unless we can reasonably believe that every child has a fair shot to live out their God-given potential. We must also recognize in this millennium that every child in America is a global citizen as well, and must be challenged to compete and cooperate with young people all over the world. Our forward thinking about education today must embrace global strategic foresight.

Education reformers around the nation have been impressed by the work of Geoffrey Canada, the founder and visionary who leads the Harlem Children's Zone.[31] Canada's work is inspiring, most especially his willingness to lead community leaders and institutions in claiming responsibility for all the children in an identifiable learning zone. Nationally, the Obama Administration has envisioned using the children's learning zone concept. "Promise Neighborhoods" would enhance public school student academic performance by bringing together community assets and wraparound services using federal seed money to drive the movement. That vision has been stalled to some great degree by federal budget battles. We will have to find ways to continue moving forward with the spirit of making every child's quality educational opportunities a broad community responsibility. In that respect, Canada's work has spurred my own imagination.

My local laboratory is the West Side of Chicago and the surrounding suburbs. As a private citizen, I have engaged education reform by challenging community leaders and stakeholders to begin to envision a Chicago West Side, western adjacent suburb regional corridor of educational opportunity for all children. Looking at the boundaries of the Seventh Congressional District of Illinois, about 51 percent African American, offers a most useful way of broadening the conversation about education reform. In our district across the western Chicago metro region, we have high quality-high schools of various governance and constitution. The public high schools in the following list are all known for their high quality:

• Whitney Young—one of the city's leading magnet high schools on the Near west side. This Chicago public high school has ranked high consistently among the elite in producing national scholars. Its seats are highly coveted, and its alumni include U.S. First Lady Michelle Obama, Santita Jackson, the oldest daughter of the Rev. Jesse Jackson, and Marcus Jordan, the son of NBA star Michael Jordan.

• Westinghouse—a highly selective East Garfield Park Chicago public high school recently rebuilt on a $40-million campus. Formerly a basketball powerhouse, it is now refashioned to attract the new urban gentry families moving into mid-West Side communities.

• Oak Park-River Forest High School—this public high school of the adjacent western suburbs is a collegiate-style institution that serves a diverse student body where graduates can access very selective colleges. The disparity in academic underperformance of the school's black students remains a continuing, perplexing problem for the district.

The Chicago western corridor is also home to high-quality, well-resourced, faith-based private high schools:

• Providence-St. Mel—an inner-city, high-achieving, private, faith-based K through 12th grade school that has had over 90 percent of its high school graduating seniors accepted at four-year colleges and universities for over thirty years. It was founded by the legendary Paul Adams, an urban educator extraordinaire in East Garfield Park in Chicago.[32]

• St. Ignatius College Prep—this august Jesuit institution, founded in 1869, has educated generations of families and sent thousands of high school students to leading universities around the nation. It is located in a diverse community of condos, stone flats, and public housing units on Chicago's Near West Side.

• Hope Christian Academy—a faith-based high school founded by Bob Muzikowski (Safe at Home author) that serves a small, diverse student body in the city's medical district on the Near West Side. This decade-old school has rescued young people from gritty backgrounds with faith and love. The school mission is to do what it takes for its most challenging students, while challenging upper-income families to consider Hope as a high school option with strong academics and Christian values.

• Christ the King—a Far West Side Jesuit College Prep high school in the city's vibrant, predominately African American Austin community. Founded in 2008, this school's $30-million campus is the living legacy of the former Park National Bank and its owner Mr. Mike Kelley. His generosity by the millions gifted this new Cristo Rey school. The mission is uncompromised academic excellence and character development for poor children. Students earn 70 percent of their tuition through a corporate job work-study program.

• Fenwick Jesuit College Prep—a very high-quality Catholic high school in Oak Park, the west suburban village adjacent to the city's Austin community. It has served mostly affluent families in the western suburbs, just ten blocks away from the urban challenges of the Far West Side.

There are quality public and private elementary schools as well that serve as feeders for the high-quality high school options in the corridor. All of these institutions, elementary and high school, are located within very diverse neighborhoods. My vision of a zone of educational opportunity for all children would ask, "Can we conceive of these schools themselves becoming as racially and socioeconomically diverse as the populations of the communities that make up the western corridor? What would it take to move us toward King's beloved community, led by and reflected through these flagship schools?" In my work as pastor, activist, and community organizer, I know most of the school leaders in these institutions. Regrettably, very few of them know or work with one another.

I have envisioned facilitating a roundtable of high-quality schools that encompasses all of the school types and builds a collaboration to provide opportunities to all families in our region. The vision would be an expansive and effective zone of educational opportunity in the Chicago urban west geographical area. It is an integrated and diverse take on the Harlem Children's Zone concept. The New York Harlem zone is still racially and class-segregated geo-space. Our west zone of opportunity would mean expanding the zone to combat segregation from opportunity and breaking down barriers among institutions and the populations they serve. Working together, these institutions can share best practices, economies of scale, staff, resources, and information. They could pursue philanthropic resources as a consortium, advantaged by the vision of philanthropic investors for wide and maximum impact. Our western corridor of educational opportunity would cross city-suburban lines and public-private divisions. The primary concern would be access to high-quality options in "zones of opportunity" for every family on the west side and the adjacent western suburbs. All families would have access to all the educational options in the zones of opportunity. In this vision, our metro region competes and cooperates in the global regional and global economy.

Globalization means the local and the global focal intensity is infused. Our local schools, public and private, cannot afford to stand in isolation. We must think of school systems as zones with diverse options. Our local systems will begin to address the global context when we take responsibility for educating every child, giving each and every child access to high-quality public and private educational options within zones of opportunity.

Collaboration for zones of opportunity requires a roundtable relationship, with each institution maintaining its distinct identity. The roundtable facilitates collaborative visioning and expanded receiving boundaries for existing high-quality schools. City and suburban, public and private, and secular and religious educational institutions working together in a zone of opportunity reflect the urgent call of our national crises. The times demand the clear focus of collaboration with the common purpose of expanding opportunity. The result could be increased resources for each institution and decreased isolation for hundreds of urban families. All children deserve to be plugged into networks that allow them access to the world. Families and children on Chicago's West Side should be integrated into the networks that afford the benefits of being citizens in a world-class city. School must be for every child what it was to me as a kid in the Jane Addams projects, a window to the world. Indeed, education is the key to the future and global power.

Chapter 4

Movement Two:
The Changing Complexion of the World Center Stage

"....And they shall be led away captive in all nations: and Jerusalem shall be overrun by Gentiles, that is, until the times of the Gentiles are fulfilled are fulfilled." **—Jesus of Nazareth, The New Testament Book of Luke Chapter 21 verse 24, around 33 A.D.**

"We are all familiar with this old world that is passing away. We have lived with it and we have seen it in all of its tragic dimensions. We have seen it in its international aspects, in the form of colonialism and imperialism. Did you know that there are approximately two billion, four hundred million people in the world? And did you know that the vast majority of them are colored?...Most of them live on two continents, Asia and Africa. About a billion, six hundred million are colored people...And all these people for years lived under the domination of either the French, the Dutch, or the British. They were dominated politically, exploited economically, segregated, and humiliated." **—Dr. Martin Luther King Jr., January 1957, at the NAACP ninety-fourth commemoration of the Emancipation Proclamation.**

"Human history has often been a record of nations and tribes—and, yes, religions—subjugating one another in pursuit of their own interest. Yet in this new age, such attitudes are self-defeating. Given our interdependence, any world order that elevates one nation or group of people over another will inevitably fail....Our problems must be dealt with through partnership; our

progress shared." —Barack Obama, the forty-fourth American President, "A New Beginning," in Cairo, Egypt, June 4, 2009.

❖❖❖❖❖❖❖

Bates College and Barack Obama 2008: *Change*

In January of 2008, I was invited to be the guest preacher for Martin Luther King Jr. weekend at Bates College in Lewiston, Maine. Bates is one of the finest liberal arts schools in America. It has the distinction of graduating the late Dr. Benjamin Elijah Mays, a former president of Morehouse College in Atlanta and mentor of Dr. King. When King attended regular chapels at Morehouse in his teens as a college student, Dr. Mays' homilies inspired the young student to envision a socially relevant Gospel and social justice ministry. In 2008, my son, Marshall Jr., was a student living on the predominately white New England campus in Lewiston. That cold January, my message would be shared in the context of the emerging presidential campaign of Illinois U.S. Senator Barack Obama. Even then I could sense that a new generation of Americans saw this national election in light of America's future in a changing new world. The new realities of globalization made Obama's candidacy both plausible and potentially transformative. My message at the school chapel, in an academic setting, facilitated the blend of spiritual insight and social commentary I enjoyed. What I shared that Sunday night before the King national holiday set in motion an ongoing reflection and prism through which I have processed the imagery and meaning of Obama's rise to the American presidency.

It was cold and dark outside, but the multiracial group of student and faculty attendees came to the service that night with a spirit of hopefulness and anticipation. Black students made up a mere 2 percent of the seventeen hundred-member student body. Almost all of the black students were present that night. A black professor was chair of the event committee that selected me for the message, and his remarks set the tone for the universality of the commemoration. Dr. King was a global citizen of the first order, and his vision was the prevailing vision for twenty-first century America. Also present were members of Atlanta's Morehouse College debate team, who were visiting Bates for the King Weekend.

Before I spoke, interracial groups of students performed gospel and jazz music with impeccable precision. I thought throughout the service, "these kids are awfully good!" One freshman young lady from California belted out a most soulful rendition of the late Sam Cooke's old civil rights movement anthem: "A

Change Is Gonna Come." I leaned over and told my son, "Boy, that girl know she can sang!" I wondered who in the world convinced that black girl to come to white Bates in the state of Maine. Maine is 96.4 percent white, and the state motto is "Life as it is supposed to be." Marshall Jr. was one of two African Americans on the basketball team and seemed very popular with students and staff. He was not the star of the team by any stretch, not even a game starter, but he was a deadly three-point specialist. The boy's got a burner. He was also clearly well-liked by students and faculty. He is a good kid. The program committee gave him the high honor of reading the scripture for the service. It was a proud moment for us. I was especially happy that I had a son who was proud of me, seemingly unashamed to be the son of a Baptist preacher. I wanted to do well and make him even prouder as a student in this high-brow academic setting.

In sharing, I stuck to the formula I had often used in the Rainbow PUSH broadcast setting. I opened with a Bible text that had arrested my attention for some time. The New Testament Book of Acts 17:6 translates in English, "These are the ones who have turned the world upside down." This is the text that gives commentary on the world of the early Christian church.[33] We call the opening years of that spiritual movement the "first century" because, in retrospect, that age ushered in a transition from an ancient world of declining empires to the rise of a new world with new peoples, new perspectives, new technologies, new global powers, and a new universal religion based upon old Judaism. The New Testament scriptures record a global shift of power and resources from the ancient peoples and their civilizations in the global south to the emerging European peoples in what we have come to know as the Northern Hemisphere. Paul's mission in the early church as apostle to the Gentiles is the main story line of the New Testament. In a real sense, the Christian faith would owe its future global growth to the European embrace of the first century Gospel.[34] The Gentiles who had been farthest from the Holy Land would be culturally transformed by the new faith, discover enlightenment, and initiate the Industrial Revolution and the contemporary global economy. It is interesting to ponder how much Paul of Tarsus understood that his pioneering mission work among European Gentiles two thousand years ago would strategically flow with the global shift and changing face of world power from south to north.[35]

The dynamics of the emerging new world order of the first century are reflective, in reverse, of a new world emerging in the twenty-first century. There is now a new power shift from the global north to the south. Dr. King was able to process this transition far ahead of others in his critique of America and the West, and his insight into the rise of people oppressed by the global European colonial system. King foresaw that the intimately interconnected new world order would not accommodate militarism, nor unrestrained capitalism or godless communism. His foresight into the central issues of the twenty-first century speaks volumes of the authentic prophetic calling on his life. In the first century and twenty-first century worlds, each generation is called to navigate and process tumultuous winds of change.[36] Like the generations succeeding the Book of Acts, we too must flow with the direction of the spiritual winds of our time.

The forward look of my message in the Bates chapel dealt with several major winds in our time: global contextualization, the emerging two-thirds world onto the global stage, the uncontainable global energies of immigration and migration, green thinking and environmental stewardship, and the continuing spiritual quest for meaning and transcendence. My premise was and is that the only way to understand anything in the world is through the context of the interconnectedness of globalization. Modernity means that the world has now literally become a global village. Village life requires mastery of relationships, mutual respect, and common values. The citizens of the village either prosper together or they perish together. If we embrace the progressive, the compassionate, the complementary, and the cooperative, we will flow with the fresh wind of the Spirit. In the first century, the witnesses of the Spirit transmitted the Gospel and laid the foundations in Europe for a global evangelical faith and universal liberties. From the Age of European Enlightenment, America arose from colonial status to an experiment with democracy that struggles to perfect itself and give light to the world.

From outer space we see the world as one, and we can conclude that proscribing parts of the world as north and south, up and down, and east and west are actually political constructs. Mapping is a matter of perspective and serves the particular interest of particular mapmakers. If we stood in the farthest northern edge of the Nile Delta, we could look southward toward Victoria Falls, the life source of the Nile River. From the Victoria Falls, the river flows down and the river source would be up the Nile. The point is, up and down are relative to origin of our perspective. So in Acts 17:6, actors in the power of the Spirit worked to dispel darkness and oppressions as witness of God's kingdom. They therefore did not so much as turn the world upside down, as they worked to turn the world right-side up. We too, in this generation, can be Spirit-led actors, impacting our world for good and for God's glory. My Baptist, preacher-style rapid delivery exhortation at the end of my message at Bates College was an admonishment to "go forth, change the world, and turn the world on its right-side up."

On that January wintery night in 2008, my message went over well. Time would prove that the Obama pollsters were right: the American people were ready for "Change." This was a political season ripe for youthful participation and fundamental change. That was the spiritual vibe I felt from the multiracial generation that brought Facebook and social networking into American politics and into the Obama campaign in 2008. A few weeks after my Bates sermon, in the middle of Maine, one of the whitest states in the nation, Obama would win the Democratic Maine caucuses over Hillary Clinton. Marshall Jr. informed me that Bates students turned out en masse in downtown Lewiston to support the Illinois Senator. A fresh new wind was blowing in America, indeed.

The "Change" theme of the Obama campaign tapped into a frustration in the American electorate and a hopefulness people wanted to feel about the future. Without fully comprehending the specifics, the people intuitively and experientially discerned that they had been disconnected from their government. The American government no longer represented their interests and government officials were removed from the experiences of common people. The American people wanted access to their government, and Obama was the perceived change agent. It was really phenomenal that the Junior Senator from Illinois, just recently released from student loan debt, was elected President of the United States. The American people were attempting to make a significant statement. The Obamas were not seen as part of the political elite, but Barack and Michelle were accessible commoners and minorities who had done well. That's how we viewed them in Chicago, as familiar neighbors and fine examples of the promise of America.

Election Night 2008: The Obama Family Tent

Election Day November 3, 2008 was unusually balmy for a fall day in Chicago. For Chicagoans, it was a national election with local feel. Early in the day Senator and Mrs. Obama had cast their ballots in their South Side Hyde Park neighborhood at the same precinct polling place that Nation of Islam leader Louis Farrakhan had used earlier in the day. They both lived less than two blocks from Dr. King's Workshop, the Rainbow PUSH national headquarters of the civil rights icon, Rev. Jesse Louis Jackson. Priscilla and I had cast our ballots on the west side in the Austin community early that day. We shared the polling place with Congressman Danny K. Davis and Chicago Mayor Richard Daley's press secretary, Jackie Heard. By early evening, Priscilla and I were headed downtown with our daughters, Joyce and Janelle, on the public transit train. We wanted to see how close we could get to history.

Arriving in downtown Chicago, we found a surreal atmosphere of unusually friendly people from every walk of life. We knew that Congressman Jesse Jackson Jr. was hosting a party at the Conrad Hilton Hotel on Michigan Avenue. I figured we could easily get in, given the relationships we had with the Jacksons and the familiarity we had with the congressman's staff members. We went up to the ballroom on the second floor. The place was jumping with music and black and white urbane partiers, mostly younger than my wife and I. At the door we were vetted and given blue party admittance adhesive wristbands so that we could come and go as we pleased. These bands were the kind that had to be cut off at the end of use to prevent attendees from handing them off to other people. We worked the room and followed early returns from the East Coast. The early numbers looked good for Obama.

Most of the black folk in the crowd hedged their hopes on Obama's election, fully aware that history had shown that whites fudged in saying they would support an African American front-runner, only to abandon the black candidate in the booth. In past years, losers Thomas Bradley for governor in California and Harvey Gantt for U.S. Senator in North Carolina were ready examples of this phenomenon in elections for high offices. The 2008 election was for the highest office in the land, and we all held our breath. After a while Priscilla and I filed out of the party room and went into the hotel lobby and mixed it up with a few friends and a lot of strangers. It was not hard at all to make new friends. Toward 8:30 p.m. central standard time, a wondrous piece of news flashed on the screen in the bar area of the Hilton. The networks were now calling Ohio for Obama. That was the state that gave George Bush a second term with all kinds of voting access irregularities in 2004.

The trends of the night were unmistakable. With excitement, Priscilla and I decided to try to use some VIP access passes to the Grant Park celebration area. The line to get in extended for blocks and it became evident that the time of calling the election was getting close. Moving to the front of a long line, we found out that our passes were for a VIP entrance three blocks away on Roosevelt Road. In a half trot, we made it to a gate with no line, made our way through security, and then herded around a crowd that was about forty yards from the stage in Grant Park where Obama would speak.

The big screen inside Grant Park flashed the report that the election had been called: "Obama wins!" The forty-fourth President of the United States of America would be the first African American to hold the nation's highest office. We could hardly contain our excitement. There were tears of joy all around. We milled near a gate to an inner standing area nearer to the stage. I finally got the courage to ask if we could get into the inner area to get closer. "You need a band to get in here," the security guy said. "You mean a band like this?" I asked, showing the blue adhesive wristband we had gotten from Congressman Jackson's party at the Hilton. "Sure, step in," he answered. I was quite sure that the party bands just happened to have been similar to the Grant Park admittance band. What a stroke of luck, I thought. Priscilla and I were in with our bands, and we began to mill around with familiar and unfamiliar folks. Then in time, the program began.

First was soulful solo singing of the National Anthem. A black African Methodist Episcopal bishop offered the invocation. It was a high time in Chicago, the heart and soul of the hope of the Great Migration. It felt like a new jubilee. Finally, the President-elect walked out with the new First Family. What a night! For the first time in my life, I felt like a full-fledged first-class American citizen. Looking with fresh eyes at the American flag, I knew the faith and sacrifices of my ancestors were not in vain. I had grown up in the Jane Addams Housing Project and attended Riis Elementary School just a mile or so to the west of this spot. There I read new World Book encyclopedias on the floor of our Ada Street apartment. From Riis and the Old Town Boys Club I had traveled to Washington, D.C. and envisioned the promise of America. I had attended high school about two-and-a-half miles to the south at Dunbar Vocational High School, then went away to college and graduate school. Indeed, I had gone out to discover the country and the world, yet the marvelous promise of America came home to me again.

After the President-elect's speech, Priscilla and I stuck around and talked to folks about the wonder of the day. As the crowd thinned out, we noticed a cluster of tents with blue letters off the stage area. Since it did not feel as if we were intruding, we milled around to take in the sights. There were wooden makeshift walkways on the grassy areas between the tents. To make myself useful, I leapt at the opportunity to assist a lady in a wheelchair onto the wooden walkway. Soon after, Joseph Biden, the Vice President-elect himself appeared in a walkway, and I instinctively went up to him and offered; "Great job, Joe!" Biden is a naturally friendly politician who treats all comers as friend and familiar. I dropped a pastor's name from his small Delaware state that I knew he would know to increase his comfort level. "I talked to my buddy, Pastor Chris Bullock the other day," I said. "Oh, he's a great guy, great guy," Biden replied. Feeling comfortable enough to pat him on his back, I retorted, "Yeah, we were close for the years he was here in Chicago. Bullock's a bright guy."

We waited around a little longer, and next to appear was Senator Claire McCaskill of Missouri. Now even more comfortable, I shared with her, "This is a great night for America." I remembered that she had been heavily influenced by her grandchildren to endorse Obama, and I mentioned that to her. "It was the youth in all of our families and the youth of the country to whom we owe this night. This is a new America," the senator added, and walked away toward Roosevelt Road.

Finally, I glanced over to the tent sign that read, "Obama Family." Priscilla and I walked over. The security guy said, "You need a security band to get in here." Holding up my wrist, I confidently replied, "Here it is." Priscilla followed, and just like that we were in a tent of about seventy-five people. Michelle Obama had a line of five to seven people waiting to speak to her, and the President-elect had a greeting line slightly longer. We meandered in, first standing near the future First Lady's mother Marian Robinson. She reminded me of the saintly, older black women I had known all my life as she expressed quite clearly that her feet were tired and that she was ready to go home. It had been a long day. Priscilla moved toward Michelle with a phone camera. "No pictures in here," Michelle Obama said forcefully without a smile. I think the point was that this was the family's tent, and the people who had access at this time of the evening would not need to burden the Obamas with picture taking. In here, the newest First Family was relieved not to have to wear its public face.

After greeting and congratulating Michelle, we moved through a short line for the President-elect. Standing in line after a kid had moved out, I moved toward the new President-elect. He was chewing gum in a way that I knew was a substitute for smoking. "Hey Rev, how ya doing?" he said, patting me on my back. "Uh, congratulations, Mr. President-elect," I uttered nervously. We shook hands and the President-elect put his arm around my shoulder. Priscilla did her best to sneak a cell phone camera shot without anyone noticing. I moved away from Obama—stunned, overwhelmed, and nervous. For some reason I was now in a hurry to get out of the tent and head home. I knew it couldn't get any better for us than the good fortune we already had. I just wanted to exit and hurriedly call our children with the amazing story of how we ended election night with a small group of people in the Obama family tent. Leaving the tent threshold, I did not want to show Priscilla just how excited I was to have the President-elect acknowledge me with the affectionate title "Rev." without any prompting on my part. Obama obviously knew me personally even though we did not have a personal relationship. I guess my years at PUSH, just blocks from his family home, and my introductions and invocations for his campaign events had registered. Walking out of the tent, I cleared my throat and muttered to Priscilla nonchalantly, "Yep, uh, he probably remembers me from the PUSH platform." It was quite a night, indeed.

The "change" I think Americans anticipated with the Obama election was a unique kind of access to their government and a restoration of faith that our system can be placed back into the service of the people. Americans know that the root causes of our economic crises are exploitation, fraud, deregulation, and greed on the part of powerful interests. As in other volatile periods of American history, we have degenerated into class warfare. But it is not a class warfare precipitated by the middle-class, working poor, or the poor; rather it is the stresses on the economic and political violence brought upon by the unbridled and unrestrained greed of the upper high-end financial class and international banking interests. The change the American people sought in the election of Obama was restoring a sense of balance in the power dynamics in our government and economy.

By electing a Chief Executive to represent the interests of common Americans, voters were looking for a champion to check the exploitations of the new robber barons. There were high hopes, not for a mandated set of policies, but for transformation and renewal of purpose. The people elected a President from the commoner class and expected a champion of the common people's interest who would use the bully pulpit of the presidency to regulate the capitalist elite and bring balance to the national government. I believe that the people sought the kind of leadership provided by Lincoln in one era and Franklin Roosevelt in another. The American people know that their nation and the world is changing. The people were and are ready for a fresh vision. The challenge remains whether we can produce executive and congressional leadership that can move us forward by our dreams, instead of taking us backward by our fears. I, too, believed in 2008 that an Obama Administration would restore balance to the body politic and could help America transition into the new global order as a moral and political leader of an emerging new world. Beyond the politics of the 2012 campaign, we still have an opportunity to cast new vision and win the future for American ideals. But make no mistake about it, there will be a short window of opportunity for the revival of America.

The Shift: The Changing Face of World Power

The twenty-first century is a time of momentous change. It is a time when the shift of world power is unmistakable and unalterable. Two thousand years ago, there was a decisive shift in global power and resources from the ancient civilizations in the Southern Hemisphere to the rising European peoples of the Northern Hemisphere. The peoples of Europe, who had been farthest away from old civilizations, embraced the Christian faith and laid the foundations for cultural transformation. In the European historical interim, Islamic civilizations and the Ottoman Empire made tremendous contributions to preserving and advancing civilization and enlightenment. The true roots and legacy of Islam in global history are as keepers of scientific discovery and as preservers of the intellectual heritage of human civilizations for the times between the fall of Rome and the modern rise of northern Europeans. European nation states emerged to initiate world exploration, the Industrial Revolution, intercontinental immigration of free and forced labor, and the contemporary global economy.

In the dawn of the third millennium, we are in the midst of a cataclysmic shift in global energy and economic dynamic from the Northern to Southern hemisphere of what has formerly been called the Third World. After World War II, the nations of the poor undeveloped Third World had two-thirds of the world's population and a disproportion of the world's poverty. In a generation-and-a-half, many of these nations are emerging as major actors on the world stage. In the post-World War II bipolar geopolitics, the United States-led North Atlantic Treaty Organization (NATO) and the Russian-led Union of Soviet Socialist Republics competed for Allies from the nations emerging from the anti-colonial movements across the globe.

By the late 1950s, the capitalist versus communist ideologies paradigm was contested by nonalignment visionaries in the developing world such as Gamal Nasser of Egypt, Jawaharlal Nehru of India, and Kwame Nkrumah of Ghana. The anti-colonial, nonalignment movement they led helped newly independent nations see beyond Eurocentric economic and cultural dominance. Intellectuals and nationalists from the Third World, or more accurately the two-thirds world, wrestled with developing blended ideologies of democratic-capitalist nationalist socialism to foster the entrance of their countries and regions into the global economy. Post-Mao Communist China emerged to compete in the global economy by embracing the profit and private property tenets of capitalism. After the collapse of the Soviet Union, China has emerged as the newest potential ideological economic rival to the United States. Global geopolitics became more focused upon the interactions of international monetary and trade dynamics than economic philosophy and ideology. All of this has served to facilitate a new world order of the rising of nations and regional economic constructs as an extension of the liberation and anti-colonial movements of peoples who had been locked out of the Eurocentric global construct.

The vision of the former colonies of Europe as nation-states across the globe rising to full participation in their own right in the world's economy and geopolitics has come to pass. The super economies of Asia, China, and Japan hold huge American government debts and have a tremendous edge with large trade imbalances. China is not only America's creditor, but it has emerged as one of the world's largest economies, looking forward to decades of outsized growth potential. The nations of the Pacific Basin, from South Korea and Indonesia, are growing in global manufacturing capacities with cheap labor and a minimum of government regulation on industries. The labor markets in these regions are highly motivated, and the region's industries benefit from a globalization of capital and low wages. The Indian subcontinent, with the world's largest democracy, adjacent to a Pakistan teeming with human creativity, has an increasingly educated workforce and dynamic markets and economic muscle.

The major challenges in these nations include managing religious fundamentalism and fanaticism, and managing Indian-Pakistan border disputes. Because economic prospects in this region have so much potential, political leaders have much incentive to pursue diplomatic resolution to conflicts. The Middle East, with decades of oil production and wealth transferred from industrial nations, is a center of global capital and investment. European and American corporations, such as Halliburton, are moving their international headquarters to exotic, stable metro areas in the region. Corporations will continue to be drawn to the region's opulence as an Organization of Petroleum Exporting Countries (OPEC) epicenter of the fuel of global industrialization.

The new future African petro-states, such as Ghana and Angola, are soon to join Nigeria as major oil producers. That means that new oil reserves and the rare minerals of the sub-Sahara will continue to attract global capital and investment and international attention to the continent.[37] Presently, Americans are being outflanked by the Chinese investments of capital and diplomacy in

117

Africa. American fallback is illustrated by the Chinese lead in building a new two billion dollar headquarters for the Organization of African States (OAS) in Addis Abba, Ethiopia. That the U.S. is losing influence in Africa during the era of the nation's first African American President, a person of recent African descent, highlights the disjointed shortsightedness of American geopolitical and international economic policy. It's hard to believe that our nation's policy strategists and government officials are properly attuned to American national interests with these kinds of tragic missed opportunities.

The emerging economies of Latin America, such as Brazil, Argentina, Venezuela, and Chile, are growing at healthy clips as this region develops greater influence on the world scene. In 2010, as the international body responsible for awarding the 2016 Olympiad deliberated on the finalists' host cities, those of us in Chicago knew of the strong efforts of then-Mayor Daley and the city's business community to win the bid. But many of us understood that as Rio de Janeiro, Brazil, emerged as an alternative to Chicago, our city would be at a distinct disadvantage for one reason: global focus was shifting from north to south. Global geopolitics were ripe for a South American Olympics. President and First Lady Obama flew to Europe with dramatic fanfare during the voting of the Olympic Committee to aid the Chicago and American pitch. While in Europe, the American President was snubbed in a meeting request with the Chinese Premier. President Obama had to barge in uninvited into a meeting that the Premier was having with Asian leaders in order to obtain an audience. The President wanted to discuss Chinese monetary policy, specifically China's refusal to help equalize trade imbalances by allowing the Chinese renminbi currency to increase in value. America's continuing declining influence was further highlighted when Chicago's bid lost on the first round to Rio, Tokyo, and Madrid. Rio, even with all of its social and public safety challenges, won the bid because of international acknowledgement of the shifting balances of global power to the emerging two-thirds world.

Brazil, with the largest population of people of African descent outside of Nigeria, has the kind of interracial and intercultural mix that attracted international support. The fact that Latin America had suffered under the heavy hand of U.S. hemispheric hegemony, I am sure, fostered additional support for Brazil's bid. Latin American nations will develop an increasingly independent foreign policy to pursue their interests and reflect their economic muscle. As Mayor Daley leaned upon the Obamas to put the prestige of the U.S. presidency on the line for Chicago's Olympic bid, those of us with better understanding of international dynamics knew that Chicago was at a distinct disadvantage. Daley and Chicago business elite investors were stunned by the magnitude of their defeat on the international stage. They did not have the capacity to process that the shifting change in the global power was at work. In the past, North America has exercised undue influence on the economics and politics of Central and South America. Going forward, Latin America is destined to exercise a much greater influence on the future of North America and the U.S. in particular.

The continuous influx of immigrants from Central and South America will profoundly impact the U.S. demographically and politically. The truth is, wall building will not be an effective long-term strategy to address immigration issues at the southern border of the United States. With up to twelve million undocumented workers in the U.S., the nation already has a substantial fusion with Latin America. The North American Free Trade Act (NAFTA), passed under President Clinton, was de facto acknowledgment that North and Central America had become a comprehensive global regional zone of labor and trade, bound together in a "single garment of destiny." The United States has already been transformed by our symbiosis with Latin America. Our economy, culture, and politics are unalterably flavored and influenced by our ties to the Spanish speaking Americas. In the last three presidential elections won by Democrats (in 1992, 1996, and 2008), Clinton and Obama both won with a minority of white voters, and a majority of black and brown minority voters. The fastest growing states, in the American Sunbelt, are attracting immigrants and migrants of color. California, with the largest number of presidential electoral votes, now has a nonwhite majority.[38] For the first time since the height of the Great Migration, more African Americans live in the southern states than in the North.[39] In 2011, for the first time, over half of America's public school children are brown and black. Before midcentury, the American people will be "majority minority."

I believe the destiny of America will be found by embracing the future and moving beyond race and ethnicity. Our future will be found by focusing upon American ideals, American principles, and the American promise. The world and the nation are shifting. In looking beyond the skin color and ethnicity of its citizens to the obligations of the American Project, America can offer the world a standard of universal human rights forged from our unique experience with democracy. A majority-minority America with a transformed foreign policy and transcended view of its role in the world could be uniquely suited to help give global leadership into the twenty-first century. The fact that America is "browning" means that we will have a unique opportunity to flow with global trends and, with our ideals, take a leading role in participating in the emerging world.

In the face of the shift of global energy and economy from north to south, America has a unique ability to move with the shift. Because of our diversity, we have the capacity to identify with the emerging world. For a Republic founded on principles of universal equality and liberty, the browning of America is a rich blessing. It has been either fortuitous or intentional that two of the U.S. secretaries of state in the first decade of the twentieth century, Colin Powell and Condoleezza Rice, were people of color. In the last thirty-five years, we have had three African American ambassadors to the United Nations—Andrew Young, Donald McHenry, and Susan Rice. Barack and Michelle Obama have radically altered the American narrative by changing the face of the presidency and American First Family. It would not be a stretch to say, in light of a shifting global geopolitical context, that there must have been some intentionality in adding color to the face of American foreign policy.

That is not to say the change in the complexion of leadership constitutes a change in American domestic and foreign policy. In many cases with the people mentioned above, policies executed from their administrations are indistinguishable from non-blacks. But the point here is that America has a unique capacity to change with the global tilt toward the two-thirds world. Toward the end of the Bush years, Americans who traveled internationally were uniquely aware of how unpopular and outdated the Bush projection of American foreign policy and imaging had become in almost every region of the world. There was simply something about the arrogance and insensitivity of the Bush Administration's presentation of America's relationship with the rest of the world that presented a real need for change. It was part of an intolerable American insensitivity and embarrassment that President Bush did not even own a passport until he was elected, or selected as it were, President in 2000. With the narrowness represented by the Bush Administration, America would be handicapped competing in the global economy of the emerging new world. Going forward, international exposure and global perspective will be absolutely indispensable for American Presidents and national leaders.

My own daughters, Joyce and Janelle, had traveled extensively to Europe, West Africa, and Asia in their late teens and early twenties. It has been a special joy watching them grow, and knowing how the breaks that I received in life are paying dividends into the next generation. Because of their sense of adventure, we have had great conversations about developing a worldview and growing as an inner-city family with a global perspective. As a family who prided ourselves on international exposure, we were excited about the prospects of traveling abroad after Barack Obama was elected President. We knew that, as African Americans, we would have a newfound pride in presenting our passports as citizens of the United States with the first black President as the fresh new face of America. We reveled in the fact that Obama had actually lived abroad as a youngster. What a comeuppance this was to the likes of George Bush.

Going to Ghana: From the West Side to West Africa

My daughters had become very influential youth leaders in our New Mount Pilgrim Church inner-city congregation in their comings and goings from college and travels. They were educators by profession, and real trendsetting young adults among young people at the church. Priscilla and I are proud of the young ladies they have become. They are quite opinionated and vocal, so we are motivated by them as well. By early 2009, my daughters had talked me into taking a youth group from the church on an African mission trip to Ghana in the summer of that year. Joyce and Janelle organized a selection process that was rather extensive with essays, research, and parental buy-in. I agreed to raise funds to subsidize the $3,000 per traveler trip expense by $2,000 per person. It's amazing the things our children can talk us into. Their conviction was that this kind of trip was real urban ministry. Inner-city kids needed the same kind of exposure that others received. To live out their true potential in the modern world, they too had to become global citizens. As black Christians, they would have to see themselves beyond neighborhood and nation, appreciating the global context. They challenged me that this is how we as a family had been called to serve our community of faith on the West Side of Chicago. They convinced me that this trip should be a priority. I was convinced. I was also now on the hook for some major fund-raising. After the youth ministry selection committee deliberated, we had a team of eleven young people, ages thirteen to eighteen, and three young adult chaperones. Interestingly, only one of the eleven young people had a passport when our planning started for this trip. And fortuitously, on the last day of our scheduled eight-day stay in Ghana, July 10th, President Obama and the First Family were scheduled to be in Accra visiting sub-Saharan Africa for the first time as the American Head of State.

It was an absolute wonder to see these young people from the families of our church grow in the processes of international travel. One of our kids had been a ward of the state. Her birth certificate arrived from California just in time to get an expedited passport and make the trip. I was amazed that the number one obstacle in preparing for the trip was helping the young people and their families overcome their fears. Inner-city parents have a great deal of anxiety daily about the safety of their children. Given the constant threat of violence in urban life, their fears and anxieties are understandable. These fears can also, I have learned, be debilitating and a real hindrance to natural processes of development and maturity for young people. Parents and guardians, forced by circumstances to be very protective, have much difficulty letting go and allowing their children exposure to a larger world. Worse yet is that the children tend to internalize their parents' anxiety.

In attempting to relieve fears, I discussed with parents and guardians that my daughter Janelle and our thirteen-year-old son Maurice would be with me on the same trip. As a high school sophomore, Janelle spent a summer in London. As a Tufts University college student, she had studied and lived abroad in Hong Kong and Ghana. She had just returned home after teaching in Japan for a year. My oldest daughter Joyce had lived in London, Ghana, and Singapore. I had been hosted by both my daughters in Asia and Europe when they lived abroad, and I had witnessed the supreme confidence and intellectual depth they developed as a consequence of their travels abroad. Because of constant urban violence, many urban parents manage risk by overprotection and limited exposure. I knew that this kind of trip could be liberating for the families and the participants involved. I wanted parents to rest assured that we had taken every safety precaution. I could not guarantee that nothing bad would happen, but we should be at least as safe traveling internationally as we would walking down Madison Street on the West Side of Chicago. The faith we live by everyday must be faith for every contingency everywhere. Healthy life prospects and fulfilled life potential require a certain confident faith in providence. That was the faith I wanted for my children and for theirs as well. On the night flight to London on the first leg of the trip, the young people settled in comfortably. By the time we arrived at Heathrow, they were calculating the weakness of the dollar to the pound and buying food at the airport. Their fears were giving way to wonder.

Within the first few days in Ghana, the kids were learning the Akan language and exchanging U.S. dollars for Ghanaian currency (cedi) like seasoned international travelers. They did some light mission work in the day and attended church services at night. They sang and danced with our host congregants and discussed how much the spirit of our worship at home was similar to our "cousins'" in Ghana. They enjoyed the local cooking at the churches and homes and remarked how the spicy Ghanaian foods delighted our taste buds. Now we knew why the black folk back home put hot sauce on everything. Yes, this was the home of the original soul food. After a couple days in Accra, we took an excursion to Cape Coast to visit the old slave castles along the Atlantic beachhead. Locals were diligently preparing for President Obama and his family's visit to these sites.

The Obamas were scheduled to be in Ghana for less than twenty-four hours, but it was clear the nation was in full-fledged preparation for a great day of national pride. The President was only stopping by this West African nation on the way home from an Asian Indian state visit. The President wanted to make a statement on African soil about Ghana's stability, their embrace of democracy, and commitment to fighting government corruption. Obama also felt the need to reaffirm U.S.-Ghanaian relations as that African nation prepared to deliver its large, newfound oil reserves from Jubilee Field to the world market. Banners with pictures of the U.S. and Ghanaian presidents had already been hoisted on streetlight fixtures. I could not help but be struck by the irony of the pictures of two black presidents with their names underneath their faces. There was President Barack Obama of the United States of America and President John Mills of Ghana: the American President had a fully African name, and the African President had a fully English name. Being black and African anywhere on the planet carries a lot of baggage and much irony and dislocation given the horrific histories of the African Diaspora. The Cape Coast slave castle tour was quite a spiritual experience and pilgrimage with our teenagers from the West Side.

The old slave-holding dungeons at Cape Coast were dark and dank. I discovered that what I had heard about these sacred spaces was true to fact. There is a very definite and inexplicable spiritual lingering in the rooms. We really could still smell the stench and feel the tragic history of centuries of the dehumanization of the Transatlantic Slave Trade. The tour guide was graphic and passionate in describing the systematic schematic of enslavement and transport from these "castles" to the New World. In his narrative, the tour guide said something that was more startling because of the ages of the young people in our group. He said that the average age of the captured person was between thirteen and sixteen years of age. The whole process of centuries of dehumanization in the slave trade became much clearer. It was not fully grown men and women who had been kidnapped and herded into ships for a hellacious journey to a new world of chattel slavery in the Americas.

———

123

The Transatlantic Slave Trade was the 350-year systematic trafficking of African teenagers. The whole episode was even more diabolical than we had imagined. More profoundly for us, there we were in the middle of a slave castle with eleven black teens from the West Side of Chicago. I thought about how far they were from their families and how easily we held sway over them and held their well-being in our hands. It all made horrific sense. The heart and soul of global black humanity, pre-adult youth, had been under continued assault for centuries.

Blacks in the Diaspora and on the Continent were still reeling from the effects of this holocaust. The contemporary global economic system was based upon the transport and labor of African teenagers. Wall Street in New York City is built on an old cemetery of African enslaved people. Our "Maafa" stained glass window at New Mount Pilgrim depicts the packing of a slave ship and is a contemporary memorial to the hundreds of thousands who did not survive the Trans-Atlantic Middle Passage. There we stood in a slave dungeon of Cape Coast. We had come back as the offspring of survivors.

One of our kids, DeAngelo, perhaps the youngest, was barely thirteen and his parents had been very concerned about his making this trip. "You have to watch DeAngelo," his mother said. "He tends to drift off." Over the course of the trip, however, we would never have a moment of trouble out of DeAngelo or any of the other kids for that matter. I would never have guessed that traveling with teens would add so much depth to our sojourn to the Mother Land. Standing in a Cape Coast slave castle that day, young DeAngelo made a most profound statement, a really keen observation. My daughter Janelle stood staring at the dark, desolate holding place where thousands had passed through on their way through a single hole in a wall. On the other side of that hole was a path that led to the shore where they would be chained and led to a ship that would take them to a tightly packed ship for a three- month voyage of unspeakable horrors.

For these young captives, it would mean a tragic end to life as they had known it. We felt the disorientation and breathed the despair. Tears streamed down Janelle's face. She was sorrowful, but also angry with fresh rage. Imagining and imaging the suffering of pitiful souls, in sacred silence, I experienced with her pain and grief. We all, I felt, sensed something very sad and spiritual about the space wherein we stood. I was certain that the young people did not, could not, have a deep understanding of the indescribable miseries our ancestors experienced in this very space. After about two minutes of sacred silence, DeAngelo nudged me and said with a hopeful disposition, "Pastor, I feel like I been here before." "Really?" I said. Perhaps in the person of an ancestor, DeAngelo really had been here before. Of course, he and we had been to these places of despair before, and we had overcome them. DeAngelo's reflection was an unexpected word of hope. As I looked at DeAngelo and the other young people we had invested in, I thought about their journey and their unlimited potential. As we further pondered DeAngelo's profundity that evening, our sorrow turned to wonder. Indeed we had all been through these painful places, and we have returned triumphantly. We have returned back through the "Door of No Return." It had been a full circle, indeed.

By the last day in Accra, the young folks had become naturals in the African marketplace. They were bargaining, calculating, speaking the language, and approaching every encounter with critical thinking and a healthy dose of skepticism. These were the same skill sets that allowed them to survive the West Side of Chicago. Yet, while they were abroad, they felt safer and freer as American tourists than at home on Chicago's West Madison Street. They carried themselves with the confidence of first-class American citizens with passports. They had the swagger of citizens whose President and First Family shared their ethnicity and hailed from their hometown. Here was more strange irony. These West Side kids had to travel to West Africa to really enjoy the blessings of security and liberty as American citizens. They shopped with a vengeance, and like all foreigners engaging local African markets, they enjoyed bargaining with the people as much as they enjoyed the bargains they purchased. They learned that a little money goes a long way in Africa, as long as you can afford to get there. In the late afternoon we headed to the airport, well ahead of our late night flight back to London. We were able to see highlights of the Obamas' visit on the television at the airport. What a coincidence, I thought. We were at the same airport the same evening that the President and his family were scheduled to return to Washington.

As the evening fell, we looked through the large windows of the airport. We still had hours before we would board our plane on schedule. Suddenly there was commotion on the tarmac, and we could see on television and through the large windows that the First Family was heading to Air Force One. We enjoyed every second of our wondrous good fortune. After the departure festivities, the American President and his family boarded. We saw it all live on television and through the large airport window at the same time. The engines revved, and we moved closer to the windows to witness the awesome sight of Air Force One with the presidential seal of the United States. We marveled as the regal plane ran the runway and took flight. We had come home to Ghana and, following our First Family, we would soon be headed back to the new home our fore-parents had forged out of the pain and promise of America. We too would soon be headed home to a twenty-first century America with unresolved challenges and an uncertain course. We had worked through old sorrows and found faith for fresh promises. Taking in DeAngelo Cottrell's revelation in the Cape Coast slave castle, we had experienced the pain of the past and glimpsed a hopeful future. The same runway that led Air Force One into the dark skies of the African night would soon lead us on the first leg of our journey back home and our struggle with Project America.

Chapter 5

The New Twenty-First Century United States and the New World Order

"And I saw a new heaven and new earth: for the first heaven and the first earth were passed away; and there was no more sea." **—the Book of Revelation, Apostle John, about 90 A.D.**

"A moment comes, which comes but rarely in history, when we step out from the old to the new, when an age ends, and when the soul of a nation long suppressed finds utterance." **—Jawaharlal Nehru, the first Prime Minister of India, (serving 1947-1964).**

"It will mark the first time in history that the non-White people of the world have held such a gathering. It could be the most important (gathering) of this century." **—Rev. Congressman Adam Clayton Powell Jr., Afro-Asian Bandung Conference, April 1955.**

"A new world order is in the making, and it is up to us to prepare ourselves that we may take our rightful place in it." **—Malcolm X, el-Hajj Malik el-Shabazz, Black Muslim Minister and Activist (1925-1965).**

We Americans have some serious work to do in our experiment with democracy and in the project of perfecting our Union. Presently, we face a most serious crisis in our economy and our values. We are in danger of selling off our freedom with choking debt and the selling of our government to corporate interests.[40] And worse, as we give up our values, we lose our soul. When families cannot envision intergenerational upward mobility, we will have moved from a class system to a caste system. The crisis in our economy was caused by greed at the top, yet the bailout is being financed by the sacrifices of the shrinking middle-class and the growing numbers of the poor. We have prosperity at the top, and austerity at the bottom. The domestic battle for the soul of the nation will be the struggle to preserve the vision of America as a land of opportunity. We will have to rethink left-wing and right-wing politics and rediscover our national purpose. We cannot allow the promise of America to be sold out by transnational capitalists. This is the most critical time in the testing of American character since the Civil War. Just as we could not survive half slave and half free, we will not be able to live out our national purpose with growing disparity between the wealthy rich and the withering rest. Lincoln's vision of high moral purpose is found in offering America as "the last best hope for mankind." We will not be able to restore our economy or reclaim our government without rediscovering our national purpose. We will not be able to reset economic or international policy in a way that advances our national interests without the reestablishment of our national purpose.

As the nation becomes predominately populated by peoples of color, we must make a concerted effort to recommit to our national purpose of perfecting the Union and recreating a nation that regards and rewards hard work, thrift, faith, and fairness. We must put supreme value upon extinguishing race-based or ethnically based classes and caste systems. To be authentically American does not mean blood relation to an ethnicity, but the embrace of ideals. It may well be our national destiny that these ideals survive for the world's benefit through an America that is made up of a majority people of color. If that be the case, it would be good for America and the emerging world. True believers in American exceptionalism seek the survival of American ideals, not an American gene pool. True American idealists believe that the world would be best served under the moral and political leadership of a multiracial, multiethnic, religiously tolerant leading power. The world needs a revived America true to its ideals and values. Time is running out for an American comeback. An American revival will depend upon how faithfully we pursue the new moral vision offered by Dr. King and the movements he led for civil and human rights.

History will judge Obama's presidency transformative, if his administration's policies reflect the values of an American exceptionalism championed by Dr. King. In that view, America is not just another country with national interests, but it is a nation called to be servant to all the nations—the salt of the earth and a light to the world. Quite simply, the U.S. at its best does not exist just for itself but to serve the higher purpose of promoting and demonstrating universal human values and universal human rights. America going forward requires a head of state whose worldview and cultural adaptability help bring our nation into line with the shifting geopolitics toward the two-thirds world. What America needs is a leadership that embraces Dr. King's vision of America's place in the world. When we reconnect with the higher ground of national purpose, national principles, national ideals, and national vision, our leaders can then be better guided in forming forward-looking domestic and foreign policies. At this vantage point, it is too soon to assess the presidency of Barack Obama. It will be interesting, if he wins a second term in 2012, to see the emergence of his true presidential personality without the constraints of a looming election.

What would a winning American international policy look like in the twenty-first century? Dr. Martin Luther King, Jr. was right on the Vietnam War question over forty years ago because he was clearly ahead of his time. He could see that the future belonged to the world that was emerging out of the release of the human spirit from the constraints of colonialism and exploitation. We honor King as a great American because he also foresaw that America could play a unique role in giving leadership to the new world. He saw that America's international policy was intertwined with our domestic policy. People of color, and the earnestness with which we embrace American ideals, must be pressed into the service of preserving American greatness as a gift to all mankind. For King, it would not be enough to have black faces in positions and offices. We need decision makers who bring a unique sense of principled self to public service. The Americans who have been victims of America, yet whose faith in American principles has been unshakeable, will have a moral authority and rectitude to speak of America's transformation and fitness for future world leadership. America as a country predominated by people of color will have the capacity to readapt the American model for the twenty-first century.

We will need an American international policy that is shaped by the worldview of minorities who have had the faith to embrace the American vision through struggle and protest. The foreign policy that would emerge from that worldview could renew and rejuvenate our national purpose in light of the global ascendency of the two-thirds world. The new American doctrine would place Dr. King's "Stone of Hope" message and renewed national purpose squarely at the center of American foreign policy. The greatest strength of America is its moral authority and the rightness and universality of ideals. With economic recovery, that moral high ground is what America's new majority must help the nation reclaim in the years moving through the second decade of the new century.

A Visionary U.S. Foreign Policy Doctrine for the 21st Century: Values That Lead the World

North and Central America

The United States shares with Mexico and Canada altogether one of the world's great economic engines and markets; yet, the U.S. government has allowed unrestrained transnational corporate and banking interests to wreck the domestic economy. Companies have enjoyed tax breaks, while they have moved American jobs overseas. The American people must take back the national government and economy. We need sufficient government oversight to restore competitiveness and fairness in the economy. Free trade among nations is good, but America needs a government and economic policy that fights for American workers and expansion of its manufacturing base. Protecting and pursuing manufacturing jobs is what every other government in the world does unapologetically. The money in our political system has made our government the servant of transnational corporate and banking interests. Federal economic policy now prospers one percent of the country and assigns austerity for the rest of us. It is the rich who have commenced class warfare, and it is up to the rest of us to engage the battle and save the nation. Simply, we need a tax policy that challenges the wealthy to pay their fair share of the tax burden. Fifty years ago, American corporations and the top 5 percent of the wealthy raised 70 percent of the federal budget, and the rest of Americans paid in 30 percent. Today the reverse is true. Corporations and the super-rich pay less than 30 percent of the federal budget, and the rest of us are on the hook for over 70 percent.

One major problem is that starving the federal government has become a political tactic and political philosophy. Nothing could be more foolish in the context of globalization. Our nation must compete globally with national governments that function with corporate efficiencies and strategic planning. Our federal government, which must compete internationally with economic zones that invest in human resource and infrastructure, is intentionally divested and drained by the political surrogates of transnational interests. We are being set up to lose the future. When our local governments cut funding for education and investments in human services, it means we have given up on the future.

The citizens who paid for the bank bailouts and who will be saddled with the national debt, are also being called upon to shoulder the load in taxes and fees for the shortages of failing cities and municipalities. In our cities and localities, bankrupt public officials offer casinos and gaming as economic development, as if our economic prospects can only be improved by creating losers to produce one lucky winner. Lottery and gaming Ponzi schemes are not the stuff true economic recovery is made of.

The recovery of our economic base requires that we play hardball with our global competitors and engage a national strategy to manufacture more of the consumer items that we purchase and use. The great success of the U.S. federal government's rescue of General Motors is a case in point. The rescue of our automobile manufacturing base shows that we can reemerge in the internationally competitive global economy as a producer and trendsetter. Strategic use of tariffs, protections for American industries and workers, and strong oversight and shepherding of the American economy are paths to maintaining the competitive edge in the global economy. We need bold leadership that unapologetically promotes the revival of American economic interests, so that American values can impact the world. Our partners in this pursuit would be the two nations closest to our national borders, Canada and Mexico.

Rather than focusing upon failing, unworkable immigration policies against our neighbors to the south, we would do better to create an economic zone of opportunity with Canada and Mexico. We could put in place a North and Central American bill of rights for workers and standards of business and corporate conduct for the three nations. It would be folly to waste energy on unworkable immigration policies that place stock on deporting millions of Mexican workers, or building walls to keep immigrants from crossing the borders of the Southwest in search of economic opportunities. We should have immigration reforms and seek to enforce the law, but we must know that these efforts are futile in the long-term, and will not be as effective as embracing Mexico as a neighbor and partner whose prosperity and well-being are in our mutual national interests.

The most pressing problem in the global economy is that we have globalized capital and corporate power, but failed at globalizing the dignity and well-being of workers and worker rights. Transnational worker rights can begin in the contexts of global regional economic development. The U.S. and our conjoining neighbors on our borders are in a position to lead the world in holding corporate interests accountable for their relationship with labor. Once we can look beyond language and ethnicity, the natural convergence of our national interests will facilitate a North American Free Trade Zone that also embraces the best of our American Project: the God-given dignity of every person, and the right of every person and family to pursue happiness and upward mobility. Labor must have the right to organize and collectively bargain to improve the standards of living for the working class. This vision and these rights should extend across national borders with the flow of transnational capital. American resurgence and restoration of national purpose must begin with our own reclamation of the American Dream and in collaborative economic relationships with the peoples and nations on our northern and southern borders. Our neighbors are our most important partners in living out our national purpose and our national values.

Central and South America

African Americans and Hispanic Americans have historically held a more progressive view of the U.S. relationship with Latin America. African Americans, because of their unique experience with the duplicity and hypocrisies of the American history, have been consistently critical of the inconsistencies between American ideals and American foreign policies. Blacks in America have been acutely aware of the double standards between the welcoming embrace of European immigrants from the east of Ellis Island and the barriers and rejections of immigrants from Africa, Haiti, and the African Diaspora in Latin America. Black Americans have critiqued U.S. foreign policy with Latin America through the eyes of, and affinity with, those with less power.

In his early years, Fidel Castro was welcomed to Harlem by the black community and Congressman Adam Clayton Powell. Hispanics have been offended by the arrogant and exploitative U.S. foreign policy in the region. From the Monroe Doctrine and "Gun Boat Diplomacy," to the Reagan Administration's Grenada invasion and beyond, Latin Americans have been subjected to the hegemonic assumptions of the United States. In the past, the United States has treated Latin America as its backyard, with the right to disregard the sovereignty of nations and demand that the rest of the world regard only U.S. national interests in dealing with any nation in the hemisphere. Consequently, deep resentment toward the United States is the backdrop as nations in Latin American have developed and projected themselves on the world stage. Shamefully, we have supported repressive regimes and sown seeds of distrust from nationalist Latin American movements and leaders.

When President Carter facilitated the transfer of the Panama Canal in 1978, the U.S. had opportunities for new directions and a new era of cooperation in the region. Sadly, the resumption of American arrogance under President Reagan reset hostilities in U.S.-Latin American relations. The continued opposition to Fidel Castro's Cuba, and nationalist progressive movements in the Caribbean and South America, spurred the formation of an anti-American coalition of Latin American leaders and governments. As Venezuela, Brazil, Argentina, and Chile emerged as strong economic actors on the world stage in their own rights, exporting oil, food products, and manufactured goods, U.S. influence waned and leftist leaders emerged who gravitated to Castro's Cuba as a nation whose defiant survival served to inspire Latin American self-determination. Latin America is a region in search of respect and its place in the world. For Brazil, landing the 2016 Olympiad is a symbolic victory of the emergence of a continent and blended culture, but the real ambitions of this region are for further ascendency in the global economy and a permanent seat on the United Nations Security Council. In the new world order, Latin America is an emerging region and our relationships with our neighbors to the south are more important than ever.

The browning of the U.S. population can give a resurging America an opportunity to realign its foreign policy with the hopes and aspirations of our hemispheric neighbors. The mutual democratic values of Brazil, the giant of South America, and others may offer the U.S. partners for progress in the Americas. The further development of a democratic future for the region would be helped along by expanding the principles of workers' rights and corporate responsibilities into Central and South America. The region already has a deep history of liberation theology, democratic socialism, and trade union movements. Historically, the U.S. has worked against these nationalist and indigenous progressive movements in Latin America. We must be consistent in our insistence on democracy, but our democratic values must also include partnering with our far south neighbors to develop economies that foster economic opportunities and economic equalities. This region would be the next logical partner in helping to expand covenants that couple globalizing workers' rights and protections with the globalization of capital. This view of the world where nations view their mutual interests in cooperative as well as competitive lenses is a uniquely Kingian way to viewing the interdependence of nations in the modern world. For the U.S., living our values must begin in our relationships with the neighbors in our own hemisphere.

Sub-Saharan Africa

The unique role of African Americans in the past and future of our national narrative gives the United States great advantages in helping to shape the future of Africa. Mineral-rich, with recent discoveries of oil reserves in southern and western Africa, the continent has attracted heavy Chinese investments. The struggle of African governments to meet their people's needs and develop their economies has left these nations open to the worst exploitation of global capitalism. While the Chinese blend a nationalist socialist capitalism domestically, they tend to deal with the outside world as raw capitalists regarding only their singular national interests. Africa's desperation, with its undeveloped natural resources, and China's rising global power and unrestrained opportunism are a recipe for disaster for the nations of the struggling Sub-Sahara. Even given Africa's troubled history of exploitation, imperialism, and colonization with the West, we would make the case that an Africa entangled with and exploited by China will be a very bad deal for Africans in the future.

African nations and Western democracies have a history together that includes development and cultural exchange that have forged strong bonds of mutual and shared values. The largest, most prosperous, and most influential nations in Africa, from Nigeria to Kenya to South Africa, share in commonwealth relationships with European nations. Moreover, Anglophone and Francophone African nations have unresolved, unrepaired moral grievances against their former colonizers that have strong support among people of conscience in the West. The debt-forgiveness movement and faith-based missions work in Africa are fueled by European and American citizens moved by powerful moral imperatives. Most importantly, with African Americans, Sub-Saharan Africans have a natural constituent and advocacy base in the middle of the political dynamics of the reigning superpower of the West. Africans will fare better in the future through a closer alignment and relationship with a resurgent United States as leader of the Free World.

Geopolitically, the United States has much to gain by competing directly with China's attempts to gain favor with African governments and peoples. Our policymakers must pay more attention to Africa and recognize that we cannot afford to give the Chinese unchecked access to Africa. Winning Africa will be an essential determinant in whether the twenty-first century will belong to the Far East or the Free West. Access to Africa will be an important factor in the global geopolitical and economic balances of power. African raw materials and markets can help fuel revived North American economies and recharge our industrial manufacturing base. The cooperation of African governments will help continued development of our military presence in strategic areas to thwart the influences and maneuvering of international terrorist groups targeting the Sub-Saharan nations as bases of operation. Helping Africa develop and democratize will add great stability to the world we would envision in a new American century. That the first African American U.S. President, Barack Obama, traces his roots to Kenya gives our nation an advantage with Africans that the Chinese could never match. We simply must use our advantages strategically for the benefit of our interests and, as I would argue, in Africa's interests as well. Africa's population increases, growing markets, rich natural resources, increasing stability, global cultural influences, and regional economic agreements altogether mean that the continent will be a key global player in the new world order. Africa can, and should, play a role in furthering the values and principles of a new American century.

The Middle East: Islam and Israel

As I found in travels to the Middle East, there is no place in the world that has as complex a set of political and religious interplay as this region of the world. Because the political and the religious intersect in regional international relations, United Nations and United States-led attempts to bring peace and stability to the region have had to deal with an extremism that works against normal processes of diplomacy. Religious conviction, so helpful in regulating personal moral and ethical conduct, lends an irrational dimension to the conflicts between Israel and her Muslim neighbors. One of the first and early successes at Middle Eastern diplomacy was led by African American diplomat Ralph Bunche. In the late 1950s, Bunche set a precedent by challenging Israelis and Palestinians with the uniquely American values of separating the political from the religious, and placing great value upon tolerance and compromise.

Over time, American presidential administrations have struggled to balance our nation's cultural and historic affinity to Israel with the need for America to function as an honest broker between the predominately Islamic nations and the Jewish state. Given the Jewish people's suffering, without question Israel has a right to self-defense and to peaceably coexist with her neighbors. The people of Palestine also have legitimate grievances and the right to self-determination in their historic homeland. In the last decade, American presidents of both parties have settled on some variation of a two-state solution

137

for Israel and Palestine, with the thorny issues of dividing Jerusalem and swaps of land for peace unresolved. The region has drifted from cold to warm to hot wars and conflict since the founding of Israel in 1948, but the rise of Arab-oil producing states, central to the global economy, has made the region's conflicts matters of global economic importance. Whoever emerges as the global superpower in the twenty-first century will have to contend with the centrality of the Middle East conflict. I would make the case here again that a new American century would benefit this region and strengthen its prospects for long-term peace. America's legacy of interreligious respect and tolerance would better serve all the parties involved. The major contributions of all the major world religions to the perfecting of the American Union means the United States can function as an honest broker in the long-standing conflict.

Much has been made of the 2011 "Arab Spring"; that is, the rise of the "Arab street" or the Muslim masses, demanding democratization and political and economic reforms. From Tunisia to Egypt to Libya to Yemen to Syria, citizens are using new technologies and social networks to oppose government repression. These movements present an unanticipated unique opportunity for the United States to influence the course of history with our ideals and vision. To the Obama Administration's credit, in 2011 they lent American support on behalf of the aspirations of the people in Egypt and Libya. We should be intentional and unapologetic in our promotion of democracy and egalitarianism. In the long-run, we cannot side with the oligarchs and win the future for our best values. The clamor for democratic values in the Arab world gives us a chance to offer a vision beyond state-sponsored religious fanaticism. The cultural exchanges between the Arab elite and the West should serve us well in influencing the future of the region. The fact that Islam has played an important role in preserving and transmitting the intellectual and scientific heritage that gave birth to the West provides foundations for fruitful engagement with the modern Muslim world. The contemporary common denominators between the Middle East and the West can and should be democracy and universal human rights.

We must continue to use our leverage to make the case that the divisions that matter most in the Middle East, as in other regions of the world, are not religious or ethnic, but the distance between the qualities of life of peoples who live in democracies as opposed to miseries of life under repressive regimes. A recalibrated twenty-first century United States of America, rescued from our own descent into oligarchy and refreshed with democratic economics, would be the one nation suited best to offer the Middle East a vision of diverse democracy, peaceful coexistence, and stability. The modern Middle Eastern conflict as we know it had its genesis in the world's attempt to address a holocaust and tragic moral failure of World War II. In the cases of Palestinians and Israelis, the culprits are intolerance and lack of appreciation for the grievances of their counterparts. Unlike conflicts in many other parts of the world, the conflict is simply not economic or territorial, but clashing moral claims. Alas, we cannot envision resolution without the lead of a values-centered continuing American Project calling the peoples of the region to higher moral common ground.

The Indian Subcontinent / South Asia

This region, as home of the world's largest democracy and a military government with nuclear weapons, is a place that has some of the most dynamic, creative energies on the planet. India and Pakistan are rivals in their region, but altogether they have peoples whose ambition and education drive continued industrialization and international investments to the subcontinent. India is a democratic miracle of several generations—a showcase of the wonders of democratic values—holding together hundreds of languages, cultural, and religious groups in a parliamentary system. India proves that democracy reconciles and covers a multitude of differences. With the spiritual foundations of Mahatma Gandhi, the nation's stable government has facilitated the emergence of a market of one billion people with one currency and one economic destiny. On the other hand, Pakistan has drifted between eras of military rule and short-lived civilian governments, and has unfortunately also gotten bogged down in Middle Eastern religious-based political conflict. Pakistan has been a staging ground of the Al Qaeda terrorist cells. Even Osama bin Laden himself was found and killed inside the borders of Pakistan in 2011. Regulating the tensions in the Middle East is a major part of the strategy of containing the political instabilities in Pakistan. But Pakistan, like India, is positioned to navigate and prosper in the twenty-first century global economy.

American foreign policy in the region has historically straddled between our democratic affinity with India and our strategic Middle Eastern interests in cultivating our relationship with Pakistan. Our support for India and the highlight of the Indian example must be the central doctrine of America for the subcontinent. American presidential administrations have used the carrot-and-stick approach to bring Pakistan's government along as an American ally against Islamic terrorism in the region. Economic incentive is the most useful instrument available in dealing with this nuclear power. The vision of democracy for the whole subcontinent provides the road to stability for the region. Again, American leadership and values offer this region what a homogenous nondemocratic superpower could not; a future that embraces universal human liberties, diversity and tolerance, and widely shared prosperity.

Western Europe

Americans who travel abroad are uniquely aware of how much cultural affinity and common values are shared between Western Europe and the United States. We share in common respect for the rule of law, constitutional democracy, and human rights. The U.S. and the West also share a common crisis of our values being overrun by the problematic effects of unrestrained, unaccountable transnational corporate capitalism. One line of reasoning is that the modern welfare state of Western Europe has led to the current need for austerity and rollbacks of entitlements in Europe and America. But the chronology of the crises is clear: it was the fraud of real estate value inflation, predatory lending, shortsighted mass mortgaging, casino derivative investment schemes, and credit rating and securities fraud in the West that caused the global recession of 2008 and beyond.

Western Europe like the rest of the world has had to react to the global bubble bust and determine which sectors of their nations would feel the pain. Sadly, the political dynamics of the European Union (EU) have led to passing the pain of economic contraction onto the working-class and the poor. This outcome and the austerity for the masses will threaten the political stability and civility of Western Europe. Even Britain's working-class, although outside of the European Union, has not escaped the redistribution of wealth upward to transnational corporate interests. Because of their history, Europeans will have a most passionate and vitriolic response to the class warfare of downward distribution of the pain of the Great Recession/Global Recession of the twenty-first century. For Western Europe, the searching for answers and scapegoats for the burdens of debt will feel eerily like pre-World War II Europe.

Americans will need a revived Western Europe as partners in the American Project. This is not the time for the European West to trade off the hard-earned qualities of life for the working-classes that emerged from the conflicts of the Industrial Revolution. Britain, France, and a united Germany as leaders of the West must be challenged to the same kind of renewal of purpose that must take place in America. The former colonialists of Western Europe still hold cultural and economic sway over many of their former colonies, especially in Africa, and they can use that influence and power to promote Western values internationally. Post-Christian Europe, with an influx of immigrants from all over the world, will need the clarity of vision and renewal of purpose offered by a revived America as a moral and economic leader of the Free World. American exceptionalism has always been grounded in an unapologetic sense that Western principles of human rights and egalitarianism are universal capstones of progressive world history. The prosperity of the West and the result of embrace of these universal rights and release of the human spirit are graces of the divine purposed to encompass the entire world. In many respects, Europeans of the West, specifically the nations of the North Atlantic Treaty Organization (NATO), will need, for their own survival, the guiding principles and renewed partnership of purpose offered by the universal dimensions of the American Project.

The governments of Western Europe will have to be reclaimed for the interests of the people, just as is needed in America. The United States must support this resurgence of Western democracies that seeks to defend the interests of the common people and restore the middle-income family as the core constituency of national government. The United States can play a major role in what Western Europe eventually becomes. The stability of a middle-class dominated society is the most important export the West can offer the rest of the world. The confluence of democratic government and wide distribution of economic viability is the defining principle of moral government in the Western world. The world needs a revived America to advance progressive universal values, and America needs a revived Western Europe as partner and ally in fulfilling this purpose.

Russia and the Old Union of Soviet Socialist Republics

In the latter years, Russian governments have moved away from ideologically pure Marxism to a blend of socialism and capitalism with protections for private property. Russia now has over 8 percent of the world's billionaires. In the European East, governments and the governed have had to distinguish between socialism and totalitarianism. With the new economic blends came liberalizations in government. Credit President Ronald Reagan in the 1980s with forcing the hand of the old U.S.S.R., but also give credit to the Russians for adapting their country to the realities of the global economy. What happened with the old Cold War rivalry between the Russian with its client-states in the Eastern Europe and the American-led Free World in the closing decades of the twentieth century demonstrates how fundamentally the world's geopolitical dynamics can change. Without a hot war, Russia moved to embrace the possibilities of the twenty-first century world. Eastern Europeans clamor to join NATO and gain access to the economic opportunities of the West. East and West Germany, united as a free nation, now serves as a bridge between Eastern and Western Europe. Time and American diligence have brought about a change.

It is ironic that a half century ago when President Nixon traveled east to "open China" as a potential bulwark against Russian-U.S.S.R. expansion, America sought the help of Communist Maoist Chinese to contain Russian Stalinist Communism. Now communism has essentially been defeated as a global ideological rival to capitalism. Both these former communist giants have proven more nationalist than ideological. Both also demonstrate that the superiority of capitalism over communism does not mean the reflexive embrace of unrestrained transnational capitalism. The new millennium global economy has ushered in a new paradigm that calls for national governments to act as regulators of the impact of transnational capitalists. The nation that can regulate the economic totalitarian dynamics of global capitalists will be more likely to retain national self-determination and have the capacities to operate in the global economy in their own national interests. Russia and China are cases in point. The American challenge in this century is understanding that our interest, our Project, is now best served by cultivating relationships with the blended national economies of Russia and Eastern Europe, and thus containing outsized influence and power of the Chinese in the new emerging global economy. That would be Nixon's China Open Door in reverse. The Russians have their own history with the Chinese, and they have many reasons to be concerned about their own interests in the global ascendency of China.

Indeed, intense old animosities can give way to new mutually beneficial friendships. Consider for example that for the last twenty years, the United States and Russia have been partners in promoting stability in the world. The Russians have clearly become more comfortable with expressing their admiration for America's accomplishments and goodwill in the world. That the Russians accepted American assistance in securing nuclear weapons in Eastern Europe is a major testament to our two nations' ability to move past the antipathies of the Cold War. The interests of the new Russia and a revived America would converge in the mutual need to contain China. Moreover, the United States has the technological capacity to help Russia exploit the vast natural resources in their huge land area. Both nations could reap large and ongoing economic bounties from the industrial exploitation of the Russian landscape.

A rapprochement with Russia is a mutually beneficial relationship that can pay great dividends moving forward. An intentional move toward solidifying the relationship would signal to the world that neither the United States nor Russia concedes the new century to Chinese hegemony. The Russians and nations of Eastern Europe, from Poland to the Czech Republic, are open to adopting free market and Western political liberalizations. With our purposeful cultivation, this region offers much potential in becoming an important partner in the globalization of Project America.

Far East and the Pacific Basin

The commonly held wisdom is that the peoples of Asia are favored to produce the leading economic powers of the new century. From Malaysia to the Philippines to Taiwan, and from Thailand to Singapore to South Korea, industrious and cohesive Asian nation-states are skillfully charting courses to productively engage and participate in the global economy. At the dawn of the new century, commentators had dubbed the twenty-first century as the rise of the Asian tigers. Before the global economic crises of 2008, I had extended visits with my daughter Janelle to Hong Kong and Japan when she lived abroad. It was quite remarkable for me to have my youngest daughter lead me around on public transportation in Hong Kong. She also allowed me to tag along with her international friends on an extensive road trip through the Japanese countryside. In the Hong Kong financial center and as we traversed across Japan, we could sense the high energy and sense of destiny from the blue and white-collar workers and the entrepreneurs in these dynamic Asian societies.

Both China and Japan are super economies that have trade imbalances in their favor with the United States; thus, they have huge dollar reserves that they use for global investment opportunities. China and Japan lead the rest of the world in holding American Treasury notes, which means that the United States of America is now a major debtor to the Chinese and the Japanese. The common values and defense treaty obligations we share with Japan tie us together ideologically with common interests. But China, with its tremendous national resources and human capital, has emerged a potential rival to American economic and political prowess as the world's reigning superpower. America's relationship with the mainland Chinese government will become increasingly destabilized and disadvantaged as the trade imbalances and debt holdings increase year after year. We have seen, and can further expect, an increased Chinese international swagger that challenges America's global influence. American military power alone cannot restore and sustain our national standing in the world. Military overspending and overextended military obligations are a part of the problem in developing a strategic response to the rise of China. America must reduce its debt to China and challenge the Japanese to pay a greater share for the military umbrella that protects Japan from the threat of Chinese militarism. Most importantly, it is the debt to China that is most disturbing and will prove most defining for the future. We must change the trade imbalances and reduce our dependency upon Chinese capital to finance our federal government deficits.

We cannot develop a strategic doctrine on dealing with China and Asia without engaging the fundamentals of our domestic policy. Conversely, we must develop our domestic policy in light of the global context and the increasing intensity of our international rivalry with mainland China. America must pay down the debt with China to help create a new American century. The current class warfare in the United States is being won by the corporate capitalists and wealthy who have purchased outsized influence over American politics and the American government. We must return to fair and just tax obligations for the highest incomes. There is a moral basis for a tax policy that places the highest obligations on the rich to fund government in a capitalist society. In America in 2011, the top 1 percent of society possessed 20 percent of the wealth.[41] The super wealthy should pay the most for government because they ultimately benefit the most from stable government. Stable government allows the rich to confidently transfer their wealth from one generation to another. The future of the American Project will require stabilizing America's financial soundness and reforming its political system. American corporate capitalists and the wealthy must be challenged to join the cause of American restoration, and they must be held responsible for paying the taxes that will help repay China and set a new American course.

What America needs are true patriots who refuse to concede the new millennium to China or any other rival. To recapture the ground that has been lost to the Far East will require a commitment to funding the American Project. One way to do this is by raising federal taxes on a top class of folk who can afford to pay more. The reality is that a homogeneously ethnic Chinese nation has arisen on the precipice of global power, but the ideals of the American Project are a more powerful and attractive vision for the world. A rediscovery of national purpose is the only way Americans can lift a vision with the capacity to call for the sacrifice and passion to challenge China's ascendency and rekindle an American sense of Manifest Destiny to give progressive leadership to the world. The new age of globalism begs for a new American century whose diversity and universality advance national interests that serve the global common good. Competition balanced with cooperation is a unique admixture of Project America. Globalism requires that even our global competitiveness seek a global economic ecology that values the spirit of inclusion and cooperation.

Zimbabwe, 1992

With Martin Luther King III and Priscilla Hatch at the dedication of the King Legacy Apartments in Lawndale, on Chicago's West Side

With Dr. Cornel West at Harvard in 1999

Being sworn in as Rainbow PUSH-West President in April 2002

Henry "Skip" Gates and Mrs. Gates at African American Institute at Harvard, 1999

With Robert Kennedy Jr. after an event at Kennedy School of Politics at Harvard in 1999

With Palestinian Chairman Yasser Arafat in Gaza in 2001

With Israeli youth in Jerusalem, 2000

With U.S. Congressman Danny K. Davis in 2003

U.S. Senatorial Candidate Barack Obama at Westside Pastor's Event, 2003

Barack Obama with members of New Mount Pilgrim after his final SEIU rally for the U.S. Senate, 2004

Pastors Press Event at Quinn Chapel AME Church fielding questions from media regarding support for Obama for President, 2008

Walking with Ambassador Ertharin Cousin at her U.S. State Department swearing in, 2010. In 2012 Ambassador Cousin became the Executive Director of the United Nations World Food Program. This former Lawndale resident grew up on Chicago's West Side.

Chapter 6

Movement Three: Environmental Stewardship

"And God saw everything that he had made, and behold, it was very good. And the evening and the morning were the sixth day."—***The Book of Genesis 1:31, Ancient Author and Date Unknown.***

"A true concept of development cannot ignore the use of things in nature, the renewability of resources and the consequences of haphazard industrialization—three things which alert our consciences to the moral dimension of development."—***Pope John Paul II, December 30, 1988, Christifideles Laici.***

"The solutions are in our hands; we just have to have the determination to make it happen. We have everything we need to reduce carbon emissions, everything but political will. But in America, the will to act is a renewable resource."—***Al Gore, former U.S. Vice President, An Inconvenient Truth, 2006.***

"And the dream we would conceived in, will reveal a joyful face; And the world we once believed in, will shine again in grace; Then why do we keep strangling life, Wound this earth, crucify it's soul; Though it's plain to see, this world is heavenly; Be God's glow."—***Michael Jackson, "Heal the World" song lyrics, The King of Pop, 1958-2009.***

The third movement of my 2008 Bates Martin Luther King weekend speech acknowledged environmental stewardship as an important spiritual wind of change that is sweeping across the world. I was clear that the highbrow crowd on this college campus would find my discussion on ecology and green economics an important part of embracing a winning future. The reality of global warming must be addressed, or all the other issues we tackle will matter less. We must have a planet to inhabit to have a future to contemplate. Former Vice President and presidential candidate Al Gore had made major contributions on the subject with his An Inconvenient Truth documentary.

The pain of Gore's lost, or stolen, election in 2000 had driven him underground for several years. I had met him several times in that campaign as I traveled with Rev. Jackson. In 2000 Jackson had a private campaign plane at his disposal, and he was very good about taking guys like me for short jaunts around the country as he conducted rallies to register voters and drum up support among blacks and progressives for the Democratic ticket. Gore's profound disappointment in the election's eventual outcome, decided by a Republican-controlled Supreme Court vote, sent him on an emotional tailspin. He disappeared, grew a beard, and apparently grew apart from his wife as well. But Gore reemerged with a new passion for the cause of environmental stewardship and gave voice to legitimate concerns about the long-term effects of industrialization and fossil-fuel driven global economics on the planet. I too had been so taken by the issue that, by 2008, I thought that stewardship of the environment was one of the most important transnational issues of the new millennium. Gore's deep pain, I thought, had given way to high purpose.

The only future that the world can have long-term is a "green future." The current calls for economic austerity could help usher in a new era of green technologies that lead humans back to a more basic and rational approach to life and human progress. Here America is well-suited to lead the way as well. Going into the new millennium, the world will be ill-served by the unrestrained and unreflective march to industrialization by the emerging economies of the two-thirds world. That includes China. In the age of global warming[42] and unprecedented impact on global ecology and climate, the world needs the leadership of a mature industrial power that is focused upon broad interests. I believe the United States is best positioned to play that role for the world. Twenty-first century industrializing nations, such as the China, already have very low air quality in their central metropolitan areas. Emerging nations singularly focused upon development have not yet built a culture or political will to hold themselves and transnational corporate capitalists responsible for environmental impact. The world will need America and Western countries to lead the way, guiding international bodies in effectively enforcing global ecological and environmentally friendly public policies. The vital issue of environmental stewardship can be an important dimension of recapturing our national purpose. Fighting the good fight for a healthy environment is another good reason we must put all our national energies toward ushering in a new American-led century.

Robert Kennedy Jr.: Champion of Environmental Justice

When I was a visiting fellow at Harvard in the spring of 1999, I had an extensive conversation with Robert Kennedy Jr., son the late New York senator who was slain after winning the 1968 California Democratic Primary. I immediately noticed how much the son resembled his late father physically, as well as in passion and humility. I was also struck by the absolute commitment he had for his work as an environmental lawyer in New England. He had given a lecture at the Kennedy School of Government in Cambridge on environmental justice. In the reception afterward, his eyes absolutely sparkled as he talked with me about what it felt like to help small communities fight corporate giants over environmental pollution and the economic and health issues that were caused by corporate pollution. I marveled at Kennedy's excitement in telling specific stories of the battles that had been won for common people. I thought it ironic that one with so famous a name and pedigree had found passion in environmental law. His cousin, U.S. Representative Joseph P. Kennedy, also attended the Harvard event to support Robert.

It was apparent that Robert had little interest in using his inherited name recognition and pedigree for elective politics. He seemed content to use his gifts and abilities to protect defenseless people in nondescript places from the abuses of powerful corporate interests, and toil with low visibility as a matter of principle on an issue that had placed him well ahead of the popular curve. I shared with Robert and attempted to inspire him to think and act broadly about the environment and the political dynamics of corporate environmental abuse. I have found that many people have the ability to get exercised over saving the planet without being engaged in the civil rights cause of environmental justice and corporate exploitation of poor and powerless communities. Poor communities, racial minorities in particular, become convenient dumping grounds for ecologically abusive industrial practices.

After sharing with Robert Kennedy, I have continued to reflect upon the civil and human rights implications of the environmental rights fights. In the Chicago area, Altgeld Gardens' residents had benefited from a young Barack

Obama, who helped the community respond to environmental justice issues caused by the steel mills' pollution. Altgeld Gardens is the Far South Side public housing project where Obama cut his community-organizing teeth before going to Harvard Law School. The development, with almost fifteen hundred units, sits at the farthest southern boundaries of Chicago's city limits.

Altgeld Gardens' residents are extremely poor, and the community is a concentrated compound of urban pathologies and subculture. Built with familiar brown project brick, the development's layout is row after row of plain, small townhouse apartments. Altgeld was built around 1945 to house the families of African American veterans returning from World War II. A close friend and fraternity brother who attended Western Illinois University with me in the late 1970s had grown up in the development. He would often talk about how isolated the project was, and the ways it was surrounded by some of the worst polluters in the Chicago metropolitan area. Southeast Chicago and northeast Indiana is a huge, old steel mill mecca and industrial zone.

"The Gardens," as it is called, had few actual gardens. Altgeld has some of the highest child asthma rates in Chicago. When the mills were humming, the air was heavily polluted with sulfur all day every day. Those days were gone. With the surrounding areas, Altgeld has become a tragic blend of discarded human capital, shuttered plants, and industrial waste. During that Robert Kennedy Jr. conversation at Harvard, we talked about how the fight for the environment is central to the ongoing American Project. Much of the corporate abuse of the environment is race and socioeconomically based exploitation. Environmental stewardship and environmental justice are core values. Because these issues deal with corporate exploitation of the powerlessness and the isolation of the poor economic ecology and environmental quality equality are important twenty-first century civil and human rights issues.

Moving toward my mid-fifties, I have found myself as a parent and a pastor increasingly concerned about the role that I can play in transferring stewardship of the planet to the next generation. My children and my future grandchildren will judge me and my generation on principles of conscious stewardship of the planet. When traveling abroad, I admire the energies and creativities of emerging nations and peoples. But like many Westerners, I am dismayed by the lack of government regulation of transnational capitalists in developing countries. The United States is a much more likely champion of universal environmental rights than newly emerging industrial powers. In America, we have built traditions

156

and trained advocates to fight corporations over environmental issues. Our legal system has also been well developed in facilitating litigation against corporate abuse of the environment and the effect of that abuse on the physical and ecological health of communities. At our best, American courts stand between the rich and powerful and the poor and exploited. Protecting the less powerful is part of our aspiring ideals of universal human rights. Environmental justice can highlight our sense of fairness that our generation owes to succeeding generations a high quality of life and healthy global ecology. What the American experience can offer better than some others on this issue is a cohesive set of principles that have emerged out of our unique history with race and class. The imperatives of Project America to progressively perfect the Union mean we must preserve quality of life opportunities for this generation and for generations to come.

Toward Comprehensive Global Principles of Environmental Stewardship

While the world community deals with countless critical issues, it would be difficult to find an issue more critical than the abuses to our common planet. The older industrialized world is going to have great difficulty attempting to counsel the emerging developing world about the environmental dangers and ecological costs of industrialization. Having a conversation about environmental stewardship after the developed world has exploited and extracted natural resources from all over the planet seems a bit unfair. I believe the world will need a revived America with outsized cultural impact and renewed moral standing to help move it toward greater levels of responsible stewardship of the earth's natural resources. What America and the West will need to lead the way is comprehensive and practical approaches to environmentally friendly and ecologically balanced public policies. Environmental stewardship requires that we change the way we think about development and modernity. New millennium development means accepting responsibility for the long-term health of our planet and blending old wisdom and new technologies. Here are some frameworks for thinking green that may help capture the imagination of the developed and developing world.

Environmental Justice

The same excesses and shortsightedness of corporate capitalists that have brought the global economic systems to the brink of disaster also endanger the health of the environment in many communities. Unregulated large corporations tend to behave the most environmentally irresponsibly in the poorest and most marginalized communities. Whether in the two-thirds world or in the lower socioeconomic areas of the developed world, the worst abuses of the environment occur in the areas where the most vulnerable people live. In Altgeld Gardens in Chicago, there has been direct correlation between problematic children's health issues and the pollution of the nation's largest steel producers. As mentioned, this issue was one of several that President Obama helped that community respond to as a community organizer. In the recent past, the National Association for the Advancement of Colored People (NAACP), with its litigation capacities, has taken up issues of environmental racism and justice on behalf of poor communities as a newly charged civil rights issue.[43] In that vein, the NAACP has tapped into an important issue that could generate new energy for the civil rights community.

There is no greater human right than the right to live in healthy environs unpolluted by violators of the public trust. I think that Robert Kennedy Jr.'s committing his life to environmental law shows he understands that his work brings a level of passion to the green movement and increases momentum around the issue of environmental stewardship. It is always more effective in fostering mass movement energy when an issue is given a face and a human rights cause. For those who see environmental stewardship as preeminent, investing resources in issues of environmental justice around the country would combine the vision of the green movement with the passion of the continuing movements for civil and human rights.

Sacred Place and Space

Traditionally, Native Americans put premium value upon living in harmony with the natural world. They regarded the land as a sacred common trust. Of course, one of the great tragedies of our history is the horrific genocide against the people who welcomed newcomers on the shores of this "New World." The Americas were new to Europeans and Africans, but it was old to the Natives. Now, after almost four hundred years, all of America will need to relearn the lessons that Native peoples attempted to teach new arrivals in 1619. If we are to survive, we will have to appreciate the wonder of the natural order of Creation. There is poetic justice in the fact that Americans will have to give honor to the spirit of those who were systematically displaced and annihilated in the movement of the American Project from New England to the West Coast.

That sad, central part of American history is diabolical and shameful. It is only right that in our rediscovery of the glories of this vast land that we recommit to welcoming Native American wisdom and peoples back into the forefront of national life. Our states and cities, from Florida and Illinois to New Mexico and the Dakotas, bear the names and legacies of Native Americans who taught environmental stewardship and fought nobly to preserve their way of life. Moving forward, we will need to embrace our Native American heritage for our own survival. America the beautiful is holy ground, just as it was before the sins committed against the first Americans. It is providential that environmental responsibility for our nation will mean bringing Native American spiritual beliefs about land from marginal reservations to the mainstream of American life. We must begin to see the land as our common inheritance and common trust, a sacred place and space. Our government has a solemn responsibility to protect our environment from corporate abuses.

Organic Urbanization

All around America, especially in the old cities of the Northeast and Midwest, urban decay is symbolic of national decline. In 2011, Detroit, Michigan, was singled out as the most glaring example of a failed city where abandoned and demolished properties over vast stretches of a once-thriving metropolis are now being reclaimed by plains and wilderness. It is a reverse process from urbanization to depopulation. Detroit has lost two million residents in the last thirty years, with its numbers down to less than seven hundred thousand.[44] From 2000 to 2010 in Chicago, the population decreased by two hundred thousand. Urban blight in Chicago's poorest neighborhoods, like Englewood and Lawndale, is as bad as anywhere.

One of the saddest realities of inner-city life is that many of these communities, while in the midst of great metropolitan cities, are places where the residents are segregated from opportunity and isolated from basic amenities. Many of these communities are called "food deserts" because residents have little access to fresh fruits and vegetables. Families without adequate resources, lacking transportation, have limited food choices. Children in poor families develop bad eating habits, eating processed snack foods and consuming sugary drinks for meals. The irony of modern poverty is that the one of the most serious health issues among poor families and poor children is obesity. I know when I am in a poor community because these communities lack healthy food options and fitness facilities. People in poverty operate in day by day survival mode.

In the midst of the bad news, there are exciting ideas and programs that seek to help poor people use the abundant vacant land in inner cities to grow organic foods and cash crops. Many of the poorest families in urban America are only a couple of generations removed from the farms and rural environments. In the city, the most expensive groceries are the foods with a minimum use of chemicals and whose origins can be traced back a specific organic grower. Among educated consumers, organic food will always be in the greatest demand. Inner-city residents re-engaging small farm agriculture responds to many needs on several levels. First, inner-city residents who skillfully grow their own fruits and vegetables will help address the issues of the urban food desert. Urban farming can be a contemporary version of the biblical vision of the "blooming desert." Second, growing one's own food brings a level of self-sufficiency and the esteem of being able to supply one's own needs. Third, some folks may be so good at urban farming that their surplus products may find markets among people who place premium value upon naturally grown foods. These creative ideas are being discussed in cities across the country. Moving these ideas along will require that local government facilitate access to vacant land, cast the vision, and perhaps provide some start-up resources. The concept could add an interesting twist to community development and micro financing for urban new agricultural entrepreneurs.

As American cities example urban agriculture, the attention of people all over the world can take note of the new ways to think of small farming and urbanization. Urbanization has been glamorized all over the world, and nations have relied on the commercial farming and global trade to provide the foods that feed their people. That has left many poorer nations food-dependent, and the world at-large vulnerable to threats of terrorists tampering with the international food supply and distribution process. As the food supply becomes more decentralized, there will be less need for chemicals and processed food. The more reacquainted people become with growing their own food, the less vulnerable families will be to wholesale contamination of the food supply. Reintroducing urban farming is a perfect example of synthesizing old wisdom and new vision.

Recycling, Recreation, and Social Cooperation

We cannot move forward into a gainful future with an endless number of garbage landfills. Treating garbage as permanent waste is an unsustainable and impractical disposal of the refuse. In the natural, nothing is ever thrown away. All matter is recycled into processes of reciprocity and renewal. The wave of the future will be found in reconnecting with fundamental ecology: creation is sustained by processes of recreation and recycling. At the outset of modern industrialization, we felt we could afford one-time uses of products and goods, while continuous production fueled the Industrial Revolution in the Western world. We are, in short order, nearing the limits of growth through disregard for the natural laws of the created order. There has been one Creation, and the genius of industrialization is recreation and refashioning the raw materials brought forth from the earth. We are quickly reaching the limits of our false sense of limitlessness. The emerging world will need philosophical and economic frameworks to guide us into a future that regards and operates new paradigms of recreation within the limits of a planet nearing ecological exhaustion.

The philosophical underpinnings of unrestrained capitalism grew from an understanding of natural law that sanctioned survival of the fittest. According to the economic model of strict laissez-faire capitalism, the weak should perish. From the works of Adam Smith in the eighteenth century to the twentieth century advocacy for social Darwinism, conservative intellectuals have promoted an economic system reflective of their view of nature. Political rhetoric, following this same line of reasoning, has often arisen to oppose support for social services and social safety. The truth is, we could never sustain pure capitalism. In times of crises and economic contraction, we have been more than willing to modify our system to deal with "robber barons"and uncompromising capitalists in efforts to preserve liberty, restart economic vitality, and extend the social safety net. We are in a new season that requires recognition anew of the virtues and vices of our economic order. Our economics are reflected in our philosophies of ecology and anthropology.

Whereas the survival of the fittest explains some processes of evolution, the human story includes the superiority of complex social structures of cooperation, self-sacrifice, and compassion. The human race, in adopting more complex social relationships such as the polis and nation-state, has populated the planet and has complete dominion over the earth. We reflect nature and our best selves when we operate in a social order that synthesizes of competition and cooperation. Our constitutional democracies function best when the core, uncompromised principles include both personal liberties and social responsibilities. There is a third way beyond left-wing and right-wing politics. Democracy can be socially responsible without being socialist. Indeed, to be self-determinative and accountable to one another is the rejection of anarchy.

Interdependent independence allows for human advancement altogether and is at the core of self-government.

How we view ecology ultimately impacts how we relate to the world and each other. We must recognize that we have entered a post-industrial era of recycling and recreation realignment with the natural world. Everything must have another use beyond its manufactured application. To a great extent, humanity has subdued everything in the world except the appetites and restlessness of humankind itself. The world is reaching the limits of absorbing our impact. Americans, with our outsized influences in global pop culture and mastery of marketing, have the capacity to help globally deliver messages of recycling and recreation. Of course, we must reign in our own consumerism and wastefulness. Thinking more accurately about the physical world can help us frame our environmental future and the future of socioeconomic relationships as well. Growing acknowledgement of the limits of exploiting the physical world can unleash re-creative energies in a future that embraces competitiveness and cooperation in new global world order. An America preserved as an example of how private rights and public responsibilities merge to fuel the greatest national economy in the world adds to our national purpose as global leaders in promoting the social compact of free people and self-government.

Capturing and Transferring Energy

We know that there will be limitations on the continued exploration and reliance on fossil fuels to drive the global economy. The reality is that there may be unknown petroleum reserves, but there is still only so much oil in the earth. The growing ecological impact of fossil fuel use raises urgent environmental stewardship issues. The ecological and economic wave of the future is alternative fuel sources. Wind, water, and geothermal energy are futuristic and a challenging way of moving toward a cleaner, greener world. The good news is that the better we become at harnessing the motion and heat inherent in the natural world, the more attuned we will be with the self-sustainable rhythms of the planet and the universe.

Nuclear energy, however, will not be the panacea for our energy needs. The problem with processing nuclear energy is that while it has the short-term benefit of producing energy, the waste from the process will increasingly become an unsolvable long-term danger. The 2011 earthquake in Japan provides a great case in point on the inherent, longer view of the dangerous nature of nuclear plants. With news reports of the Japanese earthquake and its damage to a major nuclear energy plant, there are many remaining questions on the thoroughness of the toxic waste cleanup efforts. While we focus upon the Japanese tragedy, Chicagoans have had to reflect upon the fact that their metro area has more nuclear plants than any other place on planet earth.

The Chicago area had a minor earthquake in 2011. What are the emergency plans for sudden breach in nuclear waste containment for a major American metropolitan area? Internationally, access to the technology also comes with the threat that nuclear weapons' grade waste can fall into the hands of terrorist groups and rogue governments with radical agendas. America and responsible international partners will have a major responsibility for global regulation of nuclear energy. We can best serve by leading a pursuit of energy research and technology that forgoes the dangerous waste and incumbent problems of nuclear fission.

Transferring Global Stewardship

There is much political rhetoric about government deficits and the unfairness of leaving our children to pay the bills racked up by our current lack of discipline. There is a lot of truth to that reasoning. On the other hand, because of the dynamics of economics, we can make the case that more investment now will lead to a more robust economy and larger tax base later. These are the debates for long-range economic planning. However, when it comes to ecological policies and global stewardship, we do not have the same passionate dialogue about the conditions in which our children will inherit the planet. That is one glaring inconsistency in the politics of right-wing ideologues that support balanced budgets, but deny global warming. The environmental legacy we leave will be just as important, if not more, as the economic legacy we leave. The emerging world will need new frameworks for thinking through the ecological and economic altogether as the legacy we all will pass on to our children. The days of an Adam Smith worldview and of thinking of economic growth devoid of ecology are gone. In fact, we must now let green technologies, the blending of the old and new wisdoms, drive our economic vision.

Perhaps it is the task of the one nation that has attracted immigrants from all over the world to champion the cause of intergenerational transference of the planet to succeeding generations. Those of us who have entered the middle-age years of life are developing a pronounced sense of legacy. It would be criminal to use the earth without regard to the conditions in which we will leave the planet for our children and grandchildren. America, with a global perspective and universal ideals, will be called to lead the way in reorienting the global economy to prioritize a green agenda with growth. There is no greater cause than that of preserving the earth as a habitat for the wonders of life and living organisms. This is a cause beyond our political ideologies and narrow political interests.

The charge to take seriously our environmental stewardship can lift us to a common high purpose and calling. The crisis of planet abuse has the potential to bring the world together in ways the global economy cannot. Ecologically friendly global economics will call for the kind of competition and cooperation that leads to humans remastering the earth. I would be hard-pressed to envision an industrializing nation, such as China, as a global leader in the discipline of advancing an eco-friendly economy. A revived United States of America would be best positioned, as a diverse and developed nation spurring innovations and creativity, to lead the world in transforming our approach to environmental stewardship. In the third movement of our emerging world, the world would benefit greatly from the leadership of a revived America. The green dimension of Project America is a vital part of our restored national purpose.

Chapter 7

Movement Four: Restoring Faith and Renewing the Social Compact

*"And each person will be seated under his own vine and his own fig tree, with no one to upset him, for the mouth of the Lord has decreed it."***—The Book of Micah 4:4 (737-690 B.C.)**

*"There are seven sins in the world: Wealth without work, Pleasure without conscience, Knowledge without character, Commerce without morality, Science without humanity, Worship without sacrifice, and Politics without principle."***—Mahatma Gandhi (1869-1948), the leader of the nonviolent Asian Indian Independence movement.**

*"Now, I say to you today my friends, even though we face the difficulties of today and tomorrow, I still have a dream. It is a dream deeply rooted in the American Dream. I have a dream that one day this nation will rise up and live out the true meaning of its creed: we hold these truths to be self-evident, that all men are created equal."***—Dr. Martin Luther King, the March on Washington, August 28, 1963.**

*"We serve God by serving others. . . ."***—Rick Warren, Pastor of the Saddleback Church, The Purpose Driven Life.**

Religious Pluralism and the American Project

The very nature of the systematic theological belief systems and faith traditions seems to run counter to notions of national unity and tolerance for other faiths. Faith traditions draw the allegiance of adherents because they claim particular truths about divinity and connection to the eternal and transcendent. American pluralism works precisely because citizenship does not require giving up one's particular faith. Doing away with religious distinction is unnecessary and un-American. American citizenship is designed to enable people of particular faiths, organized or not, to live out their faith in public life for the common good.

Out of the much we have gotten wrong, developing perimeters for religious pluralism is among the things we Americans have gotten right. As we look at our world torn by religious strife in every corner, we again make the case that the world needs a continuing American Project as an example of dialogue and healthy competition among faith-inspired voices in our civic life and body politic. In America, religionists are challenged to win over converts and subscribers under rules of peaceful engagement. Faith communities have had to exercise their rights and privileges under the watchful eye of a probing fourth estate and critical general public. That is as it should be. The ways in which the faithful use their religious freedoms are subjected to the critique of nonsubscribers as well. Americans believe that legitimate faith, like any good in the competitive marketplace, can stand the utmost scrutiny of its core values, utility, and durability in a diverse social and political context. Religious liberties are not exempt from healthy engagement of the civic social compact.

American Faith and the Social Movements to Perfect the Union

Wisdom for the future is almost always found in rediscovery of truths we glean from reexaminations of our past. We can only understand ourselves and perceive our future direction by giving a refreshed recollection of where we have been. In America, we learned in our genesis to regard and embrace the diversities of faith and the high commitment that comes from the public service of the faithful. We have also learned the value of protecting the rights of people who choose to live without commitment to faith communities and organized religion. By protecting the nonsubscribers to faith traditions, we reasoned that we were protecting rights of the faithful as well.

Religious liberty and freedom of assembly lie at the core of American life and the reprised American Constitution. In the nineteenth century, French chronicler Alexis de Tocqueville wrote that America's democratic experiment was uniquely effective because constitutionally protected religious assembly provided citizen space and created a power base beyond the scope of government and the rich and powerful. The fact that people could congregate in sacred settings, with norms that create community with allegiances to a higher power over human government, served as a bulwark against the development of totalitarianism. As reflected in the Federalist Papers, the phrase "separation of church and state," not mentioned in the U.S. Constitution, was not directed toward keeping people of particular faith out of government. But the "separation" discussion was about insuring an "establishment clause" in the Constitution that disallowed official government endorsement of a particular faith.[45]

It was always understood that people of religious faith and no religious faith could, and should, enter into public life and public service on behalf of the commonwealth and common good. Americans generally, among the peoples of the developed world, are probably the most accepting of public figures speaking freely and publicly of private faith. A post-Christian Europe has an uneasiness about the kinds of religious embrace and fervor that are common in much of the world. The United States has had unique successes in building foundations of peaceful, religious pluralism. For us, the passions of private faith have been a friend to democracy, social reform, and freedom.

The American Project has handsomely benefited from the witness of people of faith whose commitment to public service grew out of a personal faith nurtured in a particular religious community. Our national movements to perfect our Union and spur social change have tapped into the ready reservoir of energy, goodwill, and self-sacrifice that is fostered in faith communities. The American abolitionist movement was fueled by committed Christians who saw their work as God's work. The Great Awakening movements of the eighteenth and nineteenth centuries added the spirit of urgency to the times and national debate about the inherent contradictions of legally sanctioned human bondage in a free Republic. The revolts of John Brown, Nat Turner, and others were ablaze with apocalyptic religious visions. The Civil War "Battle Hymn of the Republic" is a religious song that gave moral impetus to war. President Lincoln's Emancipation Proclamation, enacted in the middle of the Civil War, was issued in part to appease French and English-enlightened libertarians and Christian abolitionist activists.

169

The women's rights activists of the early twentieth century found allies among Christian women temperance movement activists also concerned about family stability and child welfare. Of course, the American civil rights and antiwar movements of the mid-to-latter-twentieth century were directed and energized by people and communities of faith. Today, we are seeing the re-collections of new movement from common people within and without faith communities concerned about the moral center of our politics and our economy, as well as global issues of poverty and wealth imbalances, AIDS and disease, and environmental stewardship. The embrace of faith and values by the budding activists and social justice actors of this generation is what gives us hope for the future.

The American Project has pointed the way for the world to live with the full benefits of religious pluralism. In America, with our ideals of democratic capitalism, we have historically created a healthy competition among the particular faiths and sects of religious bodies. The American expectation for religious peoples and their communion is for them to use their particularity and peculiarity to serve the common good as they promulgate their faith. We do not tell one another what to believe about God, but we do expect every faith to be of some good to whole society. In America the real competition between faiths, sects, denominations, and communions is for the bragging rights about which groups of religionists best serve the vulnerable; who fosters the most goodwill; and who upholds our common values of respect for diversity and pursuit of the common good.

One challenge of future America in this regard is this: How can we keep these expectations as more non-Christian faiths grow and become more influential in the body politic? The case can be made that our diversity of faiths was more manageable when the overwhelming majority of the citizens identified themselves with the Judeo-Christian heritage. It was that commonality of faiths among and between Christians and Jews that Dr. King drew upon in his letter from the Birmingham jail in 1963. With the emergence of Islam in the West, as well as more openness to other non-Christian faiths, the challenges of diversity and pluralism may prove more complex. The principle of competition in serving the common good and the embrace of American values of freedom of religious expression must continue to be important national cultural norms. What we should not expect nor attempt to foster is neutralization of particular faith.

Almost all faith traditions have theological belief systems that will reflectively recoil from neutralization and nullification of dogmas, claims, and sacerdotal rites. Freedom of religion must mean that the citizens are allowed to freely serve their country from their subjective places of faith. Here I make the case for particular faith as the energy that can drive movements that improve lives. While my particular faith and the personal testimony of my journey with Christ are nonnegotiable, the American Project has found a way to absorb the particular into the plural, and place the particular into the service of the whole. Because the common good is agreed to be a great good, the highest order of life for all Americans of every creed is selfless public service. As generations to come reflect upon the meaning of the "Stone of Hope" tribute to Dr. Martin Luther King Jr. on the National Mall, the living legacy of this Baptist clergy and private citizen will continue to challenge people all over the world to ponder the difference that can be made by one life committed to public service and a cause greater than one's self.

The Twenty-First Century Search for Spiritual Meaning in Causes and Politics

There is something at the core of humanity that longs for that which transcends basic instincts for survival and materialism. While that core is often nurtured by the tenets of organized religion and systematic theologies, the innate spiritual quest can also take paths outside of religious faith communities. Secular humanists, universalists, general deists, and passionate environmentalists can take paths that engage the human spirit and address the human need for a transcendent purpose for life. Because our cognitive gifts allow for complex reasoned projection of a future without us, the urgency of transcending our mortality—the search for greater meaning of life beyond the span of our lives— grows more pronounced with our aging and maturity. The quest for spirituality, manifest in the subscription to familiar and unfamiliar religions, will be ongoing in the new millennium. Daily bread and creature comforts can never fulfill the longing of what it means to be human. For us, there must always be more. The wonder of conscious life begs for meaning and universal principles to give our lives a deeper psychological and spiritual grounding and depth. Material prosperity is not enough for the deepest places of human existence, the soul of humankind. Human beings need vision, causes, and transcendent purpose to function in our full humanity.

Impoverished families are filled with anxiety at this juncture in American history. They have accurately assessed that they and their nation are being abandoned by the people in charge of the economy and politics—corporate entities and politicians. With massive wealth being transferred out of the country as the nation's population grows browner and blacker, given our history of racism and race-based economics, it does not take complex analysis to surmise that many of the rich and powerful have accepted America's decline as a global power as a matter of course. There is evidence that the nation's youth and the children of the affluent are searching for causes of their generation that extend beyond status and material wealth. In college campuses all over the country and in the use of social networking, young people are taking up causes of poverty, education, access to health care, workers' rights, environmental stewardship, eradicating diseases, and Third World debt reduction. In 2008 they tried their hand at politics and political transformation. The youth vote was decisive and instrumental in the election of the nation's first African American President. That election was a statement of purposeful arrival for this generation that embraces the multiethnic and the multicultural. This generation was inspired in 2008, but by the midterm elections of 2010 there were signs that they had lost enthusiasm for voting and participation in electoral politics. Profound disillusionment with electoral politics by American youth, reflected in polling and low levels of participation, may be the result of the deflation that happens when idealism meets the confines of our prodding political system.

Young people were absolutely engaged in the 2008 election, and they sought a transformational presidency. The election undercurrent was "spiritual" and connected to the continuing spiritual quest of a new millennial generation of Americans. Ironically, Obama's "blackness" became a political asset because blackness in the American context had become a symbol of progressive, transformative politics, and renegotiation of the social contract. Obama's campaign was wrapped in the aura of Dr. King's legacy and vision. The year 2008 was an exact, forty-year generational shift span of time from the assassination of Dr. King in 1968 to the election of Barack Obama. In the scriptures of the Judeo-Christian traditions, forty represents a significant time of transition, transformation, and intergenerational change and transference. The election season of 2008 saw pronounced youth participation and voting as young people set out to make a statement. The Obama acceptance of the Democratic nomination in Denver was forty-five years from the date of Dr. King's "I Have a

Dream" sermon at the (August 28, 1963) March on Washington. I believe the nation, led by our youth, anticipated a new, moral vision and re-embrace of a values-based redefinition of America. The symbolism of the election suggested that we could not be more transformational for the new millennium than by sending the first African American family to the White House. Just that reality held forth a stunning visual of new possibilities for America and our place in an emerging new world.

But in short order, the realities of governing in a time of national and global distress meant that important leadership decisions were at hand. The economic course—the stranglehold of big banks over the national economy, was the immediate concern. We have, I believe, rediscovered that in a time of crises, symbolism is no substitute for substance, and political incrementalism is no substitute for core principles and resolute leadership. The first two years of the Obama presidency seemed to lack the kinds of strong leadership and political reset promised in the campaign. It seemed as if the President did not stand up to the oligarchs and corporate interests, and that he failed to communicate the class warfare dimensions of contemporary American politics in moral terms. The truth is, nothing good can come from long-term unrestrained greed and exploitation. The American Project and Constitution are about the checks and balances of interest and power, as well as balance between self-interests and the common good. The present crises are due to the fact that our system and our society are out of balance. When America is out of balance, global instability is the result.

The American Project is in great danger, and as the Founding Fathers, Lincoln, Roosevelt, and King understood, salvaging the American Project has a purpose that transcends the national interests. Fulfilling America's destiny includes the mission of being salt of the earth and light to humanity all over the world. The only thing that will save our nation for the world will be recapturing the energy and spirit that comes from reengaging a higher purpose that calls for high commitment, creativity, and selfless service. To save ourselves, we must look within ourselves and look beyond ourselves for a purpose greater than our individual self-interest. That we need the transcendent to make life better in the here and now is old wisdom, yet needed for a new age.

Chapter 8

Reigniting the American Spirit:
What We Must Do Now!

"But he knew their thoughts, said to them: Every Kingdom divided against itself is brought to desolation; and a house that is divided against itself will fail."
—The Gospel of Luke 11:17, Jesus of Nazareth, about 30 A.D.

*"Cheap grace is the preaching of forgiveness without requiring repentance, baptism without church discipline, Communion without confession, absolution without personal confession. Cheap grace is grace without discipleship, grace without the cross ..."***—Dietrich Bonhoeffer (1906-1945), German Lutheran pastor whose conscience led him to oppose and plot to overthrow Adolf Hitler. Bonhoeffer, a modern Christian martyr, was executed by the Nazis by Hitler's direct order in 1945.**[46]

*"For too many of us the political equality we once had won was meaningless in the face of economic inequality. A small group had concentrated into their own hands an almost complete control over other people's property, other people's money, other people's labor—other people's lives. For too many of us life was no longer free, liberty no longer real; men could no longer follow the pursuit of happiness.... There is a mysterious cycle in human events. To some generations much is given. Of other generations much is expected. This generation of Americans has a rendezvous with destiny."***—Franklin Delano Roosevelt, thirty-second President of the United States, June 27, 1936.**

---

*"We are faced with the fact that tomorrow is today. We are confronted with the fierce urgency of now....Now let us begin. Now let us rededicate ourselves to the long and bitter—but beautiful—struggle for a new world.... The choice is ours, and though we prefer it otherwise we must choose at this crucial moment in human history."—**Martin Luther King Jr., Beyond Vietnam: A Time to Break Silence, April 1967.***

*"No one should negotiate their dreams. Dreams must be free to fly high. No government, no legislature, has a right to limit your dreams. You should never surrender your dreams."—**Jesse Louis Jackson, Rainbow PUSH Coalition President (1941-   ).***

❖❖❖❖❖❖❖

This is one of those critical times in American history when we must renew our national purpose and recommit ourselves to the mission of the American Project. America is, and always has been, an idea that combines the political with the economic in the definition of democracy. Political freedoms are made real by economic opportunities. We cannot divorce one from the other. The Declaration of Independence is grounded upon the freedom to pursue happiness. The Project of perfecting the Union is progressive expansion of the covenant to include excluded members of the national family in the blessings of liberty and the commonwealth of our common inheritance. The current economic crisis endangers the integrity of our political system and moves us away from our national purpose. Without upward mobility for Americans and their families, America is no longer America. This is a pivotal time and a pivotal generation.

There are many who have weighed in on the dialogue of what we will need to do to renew and restore the soul and promise of America. I believe we need spiritual restoration, a new moral vision that guides our politics and our economics. The conversation must turn from what is expedient to what is right and in our long-term national interests. The following is an offering from one who has come of age through life in public housing, public schools and postsecondary education, social justice advocacy, and urban ministry. This is a season for grassroots perspective. It's a time for a common-sense perspective of what ails us and what can heal us. Common folks are the soul of America, and the health of our nation will be determined by real opportunities for average citizens to set their own course and fully participate in our politics. As a product of Project America, these are emergency interventions that describe what I think we should do now to help save America for the world.

One: Radical Campaign Reform to Purify Our Politics and Reclaim Our Government

We need serious federal and local campaign finance reform and a serious overhaul of our politics by changing the way we fund candidates and elections. There is too much money from too few people poured into the political system to have honest government that represents all of the people. The law should be used to accomplish the purposes of restoring responsiveness of government to the people. Year after year we blame ordinary Americans for their lack of participation in electoral politics. I have learned to always trust the wisdom and insight of the people. I believe that a vast number of the American people are aware that their vote matters little as long as campaigns raise enormous amounts of money from the wealthy. The politicians will do the bidding of the fat cats and lobbyists who fund this system. We must ask: Does the will of the average voting participant really matter in a political system so corrupted by the moneyed class? The system has little legitimacy and relevance to the average American, and they know that they have very little influence in the government that makes the rules. We have to restore government to the people by restoring politics and political influence to the people.

The 2010 Supreme Court decision, Citizens United v. Federal Election Commission,[47] allowed private corporate entities to spend unlimited dollars in elections. It is among the worst anti-democratic rulings in American history. It was the wrong decision at the absolute worst time, and it will further unmitigated disastrous corruption of a system already imbalanced and awash in corporate cash. President Obama lashed out at the Court publicly, unprecedentedly, during his 2010 State of the Union Address to Congress with members of the Court present. It would have been well and good for him to have gone further and rallied the nation against the Court to get this bad decision reversed. This is bad law and it will further harm the country. I would make the case that this issue—influence and money in politics—is the number one issue of our times. The Court is supposed to be insulated from partisan politics in order to do what is good and right. It should not be subject to the same short sighted political dynamics that operate in Congress and the unending campaigns of electoral politics. In this instance, as in other times in American history, the Court should feel the full weight of public opinion and the justness of this cause. The Court, by definition, is the last resort for the little guy. The voice of ordinary Americans will be further muted by this wayward decision, and overturning it should be a national cause.

177

Two: Restore Home Equity, Community Banking, and Local Access to Capital

We must make bailing out the American homeowner and restoring the fortunes of the American family top priority. There will be no economic recovery as long as millions of homes are in mortgages that are underwater. We must clear up the misconception that the current economic crisis was caused by too many mortgages issued to too many unqualified American families. That is simply not true. This crisis was caused by greed, fraud, predatory lending, and deceptive financial schemes by lenders and the mortgage aftermarket. The hopes and dreams of Main Street America did not bring us to the brink of economic catastrophe, but rather the combination of Wall Street recklessness and Washington's negligence are to blame. The fact is the American people trusted the titans of the American economy and government to steward our collective future responsibly, fairly, and in the national interest. We must now reluctantly and regretfully conclude that this trust has proven misplaced. As the abuses of Wall Street are left unrequited, the likelihood of serious political instability and social unrest in America increases.

The American people have experienced the worst exploitations of an unfair market. Financial predators created whole industries that disadvantaged unsuspecting consumers with mortgage products irresponsibly packaged for future foreclosure. Second-market Wall Street financial investors manufactured derivative schemes that allowed for insurance underwriting securities of bonds that bundled these toxic assets, infecting and affecting the integrity of the entire global financial system. When the crisis came to a head in 2008, the underwritten, artificially inflated assets of the Wall Street investors were insured through American Insurance Group (AIG) and others. Their insurance claims were eventually covered by an AIG bailout on the credit of the American taxpayer. These banks and financial institutions were bailed out to ensure the integrity of the system, while the American homeowner has been left to drown with a mortgage underwater. The people have been told that these economic matters are too complex to fully understand. The Bush and Obama Administrations had no choice but to bail out the big banks or face the calamity of collapse and foreclosure on the entire financial system. In the game of financial musical chairs, the music had stopped. The American people, who would fund the chairs, were left without a seat. We will rediscover that wisdom is at the heart of the common people. Every good pastor knows this. The people may not fully understand complex economics, but they know when they have been had. In the words of Dr. King, "There will be neither rest nor tranquility in America," as long as Main Street bears the cross of suffering and Wall Street is allowed to go free.

There will be not be an economic recovery worth having without rescuing the American homeowner and restoring the fortunes of the American family. The uniqueness of the American Project is in the wedding of political freedoms and economic prospects. From the founding of the Republic, the American idea was about an expansion of liberties for the pursuit of happiness. At every juncture in our history, expanded liberties fueled economic growth. In the nineteenth century, the push westward across the continent was driven by dreams of homesteading and family farming. Pre and post-Civil War America saw migrants and immigrants fuel the American Industrial Revolution with visions of a nation where the "right to rise" was considered an inherent human right.

The women's rights and labor movements early in the twentieth century further expressed our nation's vision of empowerment of American families, both politically and economically. In the great wars of the twentieth century, saving America and the world for democracy facilitated unprecedented economic growth. The civil rights movement in the last half of the century reflected correlations between expansions of liberty and the booming 1960s economy. The lessons of history instruct that including more people in the blessings of liberty and prosperity grows the American economy. The foundations of family prosperity are homeownership and local access to capital. Once the fortunes and equity of the American homeowner are restored, the American people will have the capital and confidence to refuel the American economy with investments in their families' futures and the consumer spending that creates long-term recovery. For our long-term economic health, the fortunes of the American homeowner must be given top priority.

A significant portion of the almost eight trillion dollars invested in the nation's largest banks and investment houses[48] should have also been designated to provide mortgage relief and principal reduction to American homeowners, the victims most harmed by the crisis. The federal government should have also placed high priority on saving community banks, because these local institutions are specifically structured to meet the banking and investment needs of Main Street America. The long-term damage done to our economy is not seen in the misfortunes of big banks and Wall Street financial houses, but the damage is seen in the further concentration of wealth and the lack of local community access to the capital needed to fuel the hopes and dreams of the common people. We have moved closer to corporate-dominated capitalism and further from a democratic capitalism that reflects our values and ideals, and helps create the stabilities of a dominant middle-class. The losses of capital foundations in homeownership and access to community banks means further erosion of access to real power in our democracy and political system. We are in danger of losing sight of the intricate intimacies between political liberties and the economic viabilities of the people made possible by decentralized democratic capitalism. Our defense of private enterprise cannot be defined as facilitating a fraudulent cornering of the marketplace, or as controlling government economic policy and monopoly. Effective democracy requires measures of decentralized political and economic power.

❖❖❖❖❖❖❖

The Park National Bank Story: Community Banking and Democratic Capitalism

Up until October 30, 2009, Park National Bank was the finest community banking institution in America. The sole owner, Michael Kelly, had built his banking empire over twenty-eight years from the single branch he founded as the First Bank of Oak Park.[49] The silver-haired, middle-aged Kelly is the quintessential, conscientious, socially responsible Catholic businessman. A Creighton University graduate, Kelly's first banking job in Oklahoma City was to find and process small business loans in the city's isolated black community. Eventually Kelly landed in the Chicago area and here again began to pursue the banking business that was in his blood. His late father had built and lost his banking business in Minnesota during the era of the Great Depression.

Young Mike Kelly began building his bank through relationships in the Village of Oak Park, the suburb adjacent to Chicago's West Side. Oak Park is a highly literate, economically and racially diverse community. It is an all-American village, known for its Frank Lloyd Wright homes and Ernest Hemingway house tours. Over almost thirty years, Kelly purchased small distressed community banks in and around Chicago. In about 2006, he purchased community banks in New Mexico, Texas, and California. Each time he shared profits with staff and employees at all levels of his corporation. From his purchases and hard work, Kelly created the "Park National Bank" brand. By 2009, with almost $20 billion in banking assets, Kelly became the largest private banker in the United States. While building one of the most successful banking empires in the nation, Kelly raised his family and remained a local resident in the western suburbs, just blocks from the gritty, urban West Side of Chicago. His philanthropy, as well as his passion for anonymity, are legendary. Kelly and his Park National Bank had proven that it was possible in America to do both well (business and family) and do good (philanthropy) at the same time.

The banking business was Kelly's profession, but community development and education are his passions. He became benefactor to a string of inner-city elementary schools on the West Side of Chicago, lining up Catholic largesse and talent to offer poor black children the benefits of a high-quality education. When the West Side Austin community was shown to have fourteen-thousand high school students and only seven-thousand high school seats, Kelly spearheaded the founding of the first Jesuit College Prep High School for West Side low-income students. Kelly recruited me to the school's board of trustees in 2006, just in time to help recruit the first class of Christ the King School. By the fall of 2008 at the onset of the nation's economic crisis, poor children from Austin were moving into a newly built $30 million state-of-the-art school facility in the heart of the community. Kelly was the catalyst, providing the capital base and institutional support for the project. It was divinely sublime good fortune. One of America's most challenging ghettos had one of the nation's wealthiest community bankers as a personally invested neighbor and benefactor. According to Mike's wife, "He was just getting started." Even then, we were all amazed at what local banking relationships could mean for the community. But within one year, the national crisis in the banking system would hit home with devastating effect.

I had heard through the grapevine that Park National Bank was "in trouble." By the fall of 2009, apparently, the trouble had come to a head. Kelly's banks were worth about $19.4 billion in assets, attracting lots of attention in the big banking world. The Illinois Park National banks were profitable to the tune of millions a year, of which Kelly was known to plow over 25 percent of his profits back into charitable causes and community development. He had demonstrated, as a conscientious Catholic businessman, that banks highly committed to the community could also be highly profitable. He had similar plans for the troubled community banks he had purchased in Texas and California. But Kelly's dream of well-resourced community banking, investing in neighborhoods and people, was about to come to a sudden end. The financial crisis of 2008 was right around the corner.

Park National's capitalization troubles began with the heavy buy-in of Freddie Mac securities. Kelly and his banks had lost $850 million in 2008 when Freddie Mac, the housing mortgage entity established by Congress, went belly-up. The "securities" held by Kelly and others were deemed worthless overnight. It was a compounded tragedy for America's economy and values. Mortgagers who exploited poor homebuyers and sold subprime products have gone unprosecuted. People who had invested in Freddie Mac and Fannie Mae, often as a matter of principle for homeownership opportunities for upwardly mobile fellow Americans, lost huge sums of money for investing in the American Dream.

It would seem logical that Park National would have been a prime candidate for recapitalization monies available through the newly minted Toxic Asset Relief Program (TARP) administered by U.S. Treasury Secretary, Henry Paulson.[50] In a page-and-a-half documented request to Congress to authorize the rescue of the entire U.S. banking system in 2008, Paulson, a native Illinoisan, had almost a trillion dollars at his disposal. This unprecedented crisis was sudden and, we were told, required immediate address. The rules for using TARP funds would have to be made up along the way. That left Paulson and the Treasury department with enormous latitude to determine which banks survived and which died.

In Kelly's case, he waited patiently for new TARP regulations on privately owned banks. He waited and waited, with assurances that the regulations would be forthcoming and he would get needed assistance. In the meantime, large corporate banks were immediately saved. If there was one bank in America it made sense to recapitalize with TARP monies, it was Park National. After all, the government's hand in the Freddie Mac fiasco should have suggested some federal responsibility to investors who followed Congress's lead by investing in the mortgager whose mission was helping American families enter the housing market. Kelly was about to discover that Washington's ways are strange. Washington works slowly, illogically, and arrogantly irresponsible. After six months of being left out to dry, he worked to bring in private investors. He needed about $500 million of investment capital to stay afloat. He had negotiated with investors, trying not to give up too much control so he could retain the ability to do his philanthropic work through Park National. Finally, as the Federal Deposit Insurance Recapitalization (FDIC) deadline schedule grew close, Kelly would need one week or so to complete the arrangements with his investors. He finally lined up private investors, and negotiated ways to maintain control to continue his philanthropy.

But ultimately for Kelly and his banks, the TARP funds regulations circular was a charade, and there would be no more time to ink the agreements with his investors. Here's what happened. After becoming low-hanging fruit in the dog and pony show with FDIC, Park National was now in the sights of the nation's fifth-largest bank, the U.S. Bank. What I would later discover as a community activist was that the FDIC "deadlines" Park National were working under were both flexible and inflexible, subject to the discretion of the bank regulators. Once the clock starts ticking with FDIC involvement and they find a favored buyer, it could be already too late. In Kelly's case, the ninety days he had to put his deal together would be a firm deadline. FDIC officials have many tools to subjectively use to their advantage, and they have the authority to be inflexible when it suits their purposes. Once they become involved, a bank's fate may be determined by macroeconomics under the fog of informal arrangements and relationships within corporate banking and government regulatory circles. As the clock ticked, Park National Bank was already a plum promised to the nation's fifth-largest bank, and Kelly's last-ditch successful efforts were not going to get in the way.

October 30, 2009 was a strange day, even surreal, in our West Side neighborhood. The Obama Administration's U.S. Treasury Secretary, Timothy Geithner, had come to our side of town to tout a community program that did good work offering vocational training to minority kids who had dropped out of high school. The West Town Vocational Center, the brainchild of Oak Park activists, was already humming with new equipment and success stories. The Secretary's presence attracted all kinds of attention. It was a media event on ten. We were all invited to a splendidly renovated warehouse that housed the program for the noon festivities. Mayor Daley arrived as the gracious host to federal officials from Treasury. Illinois' Senior Senator, Richard "Dick" Durbin, strolled in with the understated splendor of a patrician and member of the nation's most exclusive club. A buzz surrounded the arrival of two of the city's three African American congressmen, Danny K. Davis of the West Side and Bobby Rush of the South Side. Mike Kelly entered mid-program and stayed in the back, quiet and unassuming.

Ironically, a large part of Geithner's presentation was awarding Kelly's brainchild, Park National Initiatives, a $50 million tax credit to further community development in impoverished communities. After the formal program, huddles formed all over the room. The congressmen were trying to reach FDIC head Sheila Bard or one of her officials to stave off a scheduled 5:00 p.m. seizure of Park National at the flagship Oak Park headquarters. There were attempts to reach the White House, as word circulated that First Lady Michelle Obama's mother, Marian Robinson, had retired from Park National's South Side offices and still had friends working for the bank.[51] Then I overheard rumbles that the congressmen had best not push the banking regulators too hard; an FDIC official had already warned that they had the authority to contact the Federal Bureau of Investigation (FBI) for protection if congressional pressure became too hot and heavy. It was strange to witness the powerlessness of the major public officials we had lionized over the years. For us, the community activists and local pastors, we were getting a glimpse into the formal and informal nuances of dealing with this national and global crisis that had now come to the West Side. In spite of all the high power and high drama in the room that afternoon, there would be no reprieve.

The FDIC would employ a seldom used "cross guarantee mechanism" to deliver the assets of Park National to U.S. Bank.[52] They would use the recent acquisition of the troubled banks in Texas and California to take away the profitable base of banks Kelly had built in Illinois. All of this would happen without granting a week to ten days for Kelly's new investors' agreements to materialize. The seizure would happen on the same day as the Treasury Secretary's celebration of Park National's stellar community service. David Pope, the president of Oak Park Village, called this episode, "the greatest bank robbery in American history." One part of the federal government had come to town to give a measure of praise and tax credit largesse, while another part of the same administration had come to town to take it all away.

There were obviously banks and financial institutions too big to fail, no matter their market misfortunes, or even the mistakes made by their corporate officials. Here, on our side of town, was a bank we deemed too good and too valuable to our communities to fail. Our local experience with Park National is the perfect illustration of what had gone wrong in the nation. Our government and the direction of the U.S. economy were moving further and further away from the interests, needs, and aspirations of the American people and the American Project. But we were West-siders, the toughest of Chicago toughs. When Dr. King had come to Chicago in 1966, he found his organizing base on the West Side for good reason. On the West Side, we take pride in the fact that we fight back. Our goal in this fight made perfect sense to us. Simply, we wanted the FDIC to reverse its decision, and put Park National Bank back in business to continue the vision of sound community banking and giving local citizens access to capital.

The mission of Park National had, in ways intentional and unintentional, brought together the diverse communities it served. From Chicago's central city vantage point, looking far west we were gritty, urban Austin, upscale Oak Park, very wealthy River Forest, and predominately minority Maywood. We were city and suburban, poor and wealthy, postgraduate and undereducated, and black and white and Hispanic. We were all grief filled about Park National, but we were angry about what happened to Mike Kelly. For us, Kelly was more than a banker, he was our neighbor. Of course, the low-key and reserved Kelly really wanted no part of what we were up to. As a banker who still had outstanding business with regulators and the need to interact with the new owners, Kelly wanted no part of protest or agitation. He was also very concerned about the welfare of his old employees. He felt that antagonizing U.S. Bank folks would put at risk ongoing negotiations to continue bank commitments to various schools and community projects. We thought the fight was bigger than all these things. We were also certain that our activism would strengthen and make more effective whatever side door negotiations were being conducted on behalf of the schools and other projects in our community.

Two days after the takeover, on Monday, November 2nd, about thirty black clergy and activists from the South Austin Coalition (SAC) showed up at the Chicago FDIC offices. Our local SAC organization has the distinction of championing the national law, the Community Reinvestment Act, that made sure that community development and investment were a part of federal evaluation of bank performance. As pastors we had learned to give these kinds of protests a black church aura to conjure up the moral authority of the civil rights movement. When we entered the lobby, we had elderly folks from SAC singing "This Little Light of Mine, I'm Gonna Let It Shine!" When we saw security gathering, we then called for a prayer circle. We then tapped a couple of preachers to pray, specifically those we were sure would pray long, extemporaneous, rhythmic black Missionary Baptist prayers. We held hands in a large prayer circle in the lobby and made a sanctified spectacle of ourselves, while the preachers let it rip. After the ruckus of two long prayers, we were asked to have a sidebar with a couple of local FDIC officials who had come down to the lobby to meet. We hand-delivered a letter addressed to Ms. Bard, demanding reversal of the Park National decision, acting as if we thought it might just be that simple. Our first protest that day tested a theory a few of us had postulated. Our media goal was to make our local Austin neighborhood papers. Small local papers with an online presence have a huge impact, even a global audience. We banked that we could eventually garner national attention with our first aim being the front page of our neighborhood papers.

Our initial actions blossomed into the organization of a diverse "Coalition for Community Banking." The organization crossed the usual barriers of race and class. The campaign we waged was organic and phenomenal. We knew that our diversity made us stand out even more as a news story. Our sustained protests and staged actions on the Park National story attracted wide media attention, locally and eventually, nationally. We hit jackpots with New York Times features and Public Broadcasting System (PBS) news hour segments. We had also gotten the attention of U.S. Banks higher-ups, although they were not our targets. We had successfully enlisted our elected officials at all levels to support our cause. It's always difficult to gauge the authenticity of interactions with politicians. I always thought they felt less convinced of the power of the people. In many ways, I felt they pitied us poor souls who felt that truth and the power of the passionate people could reverse a FDIC decision.

After almost six months of creative and sustained protestations, we secured a congressional hearing on the Park National Bank takeover with the U.S. House of Representatives subcommittee on banking, headed by Chicago's Northwest Side congressman, Luis Gutierrez. Finally, we believed, we would see the decision by FDIC taken to task and questions asked and answered. Why could Mike Kelly not have had ten more days to save his banks? Why was the "cross-guarantee mechanism," used only six times since the 1970s in the savings and loan scandal, employed in this case? Why were TARP funds used only for Wall Street banks too big to fail, and not for community banks too good and valuable to Main Street to fail? Did anyone assess the charitable work of Park National and factor that into the decision of what would happen to our fledging communities if this resource was taken away? How much weight did the FDIC give to Park National's huge reinvestments in our communities? What will happen to our democracy if there continues to be less and less local control of access to capital? Who, by name, made this particular decision? Finally, we thought, our elected officials would get to the bottom of this. Almost seventy-five private citizens representing our diverse coalition traveled to Washington, D.C., by bus and by air at our own expense. Our hopes were high. We felt that the actions of FDIC would not stand the light of day.

Capitol Hill is impressive. Politics oozes out of the brickwork and the furniture. And the people who work and work on the Hill are political animals on steroids. Not just the elected officials, but every staffer and lobbyist exudes a sophisticated and perfected political posturing. The careful observer would discern that every word and movement is calculated for personal political utility. This is the backdrop for understanding the political theater that is a "congressional hearing." I'm afraid that the poor souls who traveled with us did not fully understand just how meaningless of an exercise in futility a congressional hearing could be. Oh, there was drama alright. There were probing and insightful questions. The Republican members of the subcommittee had great incentive and polished skills to expose the failings of Obama's Administration. It all seemed the perfect setup to get to the facts of the case. We had smart representatives, in adversarial roles, impaneled to grill witnesses. We selected the head of a large local nonprofit and Mike Kelly as the two witnesses to tell our story.[53] It was great theater, but it became clearer as time went on that this forum was designed in part to diffuse protest and dissipate citizen passion.

One last question was asked at the end of the first segment by Republican Congressman Jeb Hensarling of the Fifth Representative District of Texas. He was a fit, sharp fifty-one-year old conservative attorney and spoke with a Texas drawl. His was the central probing question of the story. It was hitting the nail on the head. "Mr. Kelly, out of all the good you have done, and given the profitability of your banks, with the investors you had lined up, why could you not have had ten more days to save your banks?" Forthrightly, in a moment punctuated with pregnant pause, Kelly the good Catholic American looked to the officials of his representative democracy with earnest blue eyes and swallowed once. Kelly finally answered: "Sir, I don't know the answer to that question." There were then a few more seconds of silence. "No further questions," concluded the congressman. Congressman Gutierrez then chimed in further, "This is the crux of what's wrong with the way we are handling the banking system. The banks dedicated to helping people in their communities are going under, while the big banks get bigger." It was time for lunch.

After lunch, next up was a senior vice president of U.S. Bank, Richard Hardnack. He solemnly explained how innocent his corporation was in what had happened to Kelly and Park National. But, Hardnack chuckled when he asserted that "we could be sure" that U.S. Bank would never match the generosity of Kelly. Hardnack wanted to be clear. They would never ever come remotely close to reinvesting a quarter of their profits back into the community. They exist entirely for the profit of their shareholders. They strive to be socially responsible, but they would not singularly focus on social service or community development as a mission of their bank. I think we got the point. We would not see the likes of Park National and its philanthropy again.

Most revealing, however, was the smugness of the nameless, faceless bureaucrats from the FDIC who appeared before the subcommittee in the late afternoon. It was obvious that for them the hearing was annoying, routine, and perfunctory. They knew the score and the real deal: their agency is imperial and impervious, and it operates beyond the purview of elected officials. Even though they had to appear, they really did not have to answer specific questions or justify their actions. It was not the verbal answers but their unspoken, body language that revealed how things really worked. The regulators and the big bank high rollers have an informal honor system. The big bank boys and girls sometimes do small favors for the regulators by taking the small, failing bank garbage off of the hands of FDIC officals. When a juicy plum like Park National is dangling, able to give a large national super-bank an immediate and impressive footprint in a major market, deadlines and seldom-used mechanisms are fair game to deliver the promised goods. Like much of life, it is the informal agreement and unspoken understanding that determine how the written rules are implemented.

These arrangements probably make perfect sense in highbrow cocktail party circles of the powerful Washington and New York elite, but it makes for lousy long-term national banking strategy. The recovery of the American economy will depend largely on policies that prioritize community interests over corporate interests. Our greatness and growth are fostered when the industrial and corporate class serves the middle-class and the poor. Ships float when the ship's bottom floats over the water. We will need to recreate our economic model from the bottom-up, not the top-down. We will need to recreate community-based democratic capitalism. Sadly, our "George Bailey, wonderful life" Park National story did not have a happy ending. Our communities now have to deal with the realities of corporate capitalism, with U.S. Bank replacing the personal and personable relationship we once had with the Park National. It has been an incalculable loss.

To be fair to U.S. Bank, they have responded to our pressure and appeals and made good on commitments Park National had made to the elementary schools, the high school, and a local university that specializes in serving first-generation minority college students. That follow-through is commendable, owing much to community organizing and Hardnack's childhood Oak Park roots as well. On the other hand, U.S. Bank behaves very much like a large, impersonal corporation. Within weeks of taking over the bank, they laid off hundreds of employees, introduced their corporate culture, and robotized remaining personnel to fit the corporate model. After about a year-and-a-half into the acquisition, U.S. Bank officials made a big splash announcing a standard community benefits agreement hashed out with the remnants of the Coalition for Community Banks. We had fought the good fight. We had gained more for our community than we would have gotten had we not fought back, but the nature of our community has fundamentally changed. The real decision makers about the kinds of access to real capital we will have for our families and our communities live in faraway places. And worst, we saw firsthand that not even our elected officials have the power to effectively regulate and influence a financial system that abuses people and operates apart from the people. These aspects of our political and financial systems must change if America is to be great again.

❖❖❖❖❖❖❖

Making whole the American homeowners and community-based banking are essential for rebuilding the American economy bottom-up. We are going to have to peel back the covering and secrecy around banking regulators and their relationships with corporate capitalists. Our freedom to self-determine politically is being compromised because we are not insistent upon the democratization of capital. Monopolies and robber barons were not good for the American economy in the years leading to the Great Depression, and they are not good today. The idea that concentrated wealth by transnational corporate capitalists is good must go the way that communism as concentrated state power has gone, into the trash heap of history. History has proven that too much political power or too much economic wealth in the hands of too few people creates corruption, economic contraction, and social instability. We need a new moral vision of democratic capitalism. That new vision begins practically with the restoration of the fortunes of the American homeowners and decentralization of banking and local access to capital. Both of these would be the right and good thing to do. We now need leadership and policies that bring the power back to the American people and restore the wherewithal of the people to pursue their hopes, dreams, and aspirations.

Three: Overhaul the Tax Code and Pay Down the National Debt

We need a radical overhaul of the U.S. tax code. Over time the wealthiest Americans and corporations have carried less of the tax burden for government and our national obligations. While more of the nation's wealth has concentrated and accumulated to the top 1 percent of Americans, tax burdens are disproportionately borne by the middle class. We need a truly progressive tax code to restore the integrity of the system. Federal government deficit spending grew substantially from 2000 to 2008 under the Bush Administration. With the Iraq and Afghanistan wars after 9-11 costing some $800 billion and counting, we incurred the expense of wars without the shared financial and material sacrifice of war. In fact, the Bush Administration pushed tax cuts and capital gains tax breaks for the wealthy in the middle of sustained military conflict in two countries. Bush Republicans also conveniently left the growing financial obligations of social entitlement programs intact. They left the tough decisions for the future. Under President Bush mortgage lenders exploited the people, government spending grew, wars dragged on, and taxes were cut. By 2008, we faced an economic day of judgment. There has never been a credible economic model that shows that nations can fund both "guns and butter" at the same time.

One of the tragedies of the all-volunteer military force we adopted after the Vietnam War is that the American people no longer have a full and deep-felt understanding of the true costs of war. Our political leadership has not been forthright to challenge the American people with the sacrifices needed to fulfill our far-flung military obligations and conduct the necessary war against the purveyors of international terrorism. The response to 9-11 provided the perfect opportunity to call for all sectors of American society to make material and financial sacrifices, but the Bush Administration did not level with us. We became simultaneously caught up in military quagmires and crises level government deficits. In 2011, the U.S. federal government received its first bond downgrade in history from a Wall Street rating agency. With $13 trillion dollars of debt and counting, the downgrade is a word of caution to our political leaders, and it reflects the shifting global balances of the world economy. America is left to engage in basic economics. We will need a period of time when we have to spend less and take in more.

Political leaders must rise to the occasion by putting entitlements and higher taxes on the table. At present there are too many loopholes that allow the wealthy and corporations to escape a fair share of the tax burden. First, the wealthy should be taxed at the highest tax brackets, with capital gains taxes taxed at the rate of income. The greater our income, the higher the percentage of that income we should pay. Warren Buffett has had the courage to say publicly what the wealthiest admit privately. Since the rich receive government's greatest benefit, the stability that allows intergenerational transfer of wealth, they should gladly bear a greater share of the tax burden for government. Second, we will have to put social security, Medicare and Medicaid, and other entitlements up for review. We will also need to operate with a smaller, smarter defense budget. Eighty percent of the budget is military and entitlement programs, so the only way to significantly reduce deficits will be to share the sacrifice and shave expenditures. Austerity for the middle-class, the working poor, and the poor is an easier case to make once we have gotten rid of the Bush tax cuts, increased the tax burden on the rich, and cut the defense budget.

Cutting the military budget means reexamining our military obligations. Our treaties and troop stations in Germany and Japan must demand shared cost with the host countries. The Obama Administration has fought smart, focused wars in Iraq and Afghanistan. The leadership of Al-Qaeda has been decimated. Taking on the remaining cells of terrorist organizations will call for high skill sets, but targeted military operations will cost less than fighting conventional armies and conquering and rebuilding occupied countries. A leaner, smarter military is more needful in the twenty-first century than a large, bloated imperial force. Third, the tax code should be simplified. Americans spend over 6.1 billion hours annually on tax preparation.[54] The code has evolved over time without rhyme, reason, or fairness. It must be simple and straightforward, with simpler categories of standard deductions. We could even entertain suspension of the basic home mortgage deductions for a time to bring balance back to the budget. Again, sacrifice that is truly shared has the best chance of being embraced and holding together our body politic.

In proper focus, we have less of a deficit problem than a political problem. We need an earnest, patriotic call for shared sacrifice to save the American Project. People are more apt to sacrifice for a transcendent purpose. In restoring the fortunes of American families and communities, we must also restore the reserves and credibility of the American government. We must bring integrity back to the tax code, take out the schemes and built-in advantages for the wealthy, and level with the American people. We will not win the trust necessary for shared sacrifice with proscribed austerity for the majority of Americans and protected prosperity for the top 1 percent. The tax code is a moral and spiritual document. It reflects our values. All Americans must have the right and opportunity to rise. And for those who do rise, they have a moral obligation pay a fair share for the government that protects their gains and promotes our mutual interests. The restoration of American greatness is contingent upon the spiritual pillars of shared sacrifice, fairness, and financial responsibility.

Four: Rebuild the American Infrastructure As Down Payment on the Future

The only reason not to commence a massive investment in rebuilding America's infrastructure would be that we have concluded that our nation's best days are behind us and that we have given up on the future. I sincerely believe that there are people in high places in our country who have reasoned that the American Project has run its course, and that the future belongs to newly emerging nations. I would be tempted to feel the same given the trends and shifts in the world, but I also believe that America's diversity means we have a unique capacity to adapt, repackage our ideals, and renew our social contract with our own newly emerging majority of minorities. Leaders in American government and industry who do not passionately share this faith in America's future forfeit the right to control our destiny. One major litmus test of patriotism and commitment to our future must be the willingness to support rebuilding the nation's roads, highways, streets, bridges, and schools.

First world status is defined by a well-developed and maintained infrastructure. The slide in America's global dominance is first seen in neglected roads and bridges, and school buildings. The history of our economic development from the Atlantic Ocean to the Pacific Ocean parallels expansion through transportation, communication, and educational development. The correlation between transportation and commerce is unmistakable. The roads and highways are the arteries that organically feed the dynamics of economic exchange. Economic systems feed on transportation systems. The steam locomotive engines of the rail transportation systems fueled the economic expansions of the nineteenth century. The transcontinental railway systems exponentially increased the industrial development dynamics that made obsolete the slave labor-based agrarian economies of the American South.

In the twentieth century, the automobile and air travel revolutionized the speed of travel and the dynamics of commerce. In America, the family automobile, the interstate highway system, and the proliferation of metropolitan airports all facilitated explosive modern market economics. Of course, the new revolution of the World Wide Web has opened cyber ways of interconnectivity that have changed the ways we market and buy every conceivable product. All of these compounding infrastructures of transportation and communication require massive investments to stay in the global competition for access to local and international markets. Included in infrastructure investment is rebuilding school facilities to state-of-the-art quality so we can develop and train competitive human capital to participate in the global economy.

In our investments in transportation, we address immediate and future needs. Today, we cannot prosper with long-term double-digit unemployment. Massive investment in capital projects means putting Americans back to work. Rebuilding roads, bridges, and schools today provides a significant jobs program at a critical time. Even with tax reforms, we would anticipate that capital projects would add to budget deficits. But the proper way to view these projects is to see them not as expenditures but as investments in America's future. Infrastructure investment is essential to future growth. As in all things economic and life, there can be no harvest without seed, and there can be no growth without investment.

First-world societies require first-class roads and first-class schools. All of America's visionaries have always seen our nation with unique capacities and responsibilities to pay extraordinary costs to maintain our calling as light to other nations. From George Washington's new nation in the New World, to Thomas Jefferson's Declaration of unalienable rights, to Lincoln's right to rise, and Franklin Roosevelt's New Deal, to John F. Kennedy's New Frontier, and Lyndon B. Johnson's Great Society, and Martin Luther King' s Dream, our national purpose has required sacrifice and the faith of a forward look. Rebuilding the nation and renewing the social contract and national purpose means having the faith to invest in an infrastructure to support America's future promise. The time to make these sacrifices and investments is now. In moving forward now, we can stimulate our economy and rebuild for the future.

Five: Radically Reform the Criminal Justice System

If there is one single thing that breeds disrespect for law and order, it is unfairness and corruption in the criminal justice system. No group of individuals are more maligned by the abuses of the American criminal justice system than African American males. The widely circulated work of Michelle Alexander's, The New Jim Crow, has well documented the ways in which the criminal justice system has served to repackage the systematic discrimination and demoralization of black males. Alexander has codified the information and facilitated dialogue around a matter that is starkly evident in every metropolitan area in America.

For a large segment of black America, the criminal justice system is not viewed as a "justice" system, but a "just us" system.

The Reagan Era's War on Drugs to some great extent has been a war against the urban, black male.[55] By 2011, almost two-thirds of urban, black males are in some stage of incarceration or supervision of the criminal justice system. While blacks make up just 13 percent of the U.S. population, they make up over 60 percent of the nation's prison population. There are more black men incarcerated in jail than enrolled in college. While drug and substance experimentation is an American pastime and a widely shared coming of age phase in almost every American community, black Americans constitute 90 percent of the nation's drug convictions. Illegal drug trafficking brings severe legal penalties for inner-city cartels, but common trafficking and use on mostly white college campuses and suburbs are handled as youthful indiscretions or personal life struggles and individual health issues. The lack of educational and economic opportunities leaves many black males without live options, and they become fodder for a ferocious criminal justice system that marks them for the rest of their natural lives. What is most diabolical, as Alexander has researched, is the historical continuum in which the contemporary wholesale criminalization of black males takes place.

The American original sin was enshrined in the "three-fifths clause" of the first compact of the U.S. Constitution. As a compromise, each person in the southern slave population were counted as three-fifths of a person for the purposes of congressional representation. The personhood of the slave was absolutely devalued by chattel bondage, but a fraction of their personhood was counted for the purposes of giving their enslavers a greater share of power in the national government. The Electoral College electoral mechanism gave outsized power to slaveholders in the seating of the national Congress and in the election of the nation's Chief Executive. It was a damnable compromise with the inherent evil of the slavocracy, and it required cleansing by a bloody civil war. The guilty stain of the three-fifths clause has perverted the American Project from the founding.

There is a lineage of perversion of our democracy from the "three-fifths clause" to the State's Rights Confederacy, to the post-Reconstruction reign of terror, to Jim Crow, to the reactionary Dixiecrats, to the Nixon-Reagan southern strategy, to the "War on Drugs" and era of mass incarceration. At each stage of American history, a race-baiting regressive political class has emerged from the disenfranchisement and suppression of the black vote.[56] The right to vote is still a state's right even after the victories of the civil rights movement. In this new era of mass incarceration, states with the largest proportions of blacks in the population are more likely to have state laws that disenfranchise offenders and ex-offenders. In the blackest states of the Union, ex-offenders cannot vote after they serve their time in jail. In the whitest states of the Union, the incarcerated can vote even while they are in jail.

As a result, some of the nation's more reactionary politicians in modern times hail from states with the largest proportions of African Americans. Jesse Helms, Strom Thurmond, Trent Lott, and others held strangleholds over their sizable black constituents and over the racially progressive public policy in the federal government by using an unfair criminal justice system to suppress black voter participation, and amassing the outsized power through the congressional seniority system. The critical presidential election of 2000 came down to voter suppression in the African American community in Florida, with drummed-up confusion over the blacks with criminal records with names similar to those names of individuals who were registered on the voting rolls. The confusion added to voting irregularities in a state whose 25 electoral votes were delivered to Bush by an officially reported plurality of 537 votes out of nearly six million votes cast. What we rediscovered in Florida in 2000 was that voting really is still a state's right is heavily controlled by county government apparatus. The confusions over individual identities, voting site changes, ballot mix-ups, and other irregularities provide the fog to cover suppression strategies by party apparatuses that control election machinery. In 2011, states are now resorting to documentation requirements at voting places to discourage poor voters. The schemes continue for the same purposes, to dissuade and prohibit free and full access to the franchise. We need strong federal enforcement of the Voting Rights Act of 1965 now more than ever. We also need to aggressively respond to the ways the criminal justice system unjustly disadvantages minorities.

We cannot overstate how the criminal justice system feeds the new Jim Crow setup. Until we reform the system and have an equally administered justice system, we will not be able to move beyond the nation's original sin. Today, with the nation in transition to a majority-minority demographic, rectifying this national travesty will determine whether we survive as a credible alternative to repressive governments and nations in the world. With just 5 percent of the world's population, we warehouse over 25 percent of the world's incarcerated people. The disproportionate victimization of minorities by U.S. drug laws and the disparities in sentencing are injustices that must be addressed immediately. We must decriminalize low-impact, self-afflicted, nonviolent drug use for all Americans. Nonviolent drug abusers are obviously more sick and despairing than they are criminal. They hurt themselves and their families most of all. Nonviolent drug abusers need treatment, opportunity, and purpose, not incarceration. Incarceration and criminalization makes a bad situation for struggling people worse. For people who are temporarily incarcerated, we need to ensure that rehabilitation, job training, and transformation are central to the mission of institutions. We must incarcerate only when necessary and do so with reentry in view.

Finally, we must have a just policy for reintegrating ex-offenders back into civil society. To permanently restrict nonviolent ex-offenders from school loans, public housing, and basic job opportunities is not only unjust, it is also bad public policy. To maintain a permanent ex-offender class is patently unjust. Every major religion holds forth some doctrine of the possibility of human redemption. In the West, we have believed that our civil law should have ethical bases upon a higher moral law. In the Judeo-Christian scriptures, we are introduced to the concept of "jubilee." Every fifty years, indebted persons and their families are given a graceful release from their debts. In the divine economy, God orders that the captives be set free from indentured servitude, and even the powerful must acknowledge God's grace to them and God's ownership of everything. The "jubilee" means that justice is balanced by mercy, and that human beings function best with the hope that they can have a new start. Think of how our criminal justice system could be refreshed by a jubilee possibility for nonviolent ex-offenders. The possibility of criminal record expungement as reward for seven or so years of clean records would be a great incentive to non-violent ex-offenders. Hope is a most powerful incentive to correct mistakes and behaviors. Our present system of permanent criminal status for minor discretions breeds despair and contempt for the law. It also tarnishes our international witness.

We cannot be the land of the free and a beacon of hope as a nation that leads the world in incarceration and disparities in the standards of justice for the rich and the poor. We also will not be able to continue the American Project with wholesale incarceration of the black and brown human capital we need to promote our national interests and values in an emerging new world. Radical reformation in the criminal justice system is among the immediate things we must do to set aright the ship of state to carry the banner of the Free World into the twenty-first century.

Priscilla and I, 2010

The Girls Grown up: Joyce and Janelle 2009

The Boys Growing Up: Marshall and Maurice, 2009

Chicago area L.E.A.D.E.R's Network Pastor's 2nd Annual Event. We styled our organization after PUSH and SCLC, 2007

Chapter 9

Sankofa: The Way Forward Always Begins by Looking Back

*"You shall receive power after the Holy Spirit comes upon you, And you will be my martyrs in Jerusalem, Judea, Samaria and even to the utmost parts of the earth." —**Jesus Resurrected, The Book of Acts 1:8, around 33 A.D.***

*"….We hold these truths to be self-evident, that all men are created equal, that they are endowed by their Creator with certain unalienable Rights, that among these are Life, Liberty and the pursuit of Happiness. That to secure these rights, governments are instituted among men, deriving their just powers from the consent of the governed. That whenever any Form of Government becomes destructive of these ends, it is the Right of the People to alter or to abolish it, and institute new Government..." —**Congress of the United States of America, "The Declaration of Independence," July 4, 1776.***

*"I should like to have it said of my first administration that in it the forces of selfishness and of lust for power met their match….I should like to have it said in my second administration that in it these forces have met their master." **Franklin Delano Roosevelt, the thirty-second President of the United States, at the final rally of his 1936 reelection campaign at Madison Square Garden in New York City.**[57]*

*"If we are to go forward, we must go back and rediscover those precious values—that all reality hinges on moral foundations and that all reality has spiritual control."—**Martin Luther King Jr., Civil Rights Martyr (1929-1968).***

"We have the opportunity to move not only toward the rich society and the powerful society, but upward to the Great Society." —**Lyndon Baines Johnson, the thirty-sixth President of the United States of America (1908-1973).**

"All Power to the People!" —**The Black Panther Party Manifesto, (1971).**

"The work goes on, the cause endures, the hope still lives and the dream will never die." —**Edward Moore "Ted" Kennedy, United States Senator from Massachusetts (1932-2009).**

"My ministry has always involved social activism. I think that every responsible ministry must be at some levels involved in the social order." —**Reverend Al Sharpton, President of the National Action Network (1954-   ).**

❖❖❖❖❖❖❖

The Day of Baptism: "The Water Chilled My Body, but it Renewed My Soul"

Whenever I have had the honor to participate in a public baptism service in the African American Baptist tradition, I reflect upon my journey of life and walk of faith. One of my greatest memories is my own baptism. I was baptized in the summer of 1963 at the age of five years old in my father's Shiloh Missionary Baptist Church on Chicago's West Side. In our tradition, eligibility for baptism begins at the age five. We view age five as the "age of accountability" for one's sins. Traditional black religious communities tend to be child centered and focus upon bringing children into the community of faith as full-fledged members very early in life. Most children raised in church look forward to an opportunity to formally join the church, be baptized, and receive the sacraments of Holy Communion on the first Sunday evening service. Entering the faith requires publicly coming forward and presenting one's self during the invitation to follow Christ as a candidate for baptism. The decision of a five-year-old would be accepted as valid testimony for baptism if the child came forward voluntarily.

In the urban context, not even children can afford to drift aimlessly, lest the powerful suction of street culture lures preteens and opportunities for a productive life "wither like a raisin in sun." Inner-city children have not had the luxuries of subsidized recovery from youthful indiscretions. Bad decisions mar and label for life. The streets of urban America are cruel and unforgiving. Churches—large and small, mega and storefront—run countercultural to street culture, and they provide an oasis in the middle of despair. I was blessed to be a part of a family that maintained spiritual moorings through the church community. I have always felt privileged to have had a father who was a pastor and a mother who provided the foundations for education in the home.

In August of 1963, I had attended a full week of our church's annual summer daily Vacation Bible School (VBS). The summer weeklong outreach ministry was geared toward children inside and outside of the congregation. It was always a fun time of arts and crafts. It was more interesting than the usual Sunday School because we wore regular clothes, played games, and usually went on a Thursday field trip. Interwoven between arts and crafts was the ministry of evangelism aimed at children. The main objective of the entire Bible school was the Friday invitation to Christian discipleship. I remember a fear and trembling after hearing so plainly about the Gospel of Jesus Christ, and that only by accepting Christ as my personal Savior could my sins be forgiven. I wanted that badly. I also wanted to be a member of the church and receive Communion. On that Friday, as the Bible school's staff sang softly, "Come to Jesus, just now," I felt an irresistible urge to say yes to the invitation. I wanted to live for God. I moved, first slowly and nervously to the front to join the church as a candidate for baptism. The Vacation Bible School teachers prayed for me. They then led me in a prayer to confess my sins and accept Christ as my personal Savior. Even at five, I was conscious of my internal flaws as a human being. In my own insecurities, I found myself gleefully putting others down. It was clear to me that I was prone to sin and disregard others in thinking only about myself. That disturbed me then, as it disturbs me still today. I wanted to be a member of the church, and I wanted to go to heaven when I died. All of those things were a part of what I was thinking and feeling at that time.

That next first Sunday was my day of baptism. In the last service of a long day, the candidates were prepped for baptism by the church elders. Shiloh had a handmade aluminum-and-wood pool carved out of the floor of a room that doubled for dining and classroom space. The pool was filled with water, often very cold, from a water hose that ran from a basement sink on the building's second floor. I was sized up for a gown made of white sheets stitched together by elderly church mothers. While we candidates stood dressed in makeshift gowns and white cotton socks, we were given the final instructions on how to audibly answer questions from the baptizer about our willingness to follow Christ for the rest of our lives.

When my turn to be taken into the water came, I remember being so nervous I wanted to cry. In fact, I did have a tear roll down my cheek. I was so small that I was not allowed to walk down the steps into the pool. A deacon handed me off to another deacon who stood in the pool. But once in the pool, I had to stand on my own two feet with the water already just below my neck. The water was very cold. That discomfort was considered part of the experience. The drama of the setting, with soulful prayers and moaning songs, and the trauma of the water temperature created a soul-stirring, transformative atmosphere. It was a moment and feeling hard to forget. I looked up as the baptizer, my own father, gave the direction for me to fold my crossed arms across my chest. I felt comforted by his voice. This was it. "In obedience to Jesus Christ, the great head of the church, . . . and upon your profession of faith," my father uttered. "I baptize you in the name of the Father, and of the Son, and of the Holy Ghost, Amen." He covered my face with his hand, and I was swept under the water face up and brought back up before I could react to the shock of it all. That was it. I was baptized into the faith.

Baptism represents the ultimate "born again" experience, as one goes back through the water as a symbol of a new birth and the newness of life. Baptism is the acting out of the West African "Sankofa," the way forward is back though. Wisdom always means we must look back to the path we have traveled to find direction for our future. The stirring of immersion baptism should only happen once in the Baptist tradition, but the spiritual baptism into greater revelation and embrace of one's life purpose unfolds over the span of a lifetime journey of walking by faith in the guiding presence of the Spirit of God. As I came of age, I never lost faith in the baptism of my childhood. I was much less than pious most of my young adult life, but I have always felt a sense of purpose and a sense of divine presence. I landed in ministry, not as a church-focused religious person, but as a follower of Jesus Christ who made a commitment to serve people on behalf of God's kingdom. For me, my faith is inseparable from daily life. I believe that authentic faith is seen in the interaction with others, the development of character, and a life of service.

The modern hero of my faith was a preacher, Dr. Martin Luther King Jr., and my life goals became selfless service and leaving a witness and spiritual legacy on the earth. My faith in Jesus Christ as an evangelical Christian is a particular theological place that I could never deny. The reality of my faith has been born out of the life experiences of my spiritual journey to date. It began with my childhood baptism, but it continued in the sense of purpose I embraced at age eight when my mother died. Discerning the special graces of choosing a high school out of my attendance area, and then having the Western Illinois University recruiter find me, I am humbled by the fact that my life reflects not just choices, but unmerited grace and favor. Through graduate schools and fellowships, and through meeting mentors and benefactors in ministry and the in the world of public service, I have realized the great debts I owe to many for having had such a fascinating journey as a part of the generation that has lived through the transition from the second to the third millennium since Christ.

I have been anchored in my faith by the inner voice of calm assurance at the most unsettling times of my life. In remembering those times when I heard the voice of the Holy Spirit within, I have been carried through the worst of times with a stable faith for the future. I believe we are now in a place of unparalleled, historic transition. These are the times that will test our faith and optimism for the future. For me, it is my faith that grounds and frees me from the debilitating anxiety that can arise in times of crises. When the nation's core values are being challenged, I rely upon my faith to yet believe these ideals for my family, for our nation, and for our world. My faith charges me to bring the ever present kingdom and justice of God to the world. Every person deserves the right to strive for their fullest potential and every person should be challenged make a contribution to the human family. I cannot give up hope on these ideals, just as I could never go back upon my personal faith in Jesus Christ for the salvation of my individual soul. I believe the good fight of faith is good for the individual as well as good for our common life together.

Civic Engagement: A New Beginning in the New Millennium

All of the evidence is pointing to substantial unraveling of the social contract that has held the nation together for the last 235 years. The 1776 Declaration of Independence outlines the nature of the "abuses and usurpations" that give human beings the right to reset the government that fails to protect their rights to live freely and pursue happiness. The stranglehold that narrow wealthy interests have over our economy and government has destabilized our body politic and created conditions that call for radical change. The 2008 Obama election, in the midst of national imminent economic collapse and corporate bailouts, was the first citizen response of activism through the electoral process. The lack of participation by young and left-leaning voters and the hyper-participation of right leaning "Tea Party" rebellion in the 2010 midterm election are opposite reactions to the same kind of citizen dissatisfaction with the responsiveness (or lack thereof) of government to the needs of the people.

The upcoming 2012 election cycle is being punctuated by the restless "occupation of Wall Street" movement that has recently swept the nation. Dissatisfaction with the direction of the nation will continue to be expressed both inside and outside of the existing electoral political system. This will be a season of high activism. There will be some very, very difficult fights for the soul of the country in the immediate future. Like the great generation of World War II and every significant generation before and since, we too have a "rendezvous with destiny."

The election of radical elected officials with narrow political interests will continue to disable our government and lessen the workability of our political system. Partisan bickering and slash-and-burn theatrics will do continual harm to confidence and respect for government and political institutions. The activism outside of the political structure will be unpredictable and volatile as well. In this environment it will be dangerously difficult to distinguish between demagoguery and populism. The patience of the American people will continue to wear thin. For believers in democracy that will be both good and dangerously unpredictable. I believe that this will be a time of volatility that will be similar to the historical periods leading up to the Civil War, the labor unrest and Great Depression, and the civil rights and antiwar movements. As in each of these periods, we too will be challenged to reinvent ourselves as a people and recalibrate the social compact for the future. In the immediate future, everything will be on the table. Everything from our political Constitution to our social contract and economic philosophy will be up for reflection and renewal. This is a new place in our national life together and a new phase in our national development. I think it will be important to maintain some grounding through this time of tumultuous change. It is also an opportunity to be at the beginning of a new creation.

In my work here, I have sought to make the case that our nation should do what we have done effectively in our past: move forward with our core principles in the flow of the spirit of human history. The place in history we are in now is new, but we have seen the scenery before. When liberty expands, economies expand. When government allows wealth to be concentrated, economies contract and the social compact unravels. Either socialism or capitalism, or our hybrid system must facilitate the democratic rights of self-determination. Democratic capitalism and local access to capital produce explosive growth in the human creativities that produce prosperity. Human competitiveness and cooperation are not mutually exclusive, but indeed, they are the complements that produce human progress. Human progresses in technology and science help create networks that bring the human family back to the kinds of closeness and interconnectedness we had when small groups of humankind moved out of Africa for the first time millennia ago. Human survival requires sophisticated organization and cooperation. Globalization means the only way to understand anything is in its global context. Globalization also means that the way forward for the world will be found in rediscovery of the values of the village. The wisdom of West African "Sankofa" is a steady guide; we can move forward resolutely once we have clearly processed where we have been.[58] In this time of changing America, I pray that we would labor to move forward by our hopes and our faith, and not backward by our fears.

Just as my personal faith anchors my personal life, it also gives me an abiding hope and faith in the American Project. I believe that America has had a special grace that gives our nation a divine purpose to be a light to the nations. The soul of America is expressed in the Declaration of Independence. Every human being has intrinsic value and an inherent right to passionately pursue their potential, dreams, and life purpose. The American Project began as a vision that every person and all families have the right to rise above their first station of life. We embrace differences in the talent and drive that allow for uneven socioeconomic classes, but we have never settled for the caste system of a trapped permanent underclass. We have never adjusted to a society that renders a child hopeless at birth, or a family hopeless and helpless perpetually. That is not an America I could stand to leave my children and grandchildren. If we fail to recover with our soul intact, we will have made vain the sacrifices of blood from Valley Forge to Gettysburg to Normandy to Selma to Iraq and Afghanistan.

This is a time for soul-searching and sacrifice, and for rising to the occasion to take our nation back by moving forward. It's a season for radical redefinition and radical reorientation. Globalism should not mean the death of democracy and loss of self-determination.[59] I believe that only American ideals and values and the American spirit stand in the way of a headlong thrust to a globalist totalitarian system that negates individual liberties and freedom. I still believe in the American Project. In the twenty-first century our task is to fight the tides, resist the waves, and recreate the meaning and manifestation of the Project America for a brand new world.

207

NOTES FOR PROJECT AMERICA

1. James Melvin Washington, A Testament of Hope: The Essential Writings of Martin Luther King, Jr. (San Francisco: HarperCollins, 1986), 226.
This work contains full sermons and speeches of King, as well as his five books written from 1958 to 1967. It is an excellent one-stop shop of King's thoughts, writings, and public pronouncements.

2. Adam Cohen and Elizabeth Taylor, American Pharaoh: Mayor Richard J. Daley: His Battle for Chicago and the Nation (Boston and New York: Little Brown and Company, 2000), 67-68.

3. Sudhir Alladi Venkatesh, American Project: The Rise and Fall of a Modern Ghetto (Cambridge: Harvard University Press, 2000), 42.

This work chronicles the rise and physical and social demise of South Side Chicago's famed Robert Taylor public housing high-rises. At the outset, the intentions of those who drove policy were less than noble. Public policy was driven more by the politics of racism and exploitation than social good. It concludes that disinvestment and isolation drove the dysfunction of social engineering gone awry.

Chicago's history with public housing policies and African Americans is particularly tragic because the policies were particularly political. Venkatesh's work is scholarly but lacks the depth of the tragedy and the profound consequences of generations lost. The current dysfunctions in Chicago's black community have deep roots in the failures of the Chicago Housing Authority and both mayors Daley, Richard J. and Richard M., effective confinement of the natural processes of black leadership development.

4. http://www.uscensus/2010/Chicago region.

5. Washington, A Testament of Hope, 555.

6. Ibid, 640.

7. Paul Krugman, The Return of Depression Economics and the Crises of 2008, (New York: W. W. Norton & Company, 2009), 28.

Krugman, the Princeton professor, is a Nobel Prize-winning economist and a prolific New York Times columnist. His has been a voice crying in the wilderness during the Obama Administration. An unabashed liberal and New Dealer, his gospel of economic recovery prioritizes job creation and massive government investment over budget-balancing and austerity. Krugman's counsel, from analysis of the Great Depression, is that we must spend and invest out of economic calamity, not budget-cut our way out.

Krugman is an unabashed disciple of John Maynard Keynes, advocate of a "mixed economy" as presented in "The General Theory of Employment, Interest, and Money." This liberal model assigns an active role for government and the public sector in responding to the cyclical downturns of privately driven capitalist economy. The failure of the "Great Depression" was that the Hoover administration did not act quickly enough to stave off the economic contraction.

8. Associated Press Report, "Majority Minority America," The Washington Times, June 23, 2011.

9. Washington, A Testament of Hope, 653.

10. Nicholas Lemann, The Promised Land: The Great Black Migration and How It Changed America (New York: Random House-Vintage Books, 1992), 70.

See also Isabel Wilkerson, Warmth of Other Suns: The Epic Story of America's Great Migration (Vintage Books a Division of Random House: New York, 2010). A New York Times best-seller, Wilkerson's book puts three characters in context with six million African American migrants who left the South for the northern and western states between 1915-1970 in search of the "promised land" of opportunity. This migration changed and flavored American urban life and culture. The 2010 U.S. Census confirms African American reverse migration trends back to the southern states.

11. Cohen and Taylor, American Pharaoh, 229-33.

12. James R. Ralph Jr., Northern Protest: Martin Luther King, Jr., Chicago, and the Civil Rights Movement (Cambridge: Harvard University Press, 1993), 56.

This book details how the Chicago campaign signaled King's growth as a broader, more radical leader. King's sharp focus on power structures and economic constructs is honed in the 1966 campaigns in Daley's Chicago. King eventually concludes that northern racism and exploitation of the black poor was more efficient and intractable than the southern variety.

See also Taylor Branch, At Canaan's Edge: America in the King Years, 1965-68 (New York and London: Simon & Shuster, 2006). This work is last of Branch's trilogy of using King's life as a metaphor for America's transition into a multicultural, multiracial modern democracy. King's life redefined America in the latter half of the twentieth century. (Branch's other King books are Parting the Waters and Pillar of Fire).

13. Cohen and Taylor, American Pharaoh, 455.

14. Riis, Jacob A., "The Making of an American," http://Bartlebu.com2000, 1901.

Riis was a late nineteenth and early twentieth century photographer and social reformer who chronicled the wretched conditions of the urban poor in New York. He is part of a generation of social reformers and socialists whose vision for America heavily influenced the Franklin Roosevelt radical presidency in response to the excesses and collapse of unrestrained capitalism.

15. Frances Kostarelos, Feeling the Spirit: Faith and Hope in an Evangelical Black Storefront Church (Columbia: University of South Carolina Press,1995), 14.

Kostarelos' work chronicles the history of New Mount Pilgrim Missionary Baptist Church as a prototypical congregation of African American southern migrants. The names of the subjects were changed in the book, an apparent standard anthropological practice, although the late church pastor Rev. James McCoy and church members preferred to have their story and cosmology told using their actual names. (My name, age, and pastoral motives are misrepresented in the book's Afterward on page 131).

16. W.E.B. Du Bois, The Souls of Black Folk, (New York: Dover Publications, Inc., 1994), 2.

Du Bois' duality in the souls of black folk describes the quandary created by the access that black people of my generation experience in an age of greater integration and access. The disorientation I would experience coming from public housing and black church culture to a place like Georgetown in the late 1970s and early 1980s was a duality that encompassed race, culture, and class altogether. Those transitions from the black world to the dominant culture in American are as real, if not more, in this century as in the last.

17. Howard Ball, The Bakke Case: Race, Education, and Affirmative Action (Lawrence: University Press of Kansas, 2000).

The 1978 Supreme Court Bakke decision was the beginning of closing the kind of doors opened for inner-city blacks like me as I came of age. It meant that aggressive affirmative action to repair African Americans from over two centuries of degeneration in chattel slavery and another century of broken promises of emancipation lasted less than about ten years from the death of King. It was painful to literally watch doors closing right behind me.

18. Roland Flint, Easy: poems (Baton Rouge: Louisiana State University Press, 1999).

Flint's other published works, Stubborn and Say It, bare the poet's soul and endeared him to Studs Terkel and Garrison Keillor, who both became Roland's long-time and close friends.

Flint wrote a poem about me called "James Wright's Briefcase," which he gave to me as a sophomore in 1977. I returned the poem gift (unpublished) with one of my own dedicated to Flint called "Say It...In the Morning," which compared my preaching with his poetry and proclaimed us as "brothers baring our souls" who helped people "overcome life's sorrows with rhythms of language and the courage to be."

19. W.E.B. Du Bois, The Souls of Black Folk, 116.

Congregants, especially in the Baptist tradition, allow clergy much latitude to engage civically and politically. Even pastors operating in electoral politics are not necessarily seen as less prophetic or less holy. It's a tough balancing act to be sure, but oppressed people tend to have much more flexible theologies than people in power and privilege. The American black preaching tradition has spawned a unique clergy activist role that sees the whole world and any issue as purview for divine pronunciation. The role is so open and fluid that it attracts the rascal and disingenuous to its ranks. There is growing resistance to clergy community leadership among some emerging community and business black leaders. In politics, however, it is more difficult to dislodge the black preacher from community leadership because folks still revere religious institutions and traditions, and churches still carry the community's largest consistent meeting of organized people and organized resources.

See also Andrew Billingsley, *Mighty Like a River: The Black Church and Social Reform* (New York and Oxford: Oxford University Press, 1999).

20. Monica Copeland, "Gulf War Protestors Get Send Off," Chicago Tribune, January, 25, 1991.

21. Marian Moore, "Gulf Survivor Murdered In Texas," Chicago Defender, May, 14,1992.

22. Kostarelos, Feeling the Spirit, 121-30.

23. Berlin, Ira, Marc Favreau, and Steven F. Miller, Editors, Remembering Slavery: African Americans Talk About Their Personal Experiences of Slavery and Emancipation (The New Press in association with the Library of Congress: Washington, D.C., 1998).

This work is a gem of invaluable captured history and passion, recorded by New Deal civilian corps interviewers. The first-person tragedy of American slavery is preserved in these tapes and transcripts. The history and tragic legacies are still an unrequited and ongoing central reality of American life and America's destiny.

See also Lerone Bennett Jr. (Forced Into Glory: Abraham Lincoln's White Dream, Chicago: Johnson Publishing Company, 2000).

Long-time Ebony Magazine editor, Bennett, takes Lincoln to task as an accidental emancipator. Of course, Lincoln must always be processed in the context of the social and political confines of his times. Bennett's work does help us recapture how marginal African American freedom was to the commencement and conduct of the Civil War for Lincoln and most white Americans. The primary clash was between the agrarian and the industrialist. The civil war was originally about the "right to rise" for white free labor. Black emancipation was a convergence of interests with those who sought to increase the market value of white, unskilled and skilled labor.

24. Ibid, p. 11.

25. Marshall, Frady, Jesse: The Life and Pilgrimage of Jesse Jackson (New York: Random House, 1996), 502.

26. Haki R. Madhubuti, Claiming Earth: Race, Rage, Rape, Redemption; Blacks Seeking a Culture of Enlightened Empowerment (Chicago: Third World Press, 1994),146.

See also Jeffery M. Levin and Kenneth A. Dachman, Ph.D., Fathers' Rights, (New York: Basic Books, a member of Perseus Books Group, 1997).

27. Paul Tough, Whatever It Takes: Geoffrey Canada's Quest to Change Harlem and America, (Boston and New York: Mariner Books-Houghton Mifflin Harcourt, 2008), 278.

28. Jonathan Kozol, The Shame of the Nation: The Restoration of Apartheid Schooling In America (New York: Three Rivers Press, 2005), 321.

See also Danizer Sheldon and Jane Waldfogel, Editors, Securing the Future: Investing in Children from Birth to College, The Ford Foundation Series on Asset Building (New York: Russell Sage Foundation, 2000).

See also Jack P. Shonkoff and Deborah A. Phillips, Editors, From Neurons to Neighborhoods: The Science of Early Childhood Development (Washington, D.C.: National Academy Press, 2000).

What we know about the absolute benefits of investment in early childhood development and education is that they far outweigh the cost. In recreating a parish campus in West Garfield Park on Chicago's West Side, New Mount Pilgrim Church has brought together community partners to focus on early childhood development. Assisting families with toddlers and small children is a substantial area where urban churches can make a major impact. Our goals include modeling this impact and twenty-first century mission of urban faith communities.

See also Charles J. Ogletree, Jr., All Deliberate Speed: Reflections on the First Half Century of Brown v. Board of Education, (New York and London: W.W. Norton & Company, 2004).

29. "Urban Prep Success," Chicago Tribune, February 16, 2011.

The first single-gender (male) public school of modern times, predominately African American, has 100 percent of its graduating class accepted into four-year colleges or universities. Remarkably, its first-ever raduating class from the Chicago inner-city Englewood community graduated vith 100 percent college acceptance; quite an accomplishment by the school's ounder, Mr. Tim King, and school staff.

:0. Tamar Levin, "Burden of College Loans on Graduates Grows," New York Times, pril 11, 2011.

In 2011 American student loan debt surpassed credit card debt and xceeded 1 trillion dollars. The cruel hoax of higher education debt and high nemployment is a recipe for social unrest and national disaster. The national eart and social and political structure will break from the betrayal of the promise f upward mobility through education..

1. Tough, Whatever It Takes, 282.

2. Samuel Casey Carter, On Purpose: How Great Schools Form Strong Character ADD City: Corwin Press, 2010).

Providence St. Mel is an inner-city gem of a school. It not only serves the rban poor, but it helps to stabilize the great west side of Chicago by allowing trong families to remain in a struggling community without sacrificing their bligations to offer their children a high-quality education. The school serves a elatively economically diverse student body. Retaining families with middle-class alues in urban communities helps all families in the community. The St. Mel ulture of excellence in education in the heart of an urban community shows how mportant class integration among African Americans is to the addressing the vorst of inner-city pathologies. Isolating poor people and segregating poor, black eople from opportunity is a recipe for a continuing and compounding disaster.

:3. Richard Horsley and Neil Asher Silverman, The Message and the Kingdom: low Jesus and Paul Ignited a Revolution and Transformed the Ancient World New York: Grosset/Putnam, a member of Penguin Putnam Inc., 1997), 187.

A great work that takes the reader through an analysis of early church aith communities as repositories of old values of ancient villages and the first ovenant in the heart of the urban centers of the Roman Empire. This book has elped tremendously in defining our inner-city ministry at New Mount Pilgrim.

.4. Edward Gibbon, abridged by Frank C. Bourne, The Decline and Fall of the

Roman Empire (New York: Dell Publishing Co. Inc., 1963), 617-20.

35. Henry Paolucci, Editor, The Political Writings of St. Augustine (South Bend, IN: Gateway Editions, Ltd., 1962), 106.

36. Horsley and Silverman, The Message and the Kingdom, 213.

37. "Africa Rising," The Economist, December 3rd-9th, 2011, 82-84.

An article entitled, "Briefing Africa's hopeful economies: The sun shines bright," makes the case that a growing African population and expanding middle-class ($3,000 household annual) means that the continent will offer one of the world's most dynamic emerging markets going forward. African households earning over $3,000 annually are expected to triple over the next few years.

Over the next forty years, Africa's population is expected to double from 1 to 2 billion people, while Europe's and China's birthrates decline. Rich in mineral and human resources, Africa, if politically and socially stable (a very big if) is poised to be a "new Asia" of global-impacting economic potential.

38. Hua Hsu, "The End of White America," The Atlantic Magazine, January-February 2009.

Prophetically, the end of one thing is always the beginning of another. America has a unique opportunity to redefine itself for the new order of the emerging world. As the nation becomes "majority minority," America can flow, with values intact, with the changing complexion of global energy and economic power. Some who are blinded by the nation's changing demographic cannot see that preservation of values matters more than preserving gene pools or racial "purity." We cannot allow the shortsighted to sell us out.

39. http:// www.uscensus2010.gov/

40. Noam Chomsky, Failed States: The Abuse of Power and the Assault on Democracy (New York: Metropolitan Books-Henry Holt and Company, 2006), 236.

41. Krugman, Depression Economics, 28.

---

42. "2011 Durbin Conference: Global Warming and Climate Change," New York Times, December 12, 2011.

43. http:// www.naacp.org, "Environmental Justice Initiative 2011."

44. http:// www.uscensus2010.gov/

45. Alexander Hamilton, James Madison, and John Jay, with an introduction by Clinton Rossiter, The Federalist Papers, (New York and Scarborough, Ontario: New American Library, 1961), 324.

46. Dietrich Bonhoeffer, translated from German by Kaiser Verlag Munchen, The Cost of Discipleship, (New York: Collier Books-MacMillan Publishing Company, 1949), 47.

   Bonhoeffer's time spent (1930-31) in Harlem's Abyssinian Baptist Church under Rev. Adam Clayton Powell Sr. stirred his interest for the passionate blend of evangelical Christianity and social justice activism. Bonhoeffer joined the black church, taught Sunday School, and became enraptured by Powell's sermons and "Negro spirituals."

   As Bonhoeffer was put to death by the Nazis weeks before the end of the war, and in his final words he called his death, "...the beginning of life." His witness was inspired by the "Negro faith" he witnessed in the black church. His prophetic ministry has in turn inspired twenty-first century evangelicals to embrace social justice issues around the world, including stemming the tides of disease around the world and debt relief for poor countries.
Also see Eric Metaxas, Bonhoeffer: Pastor, Prophet, Martyr, Spy; A Righteous Gentile vs. The Third Reich, (Nashville: Thomas Nelson Publishers, 2010), 107-111, 528.

47. http://www.supremecourt.gov/opinions/09pdf/08-205.pdf

48. New York Times, "Secrets of the Bailouts, Now Told" in Sunday Business, by Gretchen Morgenson, December 4, 2011.

49. Engen, John, "Should FBOP Have Been Saved?" The American Banker, May 1, 2010.

FBOP corporation was the holding company of Park National Bank before the banks were seized by FDIC.

50. "Secrets of the Bailout, Now Told," New York Times.

Altogether, the big banks had access to $7.77 trillion in no-interest loans from the federal government to stabilize their institutions, without any obligations whatsoever to make capital available to Main Street America. The predictable result of the bailouts was further concentration of capital, obscene Wall Street bonuses, and cash-starved local communities.

51. http://www.oak park.com/news/articles/11-3-09.

52. American Banker, January 2010.

53. FBOP, Corp. Michael E. Kelly, Testimony before the United States House of Representatives Committee on Financial Services, January 21, 2010.

54. http://www.forbes.com/taxwaste/, January 5, 2011.

55. Michelle Alexander, The New Jim Crow: Mass Incarceration in the Age of Colorblindness (New York and London: The New Press, 2010), 74-75.

56. Ibid., 188.

57. H.W. Brands, Traitor to His Class: The Privileged Life and Radical Presidency of Franklin Delano Roosevelt (New York: Anchor Books, a division of Random House, Inc., 2008), 453.

In his 1936 reelection campaign, FDR makes clear the relationship between economic self- determination and free government of, for, and by the common people. He seeks to save capitalism by fiercely fighting for a democratic capitalism that places the power of government on the side of the common folk. At this writing in 2012, President Obama is channeling the spirit of FDR in his pursuit of reelection, but Obama has not yet put forth the kinds of radical vision and policy thrust needed to set the plutocrats on their heels. In keeping with the premises and themes of Brands' book, perhaps the class warrior most equipped to take on the concentrated wealth class is a "traitor" from within its own ranks.

Also see: Lardner, James and David A. Smith, "Inequality Matters: The Growing

---

Economic Divide in America and Its Poisonous Consequences," The New Press: New York and London, 2005.

58. Erriel D. Roberrson, The MAAFA and Beyond: Remembrance, Ancestral Connections and Nation Building for the African Global Community (Columbia, MD: Kujichagulia Press,1995).

The term Maafa means "great struggle" in describing the horrors of the Transatlantic Slave Trade. The packed slave ship icon is the remaining global, public memory of the transatlantic triangular trade that is the foundation of the current global economic system. Wall Street itself is literally, physically built on a cemetery of buried bones of enslaved Africans.

The MAAFA Remembrance Window at New Mount Pilgrim, featured in the February 9, 2001 National Report section of the New York Times/"Black Church Art"(John Fountain), is the largest display the "packed slave ship" icon in the world. The challenge going forward is creation of a new world order that disallows dehumanization of people with less power in the global political and economic construct. Let the emerging world move forward in the spirit of Sankofa: remembering the holocausts of human history, embracing the emerging world, and preserving the best values forged from our human rights struggles in the fading world.

59. Brands, Traitor to His Class, 609, 701-02.

President Franklin D. Roosevelt used his leverage as savior and partner of Great Britain to help shape a United Nations that accommodated the self-determinative aspirations of colonized peoples. Roosevelt went so far as to challenge Churchill with elevating the moral purpose of World War II, siding with independence movements, and facilitating some contraction of the British Empire. Roosevelt's postwar vision foresaw expansion of Project America: the peace and prosperity of the whole world in further embrace of universal principles of human rights, democratic government, and rising standards of living for peoples in the emerging world.
Life To Legacy

Life To Legacy

Let us bring your story to life! With Life to Legacy, we offer comprehensive book production, publishing, and distribution services. Want to leave written legacies for children, grandchildren and others? We also specialize in customized family history books. Put your story in our hands, and we will bring it to literary life!

Please visit our website:
www.Life2legacy.com,
or call us at 877-267-7477
You can also email us at: Life2legacybooks@att.net

CPSIA information can be obtained at www.ICGtesting.com
Printed in the USA
BVOW03s0931181113

336599BV00011B/200/P